...ge of childhood development h...

where he experiences many peer p...

escent modeling after his parent...

conform to his peers. The adole...

his peers, plays a big role in t...

idual.

If a youth grows up in the...

ness for survival is almost a ne...

youth will become more aggressiv...

upper class area. Youths growin...

very imaginative in inventing th...

who has money to go to a show or...

Dale Iosland was
~~in~~ in. He needs a
class card for ~~#1~~
Your Ethics Class —
Winter 3 — He will
pick it up on Monday
p.m.

Norma

PSYCHOPHYSICS
Method and Theory

PSYCHOPHYSICS
Method and Theory

George A. Gescheider
Hamilton College

LAWRENCE ERLBAUM ASSOCIATES, PUBLISHERS
1976   Hillsdale, New Jersey

DISTRIBUTED BY THE HALSTED PRESS DIVISION OF

JOHN WILEY & SONS

New York   Toronto   London   Sydney

Lawrence Erlbaum Associates, Inc., Publishers
62 Maria Drive
Hillsdale, New Jersey 07642

Distributed solely by Halsted Press Division
John Wiley & Sons, Inc., New York

Library of Congress Cataloging in Publication Data

Gescheider, George A
 Psychophysics: method and theory.

 Bibliography: p.
 Includes indexes.
 1. Senses and sensation—Testing. 2. Psychology,
Physiological. 3. Psychology, Physiological—Methodology.
I. Title. [DNLM: 1. Psychophysics. BF237 G389p]
QP431.G47   612'.8   75-25913
0-470-29712-3

Printed in the United States of America

To
Betsy, Mary, and Meg

Contents

Preface

Psychophysics is the scientific study of the relation between stimulus and sensation, and therefore the problems of psychophysics constitute some of the most fundamental problems of modern psychology. For centuries thinkers have recognized the importance of understanding sensation. In fact, experimental psychology developed as an independent science largely because of the recognition that the scientific study of sensation could yield insight into the workings of the human mind.

Experimental psychology was established as an independent science when in Leipzig in 1879 Wilhelm Wundt founded the first laboratory for experimental work exclusively directed toward understanding psychological processes. The work of Wundt and other early experimental psychologists evolved from the British empiricist and associationist schools of philosophy which had firmly established the idea of the senses as the key to human understanding. This idea was reinforced by advances in sensory physiology, which suggested that the problem might yield to scientific investigation.

But perhaps the single most important historical antecedent of experimental psychology was psychophysics. Thus, for some psychologists the most significant date in psychology is not 1879, the founding date of Wundt's laboratory, but 1860, the date of the publication of Fechner's *Elements of Psychophysics*. Fechner's work, in providing methods and theory for the measurement of sensation, gave psychology basic tools for the study of mind.

Today psychophysics remains a central part of experimental psychology. Important recent changes in psychophysics are the development of the theory of signal detection and the refinements of methods for directly scaling sensory magnitude. These two advances have greatly broadened the applicability of psychophysics to areas far beyond the original problems of measuring sensory thresholds. Modern psychophysics can be credited with contributions to the solution of problems in such diverse realms as sensory processes, memory, learning, social behavior, and esthetics.

This book describes the methods and theories of classical and modern psychophysics. It was written for advanced undergraduate students with some background in statistics; graduate students may also find it useful for obtaining an overview of the field. I hope *Psychophysics: Method and Theory* will be useful for courses in perception, general experimental psychology, and quantitative methods.

I wish to acknowledge the support of my students and their special efforts in providing helpful suggestions as they read various versions of the manuscript. I am especially indebted to Michael Horn for his critical reading of the material before the writing of the final manuscript. I also wish to thank Virginia Vaughan for her excellent art work.

GEORGE A. GESCHEIDER

PSYCHOPHYSICS
Method and Theory

1

Psychophysical Measurement of Thresholds

Prior to a century ago the approach to psychological problems consisted primarily of philosophical speculation. The transition of psychology from a philosophical to a scientific discipline was greatly facilitated when the German physicist G. T. Fechner introduced techniques for measuring mental events (1860). The attempt to measure sensations through the use of Fechner's procedures was termed psychophysics and constituted the major research activity of early experimental psychologists. Since this time psychophysics has consisted primarily of investigating the relationships between sensations (ψ) in the psychological domain and stimuli (ϕ) in the physical domain.

Central to psychophysics is the concept of a *sensory threshold*. The philosopher Herbart (1824) had conceived of the idea of a threshold by assuming that mental events had to be stronger than some critical amount in order to be consciously experienced. Although measurement is not a part of this description of the threshold, scientists eventually were able to see the implication of such a concept for psychological measurement. In the early nineteenth century, for example, German scientists such as E. H. Weber and G. T. Fechner were interested in the measurement of the sensitivity limits of the human sense organs. Using measurement techniques of physics and well-trained human observers, they were able to specify the weakest detectable sensations in terms of the stimulus energy necessary to produce them. The *absolute threshold* or *stimulus threshold* (RL for the German *Reiz Limen*) was defined as the smallest amount of stimulus energy necessary to produce a sensation. Since an organism's sensitivity to external stimuli tends to fluctuate somewhat from moment to moment, several measurements of the threshold value of the stimulus are averaged to arrive at an accurate estimation of the absolute threshold. If a stimulus above absolute threshold is applied to the sense organ, the intensity of this stimulus must be increased or decreased by some critical amount before a person is able to report any change in his sensation. The difference threshold (DL for the German *Differenz Limen*) was defined as the amount of change in a stimulus ($\Delta\phi$) required to produce a *just noticeable difference* (jnd) in the sensation. If the intensity of the stimulus is 10 units and the stimulus has to be increased to 12 units to produce a just noticeable increment in the sensation, the difference threshold would be 2 units.

Sensation intensity is only one of several ways in which sensations can differ, and DLs have also been measured for other dimensions of sensation. It is generally agreed that sensations can differ on at least four basic dimensions—intensity, quality, extension, and duration. The dimension of quality refers to the fact that sensations may be different in kind. The different sensory modalities have unique kinds of sensations; for example, seeing is an entirely different kind of experience than hearing. Within sensory modalities sensations also vary in quality. A sound becomes higher or lower in pitch as the vibration frequency of the stimulus is changed. Variations of the wavelength of light are accompanied by changes in hue. A cutaneous sensation may be painful, warm, cold, or simply a pressure. If the underlying stimulus dimensions for a quality are known, the difference thresholds can be measured to find the changes in stimulus dimensions necessary to produce just noticeable changes in the quality of the sensation. For example, in auditory pitch discrimination the DL for changes in frequency has been measured and in color discrimination the DL for the perception of changes in the wavelength of light has been measured. Since sensations can also vary along spatial dimensions the DL can be measured for variation in spatial aspects of physical stimuli such as size, location, and separation. And, finally, since sensations last for varying periods of time, the DL for stimulus duration has been of interest to psychophysicists.

Much work in psychophysics has consisted of investigating how the absolute and difference thresholds change as some aspect of the stimulus (wavelength, frequency, adaptation time, intensity level, etc.) is systematically varied. The resulting relations are called *stimulus critical value functions*, since they describe how the threshold (critical stimulus value) changes as a function of other aspects of the stimulus.

DIFFERENTIAL SENSITIVITY

One of the first stimulus critical value functions to be investigated was the relation between the difference threshold for intensity and the intensity level of a stimulus. If, for example, the difference threshold is 2 units when the intensity level of the stimulus is 10 units, what would the difference threshold be for intensity when the stimulus is set at 20, 30, 40, and 50 units? Working mainly with the discrimination of lifted weights, the German physiologist E. H. Weber (1834) discovered that two relatively heavy weights must differ by a greater amount than two relatively light weights for one weight to be perceived as heavier than another, that is, heavier weights are harder to discriminate and are associated with larger DLs. More precisely, the size of the difference threshold was a linear function of stimulus intensity, with the stimulus always having to be increased by a constant fraction of its value to be just noticeably different to an observer. For weights placed on the skin this fraction is about 1/30.

The size of Weber's fraction is quite different, however, for other stimulus conditions and sense modalities. What is significant is that whether the stimulus is applied to the eye, ear, skin, nose, tongue, or other sense organs, there appears to be a lawful relationship between the size of the difference threshold and the stimulus intensity level. This relationship is known as *Weber's law:* the change in stimulus intensity that can just be discriminated ($\Delta\phi$) is a constant fraction (c) of the starting intensity of the stimulus (ϕ):

$$\Delta\phi = c\phi \qquad \text{or} \qquad \Delta\phi/\phi = c. \tag{1.1}$$

As seen graphically in our hypothetical situation, the size of the difference threshold is one-fifth of the starting stimulus intensity at all intensity levels (Figure 1.1). If Weber's law is valid we would expect to find $\Delta\phi/\phi$ to be constant as intensity level is varied ($\Delta\phi/\phi = c$). This prediction is typically confirmed for a fairly wide range of stimulus intensities. However, the Weber fraction, $\Delta\phi/\phi$, tends to increase greatly at extremely low intensities. In Figure 1.2 the relationship between the Weber fraction and intensity is shown for an experiment on lifted weights (Engen, 1971). The observer was required to successively lift weights

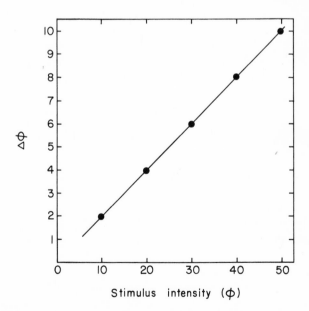

FIGURE 1.1   The relationship between $\Delta\phi$ and ϕ according to Weber's law.

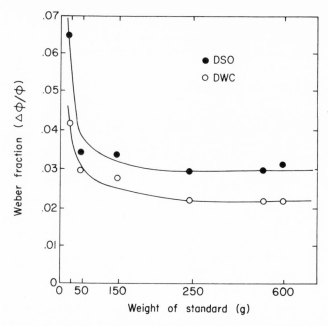

FIGURE 1.2   The Weber fraction for lifted weights. The value of $\Delta\phi/\phi$ for each of two observers was nearly constant over the stimulus range, except for the lowest stimulus values. (From Engen, 1971.)

with one hand, and the value of $\Delta\phi$ was determined for six different values of ϕ. The results for each of two observers indicate that $\Delta\phi/\phi$ is nearly constant for all but the lightest weights.

Technically, the Weber fraction is an extremely useful calculation providing an index of sensory discrimination which can be compared across different conditions and different modalities. It is impossible, for example, to compare meaningfully the $\Delta\phi$ for vision in luminosity units with the $\Delta\phi$ for audition in sound pressure units, but the relative sensitivities for the two modalities can be gauged through a comparison of Weber fractions. Some of the results from two classic studies on intensity discrimination are presented in Figures 1.3 and 1.4. In the study of König and Brodhun (1889) the observer viewed a split field in which the two sides could be made to differ in intensity by various amounts. The difference in intensity necessary for discrimination of a brightness difference between the two sides was determined for nearly the full range of visual intensities. Figure 1.3 contains data from separate experiments by König and Brodhun on the discrimination of intensity differences in white light. At low intensities $\Delta\phi/\phi$ decreased as intensity increased and then became approximately constant for the higher intensity values. In a similar study, Riesz (1928) determined the intensity increment in an auditory tone necessary for discrimination for various intensity levels and various tone frequencies. Since the frequency of 4000 Hz yielded the lowest values of $\Delta\phi$, only

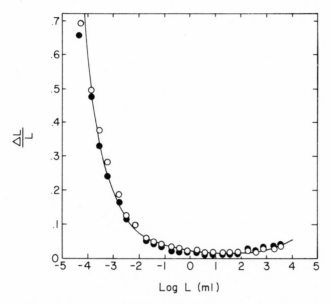

FIGURE 1.3   Relation between $\Delta\phi/\phi$ and log luminance as shown by König (open circles) and Brodhun (solid circles). (From König & Brodhun, 1889; after Hecht, 1934, Fig. 27, p. 769.)

the data for this frequency were presented in Figure 1.4. It is seen again that the value of $\Delta\phi/\phi$ first decreases as a function of ϕ and then becomes approximately constant. A comparison of the lowest Weber fractions in Figures 1.3 and 1.4 reveals that brightness discrimination is somewhat better than loudness discrimination.

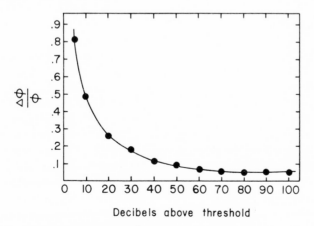

FIGURE 1.4   Relation between $\Delta\phi/\phi$ and the intensity of a 4000-Hz tone. The intensity of the tone is expressed in decibels above absolute threshold. (From Riesz, 1928.)

A modification of Weber's law more closely corresponding to empirical data states

$$\frac{\Delta\phi}{\phi + a} = c \qquad \text{or} \qquad \Delta\phi = c(\phi + a), \tag{1.2}$$

where a is a constant usually having a fairly small value. The empirical values of $\Delta\phi/(\phi + a)$ obtained in a discrimination experiment are often approximately the same for all values of ϕ when the correct value of a has been chosen. Since the original version of Weber's law does not correspond to the data for intensity values near threshold it would seem that the constant a, which brings Weber's law into line with the data, must be related to the operation of sensory systems near threshold. It is not clear what the exact significance of a may be, but it may represent the amount of sensory noise that exists when the value of ϕ is zero. The actual stimulus intensity which effectively determines $\Delta\phi$ may not be ϕ but rather ϕ plus the continuously fluctuating background noise level of the nervous system. Since sensory noise as spontaneous activity in the nervous system exists as a background for stimulation, its level may greatly influence the value of $\Delta\phi$ for very low intensity values. Perhaps when the level of sensory noise is taken into account Weber's law is essentially correct.

One advantage to the above interpretation of the constant a is that the concept of sensory noise provides a unifying principle for understanding absolute and differential thresholds. The absolute threshold can be regarded as the value of ϕ needed to increase the neural activity level above the sensory noise level by some critical amount. The difference threshold can be thought of as the change in ϕ, $\Delta\phi$, needed to produce a critical difference in neural activity level associated with two intensities of stimulation. Thus both the absolute threshold and the difference threshold involve the discrimination of differences in levels of neural activity. The importance of the concept of sensory noise will become increasingly apparent in our subsequent discussions of psychophysical theory.

FECHNER'S PSYCHOPHYSICS

It was from Weber's work on the DL that Fechner extracted the theoretical implication which led to his formulation of the program called psychophysics. Fechner's investigations, originating from an attempt to establish a precise relationship between the physical and mental, were published in 1860 as *Elements of Psychophysics*. Though Fechner was a physicist, in his later years he turned to the problems of philosophy. As a result of his background in physics and mathematics he approached these problems in a quite different manner than those who preceded him. In the last 35 years of his life Fechner's work focused on the idea that mind and matter are equal and are merely two alternative ways of regarding the universe. His psychophysics was a small, but most significant, part of this venture.

Through measurement and quantification Fechner sought to prove his ideas about the equivalence of mind and matter by finding a mathematical equation to describe the relationship between physical events and conscious experience. Fechner's first insights into the problem came when he proposed that an arithmetic series of mental intensities might correspond to a geometric series of physical energies. He later realized this principle was exactly what Weber's results seemed to imply: that as the stimulus intensity increases it takes greater and greater changes in intensity to change the sensation magnitude. Fechner proposed that sensation magnitude could be quantified indirectly by relating the values of $\Delta\phi$ on the physical scale to the corresponding values of the just noticeable difference in sensation (jnd) on the psychological scale. His central assumption was that all jnds were equal psychological increments in sensation magnitude regardless of the size of $\Delta\phi$. Fechner's proposed relationship between the size of $\Delta\phi$ in physical units (from Weber's law) and the size of the jnd in psychological units is illustrated in Figure 1.5. It is very important to understand that two independent dimensions exist in this relationship—the stimulus dimension, ϕ, and the sensation dimension, ψ. Fechner was saying that regardless of its size in physical units the jnd is a standard unit of sensation magnitude because it is the smallest detectable increment in a sensation and therefore always psychologically the same size. As is the case with any scale of measurement, once a basic unit is established one has only to count up units in order to specify the amount of a measured property. Thus, Fechner developed a scale of sensory magnitude by counting jnd's starting at absolute threshold. The intensity in physical units of a stimulus at absolute threshold, representing the transition between sensation and no sensation, was assumed to correspond to the zero point on the psychological scale of sensation magnitude. Producing a sensation by using a stimulus 20 jnd's above absolute threshold should therefore have a psychological magnitude twice as great as a sensation produced by a stimulus that is only 10 jnd's above absolute threshold.

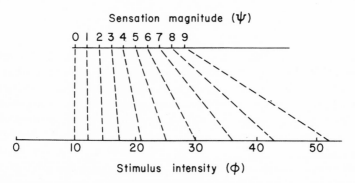

FIGURE 1.5   Relation between Weber's law and Fechner's law. Stimulus values that are marked off according to Weber's law were assumed by Fechner to result in equal steps in sensation magnitude.

If one were to determine empirically the number of jnd's above absolute threshold corresponding to values of the physical stimulus, the process would demand the arduous task of starting at absolute threshold and measuring successive values of $\Delta\phi$ along the physical continuum. The first $\Delta\phi$ above the absolute threshold would be measured and the stimulus intensity value for one jnd above absolute threshold would be recorded and would also be used as the starting stimulus for the measurement of the next $\Delta\phi$. The measurement of the second $\Delta\phi$ would provide a stimulus value two jnd's above the absolute threshold, which would be recorded and used as the starting stimulus for the measurement of the third $\Delta\phi$, and so on. Once the physical intensity values had been determined for successive jnd's over the range of energies to which the sensory system responds, the relationship between stimuli in physical units, ϕ, and sensation magnitude in psychological units (number of jnd's above absolute threshold) could be specified in terms of a graph or an equation.

Rather than employing the laborious procedure of experimentally determining successive $\Delta\phi$ values along the entire physical dimension, Fechner assumed the validity of Weber's law and was able by calculation to determine the number of jnd's above absolute threshold corresponding to specific values of the stimulus. For example, if $\Delta\phi/\phi$ is $^1/_5$ and the absolute threshold 10, the stimulus value corresponding to the first jnd would be $10 \times {}^1/_5 + 10 = 12$. The stimulus value corresponding to the second jnd is obtained by the same procedure ($12 \times {}^1/_5 + 12 = 14.4$). By this method of successive calculation Table 1.1 was developed. It contains stimulus intensity values and the corresponding number of psychological units (number of jnd's). The results of this procedure are presented graphically in Figure 1.6. If the number of jnd's above absolute threshold is a valid measure of sensation magnitude then it is apparent that increasing stimulus intensity results in smaller and smaller increments in sensation intensity. In fact, if sensation mag-

TABLE 1.1
Number of jnd's Above Threshold Corresponding to Stimulus Intensity Values

Number of jnd's	Stimulus intensity	Log stimulus intensity
0	10.00	1.000
1	12.00	1.079
2	14.40	1.158
3	17.28	1.238
4	20.79	1.316
5	24.89	1.396
6	29.86	1.476
7	35.83	1.554
8	43.00	1.633
9	51.60	1.713

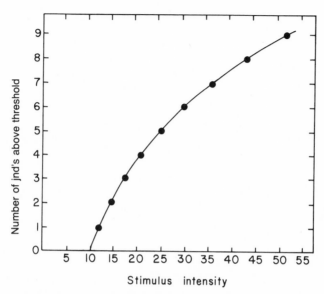

FIGURE 1.6   Number of jnd's above threshold plotted against stimulus intensity. The points are from Table 1.1, which contains the calculated values based on the assumptions that the Weber fraction is $1/5$ and the absolute threshold is 10 units.

nitude is plotted against the logarithm of stimulus intensity, the relationship is linear (Figure 1.7). A considerable amount of labor would be saved if the equation were known for this logarithmic relationship. The sensation magnitude produced by some specific stimulus intensity could then be quickly calculated. Fechner derived a general formula from Weber's law by integration over a series of ϕ values; it has become known as Fechner's law:

$$\psi = k \log \phi. \tag{1.3}$$

In the formula, ψ is the sensation magnitude, ϕ the intensity of the stimulus in units above absolute threshold, and k is a constant multiplier, the value of which depends upon the particular sensory dimension and modality.

In evaluating Fechner's law we must consider the two main assumptions that he had to make to derive the equation. First, Fechner's law is valid only to the extent that Weber's law is correct, and we have already seen that the Weber fraction is not a constant at the low end of the stimulus range. Thus the generality of the law is necessarily restricted to ranges of stimulus intensities over which $\Delta\phi/\phi = c$. In the second place, Fechner's law rests upon the assumption that the jnd is an equal increment in sensation at all levels of stimulus intensity. This assumption is basic to the entire concept of scaling sensations by using the jnd as the unit of measurement. However, experimental tests have shown that jnd's along the intensive dimension are psychologically unequal (Stevens, 1936). A sound 20 jnd's above

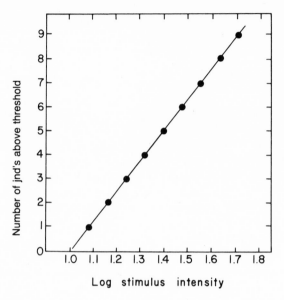

FIGURE 1.7   Number of jnd's above threshold plotted against the logarithm of stimulus intensity. The calculated values are in Table 1.1.

absolute threshold is judged to be much more than twice as loud as a sound 10 jnd's above absolute threshold.

For more than 100 years Fechner's equation was widely accepted in psychology and, to some extent, in other fields as physiology and engineering. Today it is not considered an accurate statement of the relationship between stimulus intensity and sensation magnitude. Yet the fact that experimental results have not led to the verification of Fechner's law does not detract from the overall significance of his work. The importance of his accomplishments lies in the direction he took while trying to deal with problems of the mind. The concept of measurement, a primary goal of science, became a part of psychological investigation through Fechner's work.

ABSOLUTE SENSITIVITY OF SENSORY SYSTEMS

The measurement of the absolute threshold, though perhaps not as important for the development of psychology as Fechner's insights into difference thresholds, has led to many significant advances in understanding sensory systems. Before considering in detail the various psychophysical methods for measuring DLs and absolute thresholds, let us consider examples of how measuring absolute thresholds has facilitated our understanding of vision, audition, touch, and olfaction.

The Absolute Sensitivity of the Eye

The eye is an extremely light-sensitive instrument capable of responding to almost unbelievably small amounts of light energy. However, a simple answer cannot be given to the question: How sensitive is the eye to light? The absolute sensitivity of the eye cannot be gauged by a single threshold value since the minimum amount of light necessary for vision has been found to depend on the conditions of stimulation. Therefore, the absolute sensitivity of the visual system is best understood by examining the functional relationships between the absolute threshold and the conditions that determine its value.

The value of the absolute threshold depends upon previous stimulation. Exposing the eye to intense light greatly decreases the absolute sensitivity of the eye. Sensitivity is recovered gradually if the eye is subsequently kept in darkness. Nearly complete recovery of sensitivity occurs after about one hour in the dark. The dark adaptation curve is traced out by measuring an observer's absolute threshold periodically during the recovery period and plotting its value as a function of time in the dark. The threshold at the beginning of dark adaptation may be as much as 100,000 times as high (5 log units) as the threshold after complete dark adaptation.

In an experiment by Hecht, Haig, and Chase (1937), the test stimulus was presented to a region of the retina containing both rods and cones, and the dark adaptation curve was found to be biphasic (Figure 1.8). The first phase was a relatively rapid reduction in the absolute threshold as a function of time in the dark with the threshold stabilizing after 5–8 min. The second phase, starting after about 10 min in the dark, was a relatively gradual decrease in the threshold which was complete after about 40 min. The point on the curve where the second phase begins is called the rod–cone break. The biphasic curve is caused by the intersecting of the cone and rod recovery curves which start at different intensity levels, change at different rates, and approach different asymptotes. Before the rod–cone break the absolute threshold of the rods is so high that the adaptation curve is determined completely by changing sensitivity of the cones. The rod–cone break represents the point where rod sensitivity finally begins to exceed cone sensitivity, and thereafter the remainder of the dark adaptation curve is determined by the continuing recovery of the rods.

Under most conditions the electromagnetic radiation is visible when its wavelength is between 400 nm (nanometers, millionths of millimeters) and 750 nm. However, the eye is not equally sensitive to light of all wavelengths. Spectral sensitivity curves showing the absolute threshold as a function of stimulus

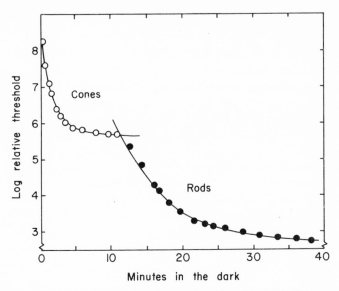

FIGURE 1.8   Biphasic curve for dark adaptation. The logarithm of the threshold intensity is plotted against time in the dark. (From Hecht, Haig, & Chase, 1937.)

wavelength have been obtained for cone (photopic) and rod (scotopic) vision. In one such experiment, Wald (1945) measured the absolute thresholds of 22 observers for detecting a 1.0°, 40-msec test stimulus of variable wavelength presented either within the fovea or 8° above the fovea. Figure 1.9 illustrates that light in the extreme blue or red regions on the visual spectrum is relatively ineffective in producing visual responses. The periphery of the retina is most effectively stimulated by light with a wavelength of approximately 500 nm, and the fovea is most sensitive when the stimulus wavelength is about 560 nm. For all wavelengths the stimulus flash at threshold appeared to be colored for foveal stimulation, indicating the operation of cones, but all threshold stimuli appeared achromatic for peripheral stimulation, indicating the operation of rods. That rods are considerably more sensitive than cones at all but the longest wavelengths is illustrated by the fact that much less energy is required at threshold for peripheral stimulation than for foveal stimulation. The difference between rod and cone thresholds is clearly illustrated by gradually increasing the intensity of a colored light presented to an extrafoveal region of the retina containing both rods and cones. When the rod threshold is reached the light appears colorless, but with continued increases in intensity a point is reached where the light is above the cone threshold and color is finally perceived. The difference between the rod and cone thresholds measured in this way is called the photochromatic interval. It is an interval on the stimulus intensity scale in which a colored light is perceived, but as colorless. As might be expected from examination of Figure 1.9, the size of the photochromatic interval varies with wavelength, being smallest for the long wavelengths and becoming larger for shorter wavelengths.

In physics it has been shown that light can be described as both a wave and a particle, or quantum. Prior to this development it was thought that energy varied on a continuum. We now know that due to its quantal nature energy, including light, changes in discrete steps. The light quantum, also known as a photon, is the smallest possible unit of light energy. It has been determined that vision occurs when the number of quanta absorbed by retinal receptors exceeds some small critical number.

The receptors are able to summate energy over space, as indicated by the fact that within certain spatial limits the total number of quanta is constant at threshold whether they are distributed sparsely over a large area (up to about 10 min of arc in the fovea and 1° in the periphery of the eye) or concentrated in a small area. Likewise, the visual receptors are able to summate energy over time up to about .1 sec since it has been found that the total number of quanta at threshold are the same when exposing the eye to a weak stimulus for a long time as when exposing it to a strong stimulus for a short time. Because the eye is unable to summate energy completely over time intervals exceeding .1 sec or areas exceeding about 10 min in

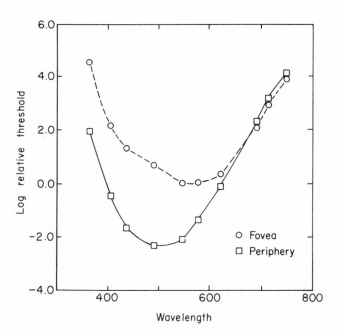

FIGURE 1.9   Relative thresholds for detection of light as a function of wavelength and location of the stimulus on the retina. (From Wald, 1945. Copyright 1945 by the American Association for the Advancement of Science.)

diameter, beyond these limits a greater number of quanta are required at absolute threshold.

In what has become a classic experiment in visual science, Hecht, Shlaer, and Pirenne (1942) determined the amount of light at the retina necessary for vision under conditions yielding optimal sensitivity. The following steps were taken to provide optimal conditions for visual sensitivity: (a) the retina was dark-adapted for at least 30 min prior to the making of threshold measurements; (b) stimuli were presented on the temporal retina 20° from the fovea since this area contains a maximum concentration of rods; (c) a very small test field (10 min in diameter) was employed to insure that within the visual system there would be complete spatial summation of the stimulus[1]; (d) similarly, the exposure time was very short (.001 sec) so temporal summation would operate; (e) a light of 510 nm was used because of the optimal scotopic sensitivity to light of this wavelength; and (f) so that he would be maximally set for each stimulus, the observer operated the shutter through which the stimulus was presented.

Stimulus intensity was measured by a thermopile which was substituted for the observer's pupil. A thermopile is a thin strip of metal which exhibits an increase in temperature when struck by light. The increment in temperature was then converted into units of light intensity. Thresholds, defined as the stimulus energy resulting in a sensation 60% of the time, measured over a period of months for seven observers, ranged between 2.1×10^{-10} and 5.7×10^{-10} ergs at the cornea. These minute amounts of energy represent between 54 and 148 quanta of blue-green light.

To specify the number of quanta absorbed at threshold by the photochemical pigment of the visual receptors (rhodopsin), the threshold values measured at the cornea were corrected for losses of light within the eye. Approximately 4% of the light reaching the cornea is reflected back instead of entering the eye. Ludvigh and McCarthy (1938) found that 50% of the light of 510 nm entering the eye is absorbed by the ocular media before reaching the retina. Finally, it has been estimated that at most only 20% of the light reaching the retina is absorbed by the rhodopsin of the receptors, the remainder being absorbed by other tissues such as blood vessels. The threshold value of 54 to 148 quanta measured at the cornea, when corrected for the above factors, is only 5 to 14 quanta absorbed by rhodopsin. In the 10-min retinal area stimulated there are approximately 500 rods, thus making it highly unlikely that more than one quantum will strike a single rod at threshold levels of intensity. On this basis Hecht et al. (1942) concluded that in order to see, it is necessary for only one quantum of light to be absorbed by a single molecule of photochemical pigment in each of 5 to 14 rods. The maximum sensitivity of the eye approaches a limit imposed by the nature of light.

---

[1]For stimuli smaller than 1° presented to the periphery of the dark-adapted eye there exists a perfect reciprocal relation between stimulus size and stimulus intensity at the threshold of detectability (Graham, Brown, & Mote, 1939); that is, the total effective energy for the eye is determined by the product of stimulus intensity and stimulus area for areas up to 1° in diameter.

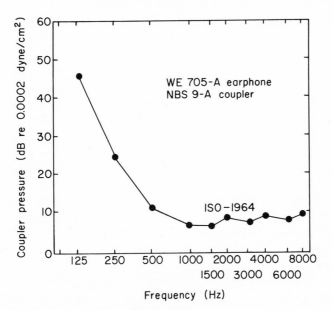

FIGURE 1.10   Absolute threshold in decibels sound pressure level for the detection of pure tones as a function of stimulus frequency. (From Davis & Krantz, 1964.)

The Absolute Sensitivity of the Ear

The remarkable sensitivity of the eye under optimal conditions of stimulation has been found to be nearly matched by that of the ear. Under normal conditions a young person can hear sound when its frequency of vibration is between 20 and 20,000 Hz. However, the auditory system is most sensitive to vibrations between 2000 and 4000 Hz and least sensitive to vibrations at the extremes of the audible range of frequencies. In Figure 1.10 the absolute threshold in decibels (dB) sound pressure level[2] is plotted for the frequencies that are employed in standard hearing tests. This graph, prepared by the International Organization for Standardization, is based on the combining of results from a number of studies in which an attempt was made to determine normal hearing for young people (Davis & Krantz, 1964). The extremely low thresholds for the middle frequencies can be better appreciated when the physical effects of such low sound pressure on the eardrum are determined. Wilska (1935) attached one end of a light wooden rod to the eardrum and

---

[2]Sound pressure is often expressed on a logarithmic scale as the number of decibels above a reference sound pressure. The most frequently used reference is .0002 dyne per square centimeter. The number of decibels can be computed by the formula

$$N_{dB} = 20 \log p_1/p_0,$$

where p_0 is a sound pressure of .0002 dyne/cm^2 and p_1 is the measured sound pressure.

the other end to a loudspeaker coil. The rod was vibrated and voltage across the speaker coil was adjusted so that a tone could hardly be heard. The vibration amplitude of the rod, and thus the amplitude of the in–out movement of the eardrum, was measured with a microscope. Direct measurements of the movement of the rods could be made only for the low frequencies of vibration. At high frequencies the movement was so slight at threshold that it had to be calculated from larger movements of the rod at low frequencies. The results of the study indicate that for frequencies of between 2000 and 4000 Hz the eardrum has to move only 10^{-9} cm in order for a sound to be heard. And this amount of movement is less than the diameter of a hydrogen molecule. By using a highly precise laser interferometer to measure vibration amplitude of the cat's eardrum at threshold, Tonndorf and Khanna (1968) were able to confirm Wilska's findings. Peak displacement amplitude at threshold was 10^{-10} cm at 1000 Hz and close to 10^{-11} cm at 5000 Hz.

Is the sensitivity of the ear limited by its construction and physiological efficiency or is it limited by the nature of air as a transmitting medium for sound? Sivian and White (1933) calculated the sound pressure generated by the constant random movement of individual air molecules within the frequency range of 1000–6000 Hz. These calculations indicate that a constant sound pressure exists which is only 10 dB lower than the average auditory threshold of approximately .0002 dyne/cm² for sounds within this frequency range. Furthermore, people with excellent hearing have thresholds which are approximately the same as the constant sound pressure from the random movement of air molecules. For people with excellent hearing, therefore, having more sensitive ears would be useless because of the normal noise continuously present in the air.

The Absolute Sensitivity for Touch

One way of measuring tactile sensitivity is to determine the smallest amplitude of vibration of the skin that can be detected by an observer. Vibrotactile thresholds depend on stimulus factors such as the locus of stimulation, the size of the stimulated skin area, the duration of the stimulus, and the frequency of vibration. An experiment by Verrillo (1963) will serve to illustrate the relationship which is found for the absolute threshold for vibration and the frequency of the vibratory stimulus. In Verrillo's experiment a stimulator attached to a vibrator was placed in contact with the skin of the prominence on the palm at the base of the thumb. The stimulator protruded up into a hole in a rigid surface upon which the observer rested his hand. There was a 1-mm gap between the circularly shaped stimulator and the rigid surrounding surface. The small gap between the stimulator and the rigid surface upon which the hand rested served to control the area of stimulation by confining the vibration to the area of the stimulator. The data presented in

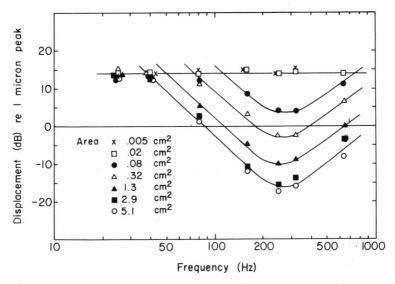

FIGURE 1.11   Vibrotactile thresholds for seven contactor sizes as a function of vibration frequency. (From Verrillo, 1963).

Figure 1.11 were obtained when the size of the stimulator was varied over a range of .005 cm² to 5.1 cm².

It can be seen in Figure 1.11 that when the stimulator was larger than .02 cm² vibrotactile sensitivity was a U-shaped function of frequency and that sensitivity was best in the frequency region around 250 Hz where the amplitude of vibration needed to exceed threshold was approximately .1 micron (μm) for the largest contactor. Thus, under the best conditions in which large areas of skin on a relatively sensitive part of the body are stimulated, vibration amplitude had to be 10^{-5} cm for the mechanical disturbance to be detected. This vibration threshold, although impressive, does not compare favorably with a vibration threshold of 10^{-11} cm for movement of the eardrum necessary for hearing a 5000-Hz tone. The superiority of auditory sensitivity may be due to the greater efficiency of the auditory system in conducting mechanical disturbances to the receptors and/or the greater sensitivity of the auditory receptors.

Variation of the size of the stimulator had an interesting effect in Verrillo's study. Increasing the size of stimulators larger than .02 cm² resulted in a proportional decrease in the threshold. This finding indicated that the tactile system is capable of summating stimulation over a relatively large area. For stimuli that were .02 cm² or smaller no spatial summation was observed. Furthermore, it can be seen that the frequency curve for these small stimulators is not U shaped but rather that the threshold is uniformly high at all frequencies. Verrillo concluded from these

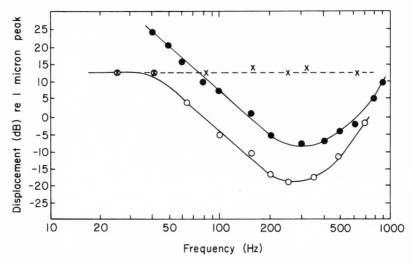

FIGURE 1.12   Human psychophysical thresholds for the detection of vibrotactile stimuli (unfilled points) compared with the electrophysiological response of the Pacinian corpuscle in the cat (filled points). The flat curve is obtained when skin containing no Pacinian corpuscles is stimulated or when very small contractors are used. (From Verrillo, 1975. From *Experimental Sensory Psychology* by Bertram Scharf. Copyright © by Scott, Foresman and Company. Reprinted by permission of the publisher.)

findings that the skin contains at least two receptor systems which are involved in the detection of mechanical disturbances. One system summates energy over space and accounts for the U-shaped frequency function obtained when all but the smallest stimulators are used. The other system, which is not capable of spatial summation, accounts for the flat frequency function when thresholds are measured for very small contactors. By comparing psychophysical data with data on the electrophysiological response of individual tactile receptors, Verrillo (1966) was able to identify the Pacinian corpuscle as the receptor responsible for spatial summation and the U-shaped frequency response curve. There is remarkable correspondence between the U-shaped psychophysical function and the neural response of a Pacinian corpuscle (Figure 1.12).

The Absolute Sensitivity for Smell

An experiment reminiscent of the work of Hecht, Shlaer, and Pirenne (1942) on vision was performed by Stuiver (1958), a Dutch investigator. After determining the smallest number of molecules of a substance that must enter the nose to be detected, Stuiver calculated the number of molecules that had to be absorbed by the olfactory receptors within the nose. Calculations were based on experiments with a physical model of the nasal cavity which revealed that only 2% of the molecules entering the nose make contact with the olfactory receptors while the remaining 98% are absorbed in mucus, are carried in air streams that never make contact with the receptor area, or are carried in air streams over the receptor area without affecting it. From his psychophysical data Stuiver estimated that 40 receptor cells must each absorb only a single molecule for a substance to be detected. The sensitivity of the nose, like that of the eye and the ear, approaches a limit imposed by the nature of the stimulus. In other words, under the very best conditions these systems are as sensitive as any sensing device could possibly be for detecting certain specific forms of energy.

2

The Classical
Psychophysical Methods

The experiments described in Chapter 1 are examples of how psychophysics has been used to determine the sensitivity of perceptual systems to environmental stimuli. In Chapter 2 the specific methods for measuring sensitivity are discussed in detail.

Presenting a stimulus to an observer and asking him to report whether or not he perceives it is the basic procedure for measuring thresholds. Biological systems are not fixed, however, but rather are variable in their reaction and, therefore, when an observer is presented on several occasions with the same stimulus he is likely to respond "yes" on some trials and "no" on other trials. Thus the threshold cannot be defined as the stimulus value below which detection never occurs and above which detection always occurs. The concept of the threshold has obviously been, and still is, useful, since it affords a technique for quantifying the sensitivity of sensory systems. But since reactions to stimuli are variable the threshold must be specified as a statistical value. Typically, the threshold has been defined as the stimulus value which is perceptible in 50% of the trials.

Fechner recognized the statistical nature of thresholds and the necessary methodological consequences. Psychologists are indebted to him for developing three methods of threshold measurement: the methods of constant stimuli, limits, and adjustment. These methods have been such valuable tools that they are used today in a great variety of psychological measurement problems. They are techniques for obtaining absolute and difference thresholds; each consists of an experimental procedure plus a mathematical treatment of data.

METHOD OF CONSTANT STIMULI

Absolute Thresholds

The method of constant stimuli derives its name from the fact that the same stimuli, usually somewhere between five and nine different values, are used repeatedly throughout the experiment. The 50% threshold is located somewhere within the range of stimulus values—the lower end of which should be a stimulus that can almost never be detected and the upper end of which should be a stimulus that is almost always detected. As the intensity level is increased within this range, the likelihood of detecting the stimulus will systematically increase. In the method of constant stimuli the percentage of detections as a function of stimulus intensity, ϕ, is determined.

Since the stimulus of lowest intensity should seldom be perceived and the most intense stimulus should always or almost always be perceived, some preliminary observations are usually made to locate these values approximately. The procedure requires that each stimulus be presented repeatedly, usually a hundred times or more, but in a random order. During the experiment a count of the number of "yes" or "no" responses for each stimulus intensity level is kept. For each stimulus value the proportion (p) of "yes" responses is then computed and a graph called a *psychometric function* is constructed. Stimulus intensity is plotted on the abscissa and the proportion of "yes" responses on the ordinate. A psychometric function for a hypothetical experiment using nine stimulus intensities is seen in Figure 2.1. In this example the absolute threshold, defined as the stimulus intensity for which the proportion of trials resulting in "yes" response is .5, does not correspond to any of the stimuli used in the experiment. Therefore a curve must be fitted to the nine data points and the threshold estimated by reading from the curve the stimulus intensity for the .5 point. In our example the threshold is 12.3 units. It should be noticed that the best fitting curve for the data points is an S-shaped function. If enough measurements are made, psychometric functions often follow a particular S shape called an *ogive*.

The procedure of fitting ogives to the points on a psychometric function is supported by theory as well as by experimental findings. Variation of biological

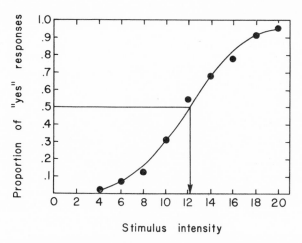

FIGURE 2.1   Typical psychometric function obtained when the absolute threshold is measured by the method of constant stimuli. An ogive curve has been fitted to the points. The threshold is the stimulus intensity that would be detected 50% of the time.

and psychological measurements tends to be normally distributed; when the frequencies or proportions of measurements of various magnitudes are plotted against the dimension on which variation is occurring (height, weight, IQ, or sensory sensitivity), the result is usually the bell-shaped normal distribution curve. The ogive curve is a cumulative form of this distribution. Various techniques for fitting ogive functions to threshold data range from simply drawing the curve by eye to various elaborate mathematical techniques.

One useful technique for fitting a particular mathematical function to a set of data consisting of pairs of numbers is to transform the data into units that should result in a linear relationship between the numbers if the mathematical function is an appropriate description of the data. An ogive psychometric function has the convenient feature of becoming a linear function when the proportion of responses for each stimulus value is transformed into a z score (Table 2.1). A normal distribution table is used to convert p values into z scores. The same result is accomplished by plotting p values on normal probability paper. This provides an ordinate marked off in p values which are spaced so that equal distances represent equal z-score distances on the normal distribution.

The ogive curve of Figure 2.2 results when the proportion of the area under a normal distribution that falls below a point, X, is plotted as a function of successive values of X on the abscissa. The units along the abscissa of the normal distribution can also be expressed in terms of z-score units. Therefore, if the p values on an ogive function are converted to z values by referring to a table of the normal curve, it must be found that z is a linear function of X. Consequently, a psychometric function where p is plotted against X can be identified as an ogive if the relationship between p and X becomes linear when p values are expressed as z scores.

TABLE 2.1
Proportion of Detections and Corresponding z Scores for Various Stimulus
Intensity Values (Hypothetical Data)

Stimulus intensity (ϕ)	Proportion detected	z score
4	.04	−1.75
6	.07	−1.48
8	.13	−1.13
10	.31	−.50
12	.55	+.13
14	.66	+.41
16	.78	+.77
18	.93	+1.48
20	.98	+2.05

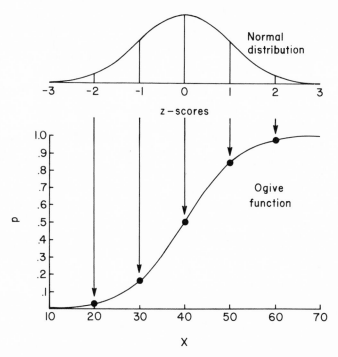

FIGURE 2.2   Derivation of an ogive function from the normal distribution curve. Each point on the ogive specifies the proportion of the total area under the normal distribution that is below a specific point.

In our hypothetical problem the proportion of detections expressed as a z score or plotted on a normal probability ordinate is seen to be a linear function of intensity, and therefore the ogive assumption seems correct (Figure 2.3). A straight line can be drawn by eye through the data points to obtain the psychometric function. Given that threshold is defined as a stimulus that is detected on half of the trials the measured threshold is the stimulus value for a z score of zero.

The psychometric function can be determined more precisely by determining the best-fitting straight line with a mathematical technique known as the *method of least squares*. In this method the constants a and b of a straight-line equation $y = a + bx$ are determined. The resulting equation describes a line through the data points which minimizes the squared deviations of the empirical y values from the line. The following equations should be used to determine a and b:

$$a = \frac{(\Sigma\, X^2)\,(\Sigma\, Y) - (\Sigma\, X)\,(\Sigma\, XY)}{N(\Sigma\, X^2) - (\Sigma\, X)^2}\ , \qquad (2.1)$$

$$b = \frac{N(\Sigma\, XY) - (\Sigma\, X)\,(\Sigma\, Y)}{N(\Sigma\, X^2) - (\Sigma\, X)^2}\ . \qquad (2.2)$$

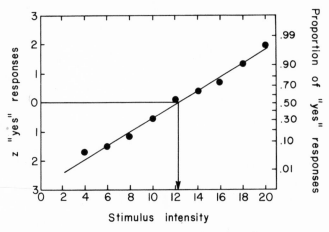

FIGURE 2.3   Psychometric function in which the proportions of ''yes'' responses are expressed as z scores or are plotted on a normal probability ordinate. The linearity of the function indicates that the relation between the proportion of detections and stimulus intensity is an ogive.

In our particular problem X would be the ϕ value, Y would be the corresponding z-score value, and N would be the number of pairs of ϕ and z-score values.

When a and b have been calculated, the equation for a straight line that best fits the plot of z scores against stimulus intensity is given by the formula

$$z = a + b\phi. \tag{2.3}$$

The ϕ values for particular z scores can be determined by

$$\phi = \frac{z - a}{b}. \tag{2.4}$$

The threshold value would then be determined by solving for ϕ when $z = 0$.

Difference Thresholds

The method of constant stimuli can also be used to measure difference thresholds. The observer's task is to examine pairs of stimuli and to judge which stimulus produces a sensation of greater magnitude. One of the stimuli of the pair has a fixed value and is called the *standard stimulus* (St). The value of the other stimulus, called the *comparison stimulus* (Co), is changed from trial to trial, being sometimes greater than, sometimes less than, and sometimes equal to the value of the standard stimulus. Usually five, seven, or nine values of the comparison stimulus, separated by equal distances on the physical scale, are employed. The values of the comparison stimuli are chosen so that the stimulus of greatest magnitude is almost always judged greater than the standard and the stimulus of least magnitude is almost always judged less than the standard. There are usually an equal number of

· comparison stimulus values above and below the value of the standard stimulus. In a random sequence, each of the comparison stimuli is paired several times with the standard stimulus and the observer reports which stimulus has the greater sensory value.

One might think that ideally standard and comparison stimuli should be presented together in space and time for optimal discriminability. This is impossible, however, because sensations occurring at the same time and initiated at the same receptive areas would blend together and become completely indiscriminable. Therefore the two stimuli must be presented to different receptive areas at the same time, or to the same receptive areas, but at different times. The particular circumstances of an experiment usually determine whether the stimuli are presented simultaneously or successively and to the same or different receptive areas. In experiments on visual brightness discrimination, for example, stimuli are often presented simultaneously to adjacent areas of the retina; but loudness discrimination is frequently measured by successively presenting the standard and comparison stimuli.

The necessity of presenting stimuli for comparison to different receptors or at different times may lead to certain errors of measurement unless special precautions are taken in the designing of the experiment. If stimuli are presented to different receptive areas, judgments may be affected by differences between the receptive areas as well as differences between stimuli. In other words, it may be difficult or impossible to conclude anything about an observer's ability to discriminate stimuli. To control for the effects of the *space error,* the standard stimulus may be presented on half of the trials to one receptor area and on half of the trials to the other receptor area. In an experiment on the discrimination of line length, for example, the standard line would be presented equally often to the left and right of the comparison line so that the effects of spatial location would be neutralized when the DL (difference threshold) was determined. A *time error* may also confound experimental results when the standard and comparison stimuli are presented successively. In one form of the time error the proportion of times the comparison stimulus is judged greater than the standard stimulus is found to be higher when it is presented second than when it is presented first. Successive presentation makes it necessary for the observer to compare the second stimulus with the memory image of the first. In one interpretation of the time error it is assumed that since the memory image may rapidly fade, the first stimulus may be judged less than the second stimulus even though the physical intensities of the two stimuli are identical. Again, since the aim of the discrimination experiment is to study the ability of observers to detect differences in stimuli, certain measures must be taken to eliminate the biasing effects of time errors. The most common procedure is to present the standard stimulus first on half of the trials and second on the other half of the trials. The method of counterbalancing spatial location or temporal order of standard and comparison stimuli is based on the assumption that when the results from all of the trials are combined the effects of the space or time errors will cancel, providing an unbiased estimate of the DL.

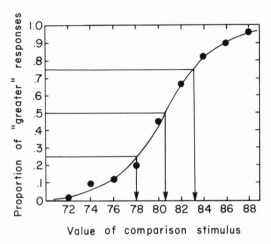

FIGURE 2.4   Typical psychometric function obtained when the difference threshold is measured by the method of constant stimuli. An ogive curve has been fitted to the points.

To illustrate the application of the method of constant stimuli, consider a hypothetical example where the purpose of the experiment is to measure the DL for weight discrimination when the standard stimulus is 80 gm and the comparison stimuli are 72, 74, 76, 78, 80, 82, 84, 86, and 88 gm. In this kind of experiment care is taken to make the weights identical in size and shape so that the observer's discrimination will be based exclusively on heaviness. A blindfolded observer is asked to lift a weight placed in his hand. After the weight is removed he is required to lift a second weight and to compare it with his impression of the first. Since the stimuli are presented successively, it is necessary to control for the effects of time errors by presenting the standard stimulus (80-gm weight) first and the comparison stimulus second on half the trials and by using the reverse order on the other half of the trials. The standard stimulus is paired with each comparison stimulus a sufficient number of times to obtain a reliable estimate of the proportion of "greater" responses for each comparison stimulus. The psychometric function with the proportion of greater responses plotted against values of the comparison stimuli is usually an ogive curve, as seen in Figure 2.4.

In a discrimination experiment, where the observer is required to say "less" or "greater" even when he cannot perceive any difference, we expect the observer to say greater and less about an equal proportion of times when no discrimination can be made. This .5 point on the psychometric function is called the *point of subjective equality* (PSE), and represents the value of the comparison stimulus which over a large number of trials is subjectively equal to the standard stimulus. In most cases the PSE does not correspond exactly to the physical value of the standard stimulus. In our present example the standard was 80 gm, but the PSE was 80.6 gm. The difference between the standard stimulus and the PSE is a psychophysical quantity called the *constant error* (CE):

$$CE = PSE - St. \qquad (2.5)$$

A constant error reflects the effects of some uncontrolled factor which systematically influences that which is being measured, making numbers either too high or too low by a certain amount. Space and time errors are constant errors since they systematically affect the observer's judgments. In the present example a large negative constant error would probably occur if the standard weight were always presented first and the comparison weight second. The proportion of "greater than" responses for all comparison stimuli would tend to be too high because of a tendency to underestimate the sensory magnitude of the previously presented standard stimulus. The PSE would therefore have a value lower than that of the standard stimulus.

Because the PSE represents a complete lack of discrimination and because 0 or 1.0 greater than responding is perfect discrimination, the intermediate proportion points of .25 and .75 have been used to find the DL. It is possible to determine two DLs, an upper and a lower. The upper difference threshold (DL_u) is the stimulus range from the PSE to the .75 point. In our example, $DL_u = 83.3 - 80.6 = 2.7$ gm. The difference between the .25 point and the PSE yields a lower difference threshold (DL_l) of 2.6 gm. The method provides a measurement of one DL above the PSE and one below; therefore the two are often averaged to give one DL for a particular standard stimulus.

The steepness of a psychometric function depends on the observer's differential sensitivity. By the manner in which the DL is derived from plotted data it should be evident that psychometric functions with steep slopes yield small DLs. Therefore the slope of the psychometric function and the DL are sometimes used interchangeably as measures of sensitivity.

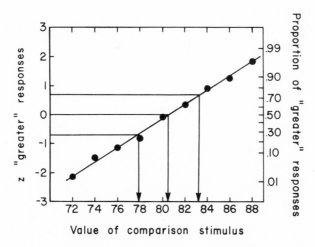

FIGURE 2.5 Psychometric function for the measurement of the difference threshold in which the proportions of "greater" responses are expressed in z scores or are plotted on a normal probability ordinate. The linearity of the function indicates that the relation between the proportion of greater responses and the value of the comparison stimulus is an ogive.

As was true for measuring absolute thresholds, the psychometric function for the difference threshold can be expressed in z-score units as well as in response proportions. The advantage of the z-score plot, again, is in the ease of curve fitting, since the data points almost always form a straight line. The linear z-score psychometric function of Figure 2.5 indicates that our hypothetical data have the ogival form of the cumulative normal distribution. When this is obtained experimentally the most common interpretation is that fluctuations in differential sensitivity are normally distributed.

The line can be fitted to the data by eye or by a more precise technique such as the method of least squares. The PSE corresponds to a z score of zero. By drawing vertical lines from the psychometric function when z is $-.67$ (.25 point) and $+.67$ (.75 point) the values of the lower and upper DLs can be determined. If the values of a and b for the equation $z = a + b(Co)$ have been calculated by the method of least squares, then the Co values corresponding to z values of zero, $-.67$ and $+.67$, can be determined by the equation

$$Co = \frac{z - a}{b}.$$ (2.6)

METHOD OF LIMITS

The method of limits is perhaps the most frequently used technique for determining sensory thresholds. It is an extremely efficient means of threshold measurement and, if proper controls are used to correct for certain constant errors characteristic of the method, satisfactory results are usually obtained. The method is less precise than the method of constant stimuli, but it is far less time consuming and therefore used much more extensively. Furthermore, in choosing the values to be used when applying the method of constant stimuli, a few minutes taken to estimate the location of the threshold by the method of limits would be well spent.

Absolute Thresholds

In the measurement of absolute thresholds by the method of limits the experimenter starts by presenting a stimulus well above or well below threshold; on each successive presentation the threshold is approached through changing the stimulus intensity by a small amount until the boundary of sensation is reached. The stimuli are manipulated in either an *ascending series* or a *descending series*. If the series is ascending, the experimenter begins by presenting a very weak subthreshold stimulus to the observer. On each successive trial the intensity of the stimulus is increased by a small amount until the observer eventually reports the presence of the sensation; at this point the series is terminated. A descending series consists of decreasing the value of the stimulus in successive steps until the observer reports the disappearance of the sensation. Each transition point obtained in a number of ascending and descending series can be considered an estimation of the threshold, and the threshold is the average of these values.

The method of limits is often used in audiometry, the measurement of hearing, to determine the absolute threshold for hearing pure tones of various frequencies. Measurement of the threshold for perception of a 1000-Hz tone might be accomplished by applying a 1000-Hz signal generated by a pure tone oscillator to earphones worn by an observer. The intensity of the signal, as measured in decibels (dB), could be varied systematically by the experimenter. Typical results of the determination of an observer's hearing threshold for a 1000-Hz tone are shown in Table 2.2. Alternate ascending (A) and descending (D) series were administered for a total of ten series. The transition point between sensation and no sensation is taken as the point on the physical dimension midway between the stimuli for the last "no" response and the first "yes" response in the case of an ascending series or the last "yes" response and the first "no" response for a descending series. The mean of the transition points was 4.1 dB and the variability was considerable—the highest value being 5.5 dB and the lowest 2.5 dB. Here

TABLE 2.2
Determination of the Absolute Threshold for Hearing by the Method of Limits[a]

Stimulus intensity (dB)	A	D	A	D	A	D	A	D	A	D
10						Y				
9		Y				Y				Y
8		Y				Y				Y
7		Y			Y	Y				Y
6		Y		Y	Y	Y		Y		Y
5	Y	Y		Y	N	Y	Y	Y		Y
4	N	Y	Y	N	N	N	N	Y	Y	N
3	N	N	N		N		N	Y	N	
2	N		N		N		N	N	N	
1	N		N		N		N		N	
0	N		N				N		N	
−1	N		N				N			
−2	N						N			
−3	N						N			
−4	N									
−5	N									
−6	N									
−7	N									
−8	N									
−9	N									
−10	N									
Transition points =	4.5	3.5	3.5	4.5	5.5	4.5	4.5	2.5	3.5	4.5

[a]Mean threshold value = 4.1

again, as is the case for the method of constant stimuli, the observer's behavior is characteristically variable.

Two constant errors may influence results obtained in using the method of limits. Since the stimulus is gradually changed in the direction of threshold over several trials, there may be a tendency for an observer to develop a habit of repeating the same response. This habit may result in his continuing to make the response for a few trials after the threshold point has been reached. The constant errors resulting from this tendency are called *errors of habituation* and affect the data by falsely increasing ascending thresholds and decreasing descending thresholds. In opposition to this constant error, an observer may prematurely anticipate the arrival of the stimulus at his threshold and report that the change has occurred before it really has, thus making *errors of expectation*. In this case ascending thresholds will be deceptively low and descending thresholds too high. If errors of habituation and expectation were of equal magnitude they would cancel each other, but this is unlikely in most experimental situations. A technique to prevent anticipatory tendencies is to vary the starting point for successive series so that the observer does not expect a certain number of trials to be necessary for reaching his threshold. To minimize habitual tendencies experimenters often try to avoid the use of excessively long trial series. Preliminary training and careful instructions may help to eliminate, or at least to minimize, the effects of these tendencies.

Difference Thresholds

The method of limits is also frequently used to measure difference thresholds. Standard and comparison stimuli are presented in pairs, and on successive presentations the comparison stimulus is changed by a small amount in the direction of the standard stimulus. If the standard is a 20-dB tone, the experimenter might start with a 15-dB tone and move in .5-dB increments or start with a 25-dB tone and move in .5-dB decrements. During each series, whether ascending (A) or descending (D), two transition points are obtained which are termed the *upper limen* (L_u) and *lower limen* (L_1). The upper limen is the point on the physical dimension where "greater" responses change to "equal" responses. Similarly, the lower limen is the point where the "less" responses change to "equal" responses. If an ascending series is given, for example, the first tone would be obviously weaker than the standard and the observer would say "less." He would continue to say "less" until the experimenter had increased the comparison stimulus sufficiently to be indiscriminable from the standard, at which point the observer would say "equal." The physical value of the stimulus at this point would define the lower limen. As the experimenter further increased the intensity of the comparison stimulus, the observer would continue to say "equal" until the comparison stimulus became discriminably louder than the standard. His response would then change to "greater," which would establish the upper limen and end the series.

TABLE 2.3
Determination of the Difference Threshold for Hearing by the Method of Limits[a]

Stimulus intensity (dB)	A	D	A	D	A	D	A	D	A	D
24.5						G				
24.0		G				G		G		
23.5		G				G		G		G
23.0		G		G	G	G		G		G
22.5		G	G	G	E	G	G	G		G
22.0	G	E	E	G	E	G	E	G	G	E
21.5	E	E	E	E	E	G	E	E	E	E
21.0	E	E	E	E	E	E	E	E	E	E
20.5	E	E	E	E	E	E	E	E	E	E
20.0	E	E	E	E	E	E	E	E	E	E
19.5	E	E	E	E	E	E	E	E	E	E
19.0	E	E	E	E	E	E	E	E	E	E
18.5	E	L	E	E	E	E	E	E	E	E
18.0	E		E	L	E	L	E	L	E	E
17.5	L		L		E	L	L		L	L
17.0	L		L		L	L	L		L	
16.5	L		L		L	L	L		L	
16.0	L				L				L	
15.5	L				L				L	
Upper limen	21.75	22.25	22.25	21.75	22.75	21.25	22.25	21.75	21.75	22.25
Lower limen	17.75	18.75	17.75	18.25	17.25	18.25	17.75	18.25	17.75	17.75

[a]Interval of uncertainty = IU = $\bar{L}_u - \bar{L}_l$ = 22.00 − 17.95 = 4.05. Difference limen = DL = ½IU = ½(4.05) = 2.025. Point of subjective equality = PSE = ½($\bar{L}_u + \bar{L}_l$ = ½(22.00 + 17.95) = 19.97.

Table 2.3 contains results of an experiment in which the DL was measured for loudness when the standard stimulus was a 20-dB, 1000-Hz tone. The mean upper limen was 22.00 dB, indicating that on the average the observer perceived a 22.00-dB tone as just noticeably louder than a 20-dB tone. On the average, a tone of 17.95 dB (the lower limen) was perceived as just noticeably weaker than the 20-dB standard. The range on the stimulus dimension over which an observer cannot perceive a difference between the comparison and standard stimuli is called the *interval of uncertainty* (IU) and is computed by subtracting the mean lower limen ($\bar{L}_l$) from the mean upper limen ($\bar{L}_u$). The best estimate of the difference limen (DL) is taken as half the IU, and the point of subjective equality is obtained by finding the midpoint of the IU [PSE = ½($\bar{L}_u + \bar{L}_l$)]. In the present example the IU was 4.05; the DL is therefore half of this value, or 2.025, and the PSE is 19.97.

It is important to note that in measuring the DL, as in measuring absolute thresholds by this method, care must be taken to control for the effects of errors of habituation and expectation. In addition, since two stimuli are presented to the observer for comparison when the method is used to measure DLs, controls must be employed to prevent contamination of results by space and time errors. The same procedures suggested for use with the method of constant stimuli—counterbalancing spatial position or temporal order of stimuli—should also be sufficient when using the method of limits.

Variations of the Method of Limits

A variation of the method of limits is the *up-and-down* or *staircase method* (Cornsweet, 1962). One begins by presenting a sequence of stimuli which progressively increase or decrease in value. When the observer changes his response, the stimulus value is recorded and the direction of the stimulus sequence is reversed from ascending to descending, or vice versa. For example, when the observer first says "yes" in an ascending sequence, the experimenter will start a descending sequence which is terminated when the observer first says "no," at which time the sequence is reversed again. This procedure continues until a sufficient number of response-transition points has been recorded. The threshold is taken as the average of the transition points. This method saves time because stimuli that are much below or above threshold are never presented. Because of its efficiency the staircase method has been of value to clinicians.

The staircase method resembles the *threshold tracking method* used by von Békésy (1947) with an audiometer to test hearing. However, in the threshold tracking method the stimulus is continuously variable, the observer controls its intensity, and the results are usually recorded by a graphic recorder. The observer's task is to track his own threshold continuously. As long as the observer presses a switch the stimulus will gradually decrease in intensity and as long as he keeps the switch open the stimulus will gradually increase in intensity. If he starts by pressing the switch he will keep it depressed until the sensation first disappears, at which time he releases the switch causing the intensity of the stimulus to begin to gradually increase. When the stimulus is again detected the observer presses the switch and keeps it closed until he can no longer detect the stimulus. The observer continues in this manner until his performance becomes stable for some specified period of time. A record of the up and down fluctuations in stimulus intensity produced by the observer's tracking is made by a graphic recorder. A sample record from a von Békésy audiometer is seen in Figure 2.6. Since the output of the audiometer that is applied to an earphone can be made to change frequency continuously over a 125–10,000-Hz range in a period of a few minutes, a complete record of the observer's threshold as a function of frequency can be made in a very short time. The method has been extremely useful in clinical audiometry but it also has been successfully adapted to measure thresholds in modalities other than hearing.

The method of threshold tracking has been useful in animal psychophysics inasmuch as animals can be trained to make a different response when a stimulus is

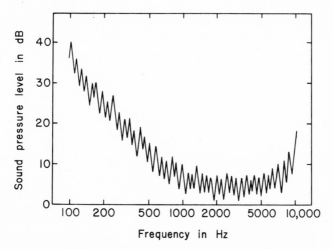

FIGURE 2.6   Record of observer's responses as he continuously tracked his auditory threshold as the frequency changed.

detected than when it is not detected. After training pigeons to peck one key when a light was visible and another key when it was not visible, Blough (1958) obtained a dark-adaptation curve as the bird tracked its threshold in a dark chamber following exposure to intense light (Figure 2.7).

Another variation of the method of limits is the *forced choice method* first used by Blackwell (1953) for experiments on vision and by Jones (1956) for experiments on taste and smell. The observer's task is to choose among several carefully

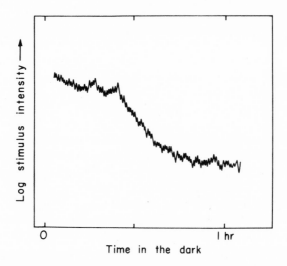

FIGURE 2.7   Record of pigeon's responses during dark adaptation. (From Blough, 1958. Copyright 1958 by the Society for the Experimental Analysis of Behavior, Inc.)

specified observations, only one of which contains the stimulus. Observations may be sequential, as in *temporal-forced choice,* where observations are made one after another, or simultaneous, as in *spatial-forced choice,* where observations are made of several different locations. In a four-interval, temporal-forced choice experiment the observer would be required to make a series of four observations followed by a choice of which observation contained the stimulus. If the task became a spatial-forced choice task the observer might be required to view a display on which a stimulus would be presented in one of four quadrants and would be asked to choose which quadrant contained the stimulus. In both cases, stimulus intensity is increased by discrete steps on successive trials. The stimulus intensity corresponding to a specified performance level, such as two correct responses in succession, is defined as the threshold. The method can be used to measure the DL as well as the absolute threshold by presenting the comparison stimulus for one observation and the standard stimulus for all other observations. The observer is required to pick the comparison stimulus from among the several observations.

METHOD OF ADJUSTMENT

The method of adjustment has been used primarily for measuring difference thresholds but can also be applied to problems of absolute sensitivity. One of the main features of this method is the opportunity afforded an observer to control the changes in the stimulus necessary to measure his threshold.

Absolute Thresholds

In measuring absolute thresholds by the method of adjustment, the general procedure is to set the stimulus intensity level either far below or far above threshold and to have the observer either increase the intensity level until it is just perceptible or decrease the intensity until the sensation just disappears. Usually the stimulus intensity is continuously variable. Experiments generally require an observer to make a fairly large number of ascending and descending settings, and the absolute threshold is taken as the mean of these settings. One of the advantages of this method is that it gives the observer an unusually large amount of active participation in the experiment, which may help to prevent boredom and therefore to maintain high performance.

Difference Thresholds

When the method of adjustment is applied to measuring difference thresholds, the observer is instructed to adjust a comparison stimulus until it seems equal to some standard stimulus. This is often called the *method of average error,* since the

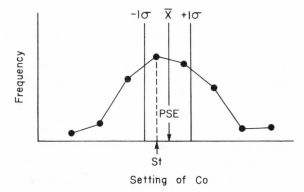

FIGURE 2.8   Frequency distribution of setting of the comparison stimulus when the method of adjustment is used to measure the difference threshold. The mean of the distribution is the point of subjective equality and the standard deviation is used as the difference threshold.

experimenter is primarily interested in the discrepancies between the observer's settings of the comparison stimulus and the physical value of the standard stimulus. In a large number of settings an observer will sometimes underestimate and sometimes overestimate the standard by a considerable amount, but typically most of the matches tend to cluster closely around the value of the standard stimulus. As is true for the hypothetical data of Figure 2.8, a frequency distribution of the results will most likely be symmetrical and, if enough trials have been administered, will approximate a normal distribution.[1] The mean ($\bar{X}$) of this distribution (the mean of all the settings of the comparison stimulus) is the PSE. If there are no constant errors, the PSE should correspond closely to the value of the standard. The constant error (CE) is computed by subtracting the value of the standard from the PSE (CE = PSE − St).

Whether or not there is a constant error, the frequency distribution will have a high degree of central tendency when discrimiation is good; when discrimination is poor the settings will tend to be quite variable. A measure of dispersion such as the standard deviation (σ), therefore, is used as the DL. One frequently used formula for the standard deviation is

$$\sigma = \sqrt{\frac{N \sum X^2 - (\sum X)^2}{N^2}}. \qquad (2.7)$$

where X is the value of a particular Co setting and N is the number of settings. If the standard deviation is large it would indicate that over a wide range of stimulus values the two stimuli appeared equal and that discrimination was poor. If dis-

[1] A normal distribution of comparison stimulus setting is sometimes obtained only after some transformation is made on the stimulus units. Often a logarithmic transformation of the stimulus values results in a normal distribution of responses.

crimination is precise, the two stimuli will appear equal only over a narrow range of stimulus values. Judgments will tend to cluster together, and the standard deviation of the distribution of judgments will be relatively small.

The method of adjustment is difficult to apply when stimuli are not continuously variable and when pairs of stimuli cannot be presented simultaneously. When stimuli are varied in steps rather than continuously, measuring the DL is somewhat inaccurate. When the standard stimulus must be presented first and is followed by the comparison stimulus for the observer to adjust, it is impossible to counterbalance or measure stimulus order effects. A final shortcoming of the method results from giving the observer control of the stimulus: maintaining constant conditions during threshold measurement may thereby be made difficult.

APPLICATION OF CLASSICAL PSYCHOPHYSICAL METHODS TO PROBLEMS OF STIMULUS MATCHING

A stimulus critical value function in which absolute threshold is plotted against some property of the stimulus can be thought of as an *equal sensation contour*. The function describes how stimulus intensity must be adjusted to maintain sensory intensity at absolute threshold as other properties of the stimulus are changed. Figure 1.10 illustrates how sound pressure must be changed in order to keep the sensory magnitude of the sound at a just audible level as the frequency of the stimulus is changed. Often it is of interest to determine an equal sensation contour for suprathreshold levels of stimulation. In the case of hearing the function would specify the sound pressure at various frequencies necessary to keep the psychological loudness of the sound at some constant level.

Figure 2.9 illustrates equal loudness contours obtained by Robinson and Dadson (1956). Each contour represents a different loudness level. Loudness level, in units called phons, is the sound pressure level in dB of a 1000-Hz tone which sounds equal in loudness to a given tone. In determining equal loudness contours, a 1000-Hz tone is set to a particular loudness level and the intensity of a comparison tone of another frequency is adjusted so that its loudness matches that of the standard 1000-Hz tone of fixed intensity. This procedure is repeated for a number of comparison tones of different frequencies and the plotted results constitute one equal loudness contour. The results of Robinson and Dadson indicate that to maintain sound at the same loudness level both low- and high-frequency tones must be considerably more intense than those in the midrange of frequencies. The shapes of the equal loudness contours are not unlike that of the threshold curve measured in a free field situation as indicated by the minimal audible field (MAF) curve of Figure 2.9. However, it can be seen that the equal loudness contours become somewhat flatter at higher loudness levels. The results of this experiment indicate that the relative deficiency of the auditory system at low frequencies is

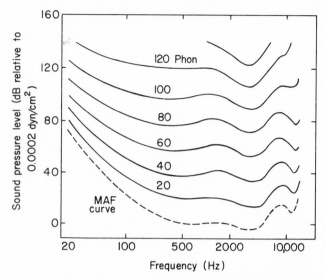

FIGURE 2.9   Equal loudness contours. Each curve describes the intensity levels to which tones of various frequencies must be adjusted to keep loudness constant. Each curve was obtained at a different loudness level. (From Robinson & Dadson, 1956. Copyright 1956 by the Institute of Physics.)

much more severe at low intensity levels of stimulation. For this reason high quality stereophonic sound equipment is usually designed to produce a relatively more intense bass response when the volume control is turned down.

Perhaps the method of adjustment provides the most efficient technique for determining an equal sensation contour. As in measuring the DL, an observer is required to adjust the value of a comparison stimulus to match that of the standard stimulus. The values plotted on the equal sensation contour would consist of PSE values for several different stimuli that had been matched to the standard stimulus. The PSE values could also be obtained by other psychophysical methods such as the method of limits or the method of constant stimuli.

In constructing equal sensation contours, psychophysical matching procedures are employed to determine the stimulus values necessary to keep sensation magnitude constant for various conditions of stimulation. All matches of a number of comparison stimuli are made to a common standard stimulus of constant value. Therefore, each match should yield a value of the comparison stimulus that produces the common sensation magnitude of the standard stimulus. Another equally useful matching method is to employ a single comparison stimulus which is adjusted by the observer to match changing sensation magnitude as some parameter of the standard stimulus is changed. For example, increasing loudness of a tone as its duration is increased could be specified in terms of the intensity of a comparison stimulus of fixed duration needed to match the loudness of tones of fixed intensity and variable duration.

CONCLUSION

The temptation to conclude that sensations can be directly measured by the procedures outlined in this chapter must be avoided; sensations cannot be measured in units of sensory magnitude by using these methods. Instead, sensation must be expressed in terms of the amount of stimulus energy necessary to produce certain changes in the observer's behavior. Sensation is thus treated as a concept which must be defined in terms of stimulus–response relationships. The extent to which the threshold or value of the matching stimulus has been carefully measured under controlled conditions will determine the extent to which the measurements can be validly used to infer the operation of sensory processes within the observer.

3

Psychophysical Theory

The application of the methods described in Chapter 2 yields a quantity, expressed in physical units, called the threshold. The concept of the threshold as an index of absolute and differential sensitivity has been extremely useful in the study of sensory systems. Through the use of this quantity investigators have been able to discover the stimulus conditions to which our sensory systems are the most and the least sensitive. But psychophysicists, not content to work exclusively at this descriptive level, have proposed theories concerning the underlying mechanisms of sensory thresholds. Each theory was proposed to account for empirical data obtained in psychophysical experiments and consists of a description of neurophysiological or psychological processes within the observer which could determine the observer's behavior. The validity of each theory must be evaluated by determining the degree to which precise quantitative deductions from the theory are confirmed by experimental data.

CLASSICAL THRESHOLD THEORY

Early threshold theories were based upon the assumption that the measurements obtained in psychophysical experiments were estimates of a threshold in the observer which could not be measured directly. It was thought that the threshold was a sharp transition point between sensation and no sensation and that a specific, critical amount of neural activity must result from stimulation to exceed threshold. The value of the threshold was assumed to vary with properties of the stimulus (such as duration, area, and wavelength) and also to vary according to the condition of the sensory nervous system (such as state of adaptation and level of background activity). If all the factors affecting the threshold level could be maintained exactly the same from measurement to measurement and if the application of the stimulus energy to the receptors could be exactly replicated, a particular stimulus would be expected either always or never to produce a sensation, depending upon whether the stimulus produced enough neural activity to exceed threshold.

Since the level of neural activity increases with the intensity of the stimulus, the predicted psychometric function using the method of constant stimuli would jump sharply from 0 to 100% detection when the stimulus intensity was set at a level that produced the threshold amount of neural activity (Figure 3.1). Empirical psychometric functions do not follow this form but are typically ogive curves, where the proportion of "yes" responses gradually increases with stimulus intensity. The steplike function of Figure 3.1, however, is a theoretical curve representing predicted results in a hypothetical situation where perfect control is maintained over all of the stimulus and biological variables affecting the level of neural activity in the sensory system. Since perfect control cannot be achieved, the function remains a theoretical formulation and must be considered the idealized outcome if the assumptions of the classical threshold theory are correct.

Inasmuch as it has been impossible to test the theory by examining the relationship between proportion of detections and stimulus intensity when all stimulus and biological factors are perfectly controlled, proponents of the theory are obliged to

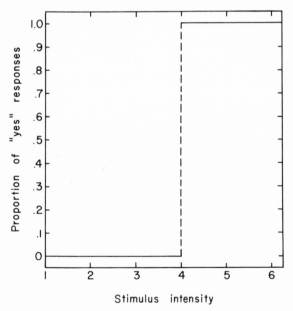

Stimulus   intensity

FIGURE 3.1   Psychometric function predicted from classical threshold theory for an idealized situation in which all stimulus and biological factors are under perfect experimental control. Under these conditions the threshold is represented as the stimulus intensity corresponding to an abrupt increase from zero to one in the proportion of "yes" responses.

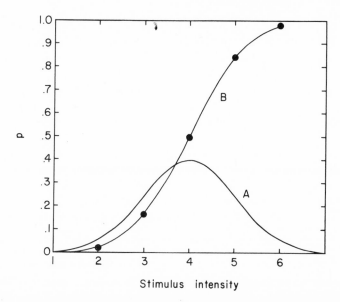

FIGURE 3.2   Derivation of the ogive psychometric function from classical threshold theory. Curve A is a theoretical normal distribution of momentary thresholds. Curve B is the predicted proportion of "yes" responses for each stimulus intensity value. The predicted proportion of "yes" responses corresponds to the proportion of the area under curve A that is below a particular stimulus intensity value.

account for results obtained under imperfect conditions. The basic notion in classical threshold theory is that the threshold varies over time. Although an observer's threshold may be a sharp boundary at a particular instant in time, in an experiment it acts as though it were always changing. Factors affecting the threshold fluctuate randomly from moment to moment, and therefore repeated applications of a stimulus of a particular intensity should result in a detection response only on those trials when the *momentary threshold* is exceeded. The proportion of trials where the momentary threshold is exceeded should increase as an ogival function of stimulus intensity if the variation of momentary thresholds is normally distributed. Curve A of Figure 3.2 illustrates a hypothetical frequency distribution of momentary thresholds expressed in units of stimulus intensity. A detection response should be produced only when stimulus intensity is equal to or greater than the momentary threshold value. The proportion of time that a stimulus will exceed threshold is equal to the proportion of the area under curve A below the value of the stimulus. For example, a weak stimulus of 2 units would exceed momentary thresholds of 2 units or less only 2% of the time because on only 2% the trials will the momentary threshold be lower than 2. The first point on the psychometric function, curve B of Figure 3.2, would be .02 for a stimulus of 2 units. A stimulus of 3 units should be detected on .16 of the trials, since momentary

thresholds are 3 units or less on 16% of the trials. The second point on the
psychometric function can then be plotted. When stimulus intensity is 4 units, the
momentary threshold will be equal to or less than this value on exactly 50% of the
trials and this stimulus will be detected on .5 proportion of the trials. Thus, the .5
point on the psychometric function corresponds to the mean of the momentary
threshold values. It should now be clear why the early psychophysicists chose 50%
detection as the best estimate of the threshold. The proportion of trials on which
stimulus intensity is equal to or above momentary threshold is .84 for a stimulus of
5 units and .98 for a stimulus of 6 units.

Classical threshold theory is often identified as the *phi–gamma hypothesis,* with
phi referring to the probability of a response and gamma referring to stimulus
intensity. The phi–gamma hypothesis states that the psychometric function in
which response probability is plotted against stimulus magnitude should have the
ogival form of the cumulative normal distribution. The prediction of an ogive
psychometric function follows directly from the assumption that momentary
thresholds are normally distributed over time. The unit of measurement of the
stimulus is sometimes an important consideration when testing the phi–gamma
hypothesis because intensity can sometimes be measured on several different
physical scales which are not always linearly related to each other. Sound energy is
not proportional to sound pressure, for example, but is instead proportional to
sound pressure squared. The cumulative normal distribution cannot possibly
describe the psychometric function both when sound intensity is expressed in
pressure units and when it is expressed in energy units.

Which unit of stimulus intensity is appropriate for testing the theory? Whenever
possible stimulus intensity should be expressed in units that best reflect the
operating characteristics of the sensory system. Thurstone was aware of this
problem as early as 1928. He noted that for classical threshold theory to predict
correctly an ogival psychometric function the stimulus should be expressed in
psychological units instead of in physical units. If fluctuations in sensitivity were
normally distributed along a psychological dimension of intensity they would not
be normally distributed when expressed in units of stimulus intensity unless
stimulus values were transformed to reflect psychological intensity. Thurstone
made the assumption that Fechner's law is correct and proposed the *phi–log–
gamma hypothesis.* According to this hypothesis the psychometric function should
have the ogival form of the cumulative normal distribution when response probability is plotted as a function of log stimulus magnitude. Since the range of stimulus
values is unfortunately so small, the predicted psychometric functions from the
phi–gamma hypothesis and the phi–log–gamma hypothesis are so similar that data
precise enough to differentiate between the two hypotheses have not yet been
obtained.

Because similar ogival psychometric functions have been obtained in detection
and discrimination experiments, classical threshold theory has been applied to the
measurement of the difference threshold. Investigators assumed that the neural
activity for two sensations must differ by some threshold amount to be perceived as

different. The size of the stimulus difference required to exceed threshold was assumed to vary randomly from trial to trial, and therefore the probability of detecting a difference should increase as an ogival function of the size of the stimulus difference. A detailed description of the application of classical threshold theory to the problem of sensory discrimination can be found in Boring (1917).

In summary, classical threshold theory was the first attempt to make inferences from psychophysical data about the nature of processes within the observer. Empirically determined psychometric functions have thus been used to make inferences about the underlying nature of sensory mechanisms. The ogival psychometric functions so frequently observed in psychophysical investigations have led to the logical inference that fluctuations in momentary sensory thresholds are normally distributed along some sensory continuum within the observer.

NEURAL QUANTUM THEORY

The central assumptions of classical threshold theory are that fluctuations in threshold are random and that the sensory dimension is continuous. The sensory dimension, however, may not be a continuum but instead may be a series of discrete steps. Under these circumstances psychometric functions for difference thresholds could deviate from the ogival form. In fact, not all psychometric functions obtained during measurement of difference thresholds follow the ogival form. Infrequently obtained psychometric functions, where response probability increases from 0 to 1.0 as a linear function of stimulus magnitude, therefore became the basis of a new theory of sensory discrimination. The *neural quantum theory*, first made explicit by Stevens, Morgan, and Volkmann (1941), is an attempt to derive a linear psychometric function from the assumption that discrimination occurs along a sensory dimension within the observer which is made up of small discrete (quantal) steps. Neurophysiology provides no clear evidence as to the nature of the sensory dimension. In the nervous system receptor potentials and postsynaptic potentials vary as a continuous function of stimulus intensity while action potentials constitute all-or-none responses to changes in stimulus intensity. Neither have any final answers been supplied by psychophysics, but it is significant that the psychometric functions of a handful of investigators are remarkably consistent with the neural quantum concept.

In the simplest form of neural quantum theory it is assumed that an observer can detect an increment in a stimulus only when it is large enough to excite one additional neural unit. The size of the necessary stimulus increment will depend on how much the first stimulus is above the threshold of the last excited neural unit. The greater the excess over the threshold of the last unit, the smaller the required stimulus increment to excite the next unit will be.

The first evidence in support of a quantal theory of discrimination was reported by von Békésy (1930). A standard tone lasting .3 sec was presented to an observer and was followed immediately by a .3-sec comparison tone of a different intensity.

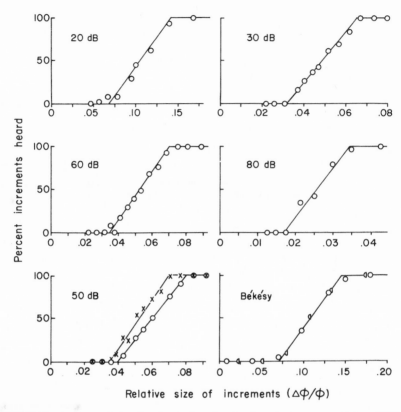

FIGURE 3.3   Psychometric functions for the detection of an intensity increment added to a 1000-Hz tone of five different intensity levels. Von Békésy's data are also presented for the detection of increments (circles) and decrements (half circles). The theoretical curves were drawn with the restrictions that they be straight lines with intercepts that stand in a 2-to-1 relation. (From Stevens, Morgan, & Volkmann, 1941.)

On each trial the observer reported whether or not he detected a loudness difference between the two tones. The linear psychometric functions in this experiment were interpreted as support for the quantal nature of loudness discrimination. Similar results were obtained by Stevens, Morgan, and Volkmann (1941) for both loudness and pitch. Some of the linear psychometric functions found in these experiments are presented in Figure 3.3.

Stevens (1972a) reviewed the data from about a dozen investigations carried out over a span of 40 years. Some 140 steplike functions for auditory loudness and pitch and for three types of visual patterns were reproduced in Stevens' paper as support for neural quantum theory. In the experiments that were reported, observers were presented with a standard stimulus followed immediately by a comparison stimulus which produced an incremental change in stimulation. Observers were required to respond when they detected the incremental change between the first and second stimulus. During a single session sufficient data were obtained to determine the proportion of detections for several sizes of stimulus increment.

Stevens pointed out that there are three features of the data from these experiments which have special importance for neural quantum theory: (a) stimulus increments below a critical size produce no response; (b) above that critical value, the number of increments detected is a linear function of the size of the increment; and (c) increments are always detected when the increment reaches a second critical size, which is twice the size of the largest increment that is never detected. These characteristic results are clearly seen in the data of Stevens, Morgan, and Volkmann (1941) presented in Figure 3.3. The importance of these findings should become clear when the elements of the neural quantum model are understood.

According to the neural quantum model a stimulus of a particular intensity stimulates a certain number of neural quantum units and, as illustrated in Figure 3.4, there may be a stimulus surplus (p) which is insufficient to exceed the threshold of the next unit but is available to combine with a stimulus increment ($\Delta\phi$). When a stimulus increment occurs it adds to p, and if their sum is large enough to excite one or more additional quantal units the stimulus increment is detected.

The present form of the theory requires the assumption that the observer's random sensitivity fluctuations are large compared to the size (Q) of the neural units and slow compared with the time needed for the stimulus increment to be made. The relatively large fluctuations in sensitivity cause considerable variability

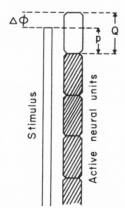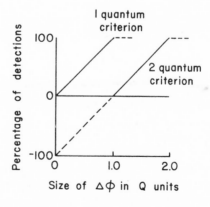

FIGURE 3.4   The diagram on the left illustrates the basic concepts of the neural quantum model. The stimulus activates a certain number of neural units. The stimulus has a surplus p that is insufficient to exceed the threshold of the next unit unless the stimulus increment $\Delta\phi$ is added. (From von Békésy, 1930.) The diagram on the right is the psychometric function predicted for a 2-quantum criterion. (From Stevens, 1972a. Copyright 1972 by the American Association for the Advancement of Science.)

in the *total number* of excited neural units. As a result of this large random variability over a range of many neural quantal units one value for the stimulus surplus p is as likely as any other for the presentation of a particular stimulus and consequently the frequency distribution p for a particular standard stimulus is rectangular. Thus, if Q is the stimulus increment that will always succeed in exciting an additional neural quantum, the value of $\Delta\phi$ that is just sufficient to excite one additional neural quantum is given by

$$\Delta\phi = Q - p. \tag{3.1}$$

A given $\Delta\phi$ will excite an additional neural unit whenever $\Delta\phi = Q - p$. Since p is uniformly distributed over the neural quantum and since the greater the value of $\Delta\phi$ the more likely $\Delta\phi$ plus p is to exceed threshold, the proportion of times that $\Delta\phi$ will excite one additional neural quantum is given by

$$r_1 = \Delta\phi/Q. \tag{3.2}$$

Equation (3.2) indicates that for a particular Q size the proportion of increment detections (r_1) increases as a linear function of $\Delta\phi$. The function starts at the origin and reaches 1.0 when $\Delta\phi$ is equal to Q, as seen in Figure 3.4 for the one-quantum criterion. When $\Delta\phi/Q$ is .8 on 80% of the trials, p will be equal to or greater than the value necessary to exceed threshold when combined with $\Delta\phi$. When $\Delta\phi$ is further reduced so that the value of $\Delta\phi/Q$ is only .5 on only 50% of the experimental trials, the value of p should be equal to or greater than the value necessary to exceed threshold when combined with $\Delta\phi$.

The use of Equation (3.2) predicts the behavior of the observer as he adopts a judgment criterion for reporting an increment in stimulation whenever one additional neural unit is excited. Psychophysical data, however, are more consistent with the hypothesis that the observer reports a stimulus increment when two additional neural quanta are excited. According to Stevens (1972a) the two-quantal criterion is necessary because the random fluctuations in sensitivity produce randomly occurring one-quantum increments and decrements in neural activity. The observer needs to adopt a two-quantum criterion in order to distinguish the presence of the stimulus from the background activity of the nervous system. The prediction from the neural quantum theory for a two-unit threshold is given by

$$r_2 = \frac{\Delta\phi - Q}{Q}. \tag{3.3}$$

In Equation (3.3) the proportion of detections first exceeds zero when $\Delta\phi$ is equal to Q and becomes 1.0 when $\Delta\phi$ is equal to $2Q$ (see Figure 3.4). Thus the value of $\Delta\phi$ when the proportion of detections first becomes 1.0 should be exactly twice the value of $\Delta\phi$ when the proportion of detections first becomes greater than zero. The data reviewed by Stevens (1972a) are remarkably consistent with this prediction.

It is significant that data in support of neural quantum theory have been obtained under a variety of conditions using both auditory and visual stimuli. Stevens argued that the generality of this finding is consistent with the hypothesis that the operation of the neural quantum may be a central neural mechanism of sufficient generality to process information from all sensory modalities under a great variety of stimulus conditions. According to this hypothesis sensory inputs would eventually converge on the same neural center in the brain. The reticular formation of the brain stem is a possible candidate for such a center in that it receives inputs from all sensory modalities. A quantal jump in neural activity level would occur when $\Delta\phi$ is large enough to exceed the threshold of some switching mechanism in the center.

The difficulty of obtaining linear psychometric functions has been attributed to a lack of precise experimental control over such randomly fluctuating factors as the observer's motivation, attention, and fatigue. Since neural quanta are very small, their operation in the detection or discrimination experiment is often masked by the much larger effects of the fluctuation of these uncontrolled factors on the observer's judgments. Fluctuation of the uncontrolled factors is likely to be normally distributed, and the ogive psychophysical function is therefore obtained. Because it is not precisely clear in this instance what constitutes an acceptable experiment, neural quantum theory is difficult to reject. When the data do not fit the theory one can argue that something was wrong with the experiment. Stevens, however, identified some conditions that seem to be necessary for the production of linear psychometric functions:

1. The stimulus must be carefully controlled. When the standard and the comparison stimuli were bursts of white noise and thus varied randomly over time, a normal ogive rather than a linear function was obtained (Miller, 1947). A jittering stimulus, such as white noise which is constantly changing in amplitude and frequency spectrum, should obscure the stepwise quantal function since large random variations between presentation of standard and comparison stimuli would greatly influence the observer's judgments.

2. If the observer is unable to maintain a constant criterion during an experimental session the psychometric function will tend to be an ogive rather than a straight line. It is no easy task to maintain a fixed criterion during a one- or two-hour session in which a thousand or more stimuli are presented. According to Stevens, some observers simply cannot concentrate well enough to produce linear functions. Best results are often obtained when highly motivated investigators serve as observers.

3. If the size of the neural quantum changes within a session the function will become an ogive. In Figure 3.5 are data obtained by Miller and Garner (1944) for the discrimination of loudness increments of a 1000-Hz tone. Plots A and B clearly support the hypothesis of quantal discrimination with a two-quantum criterion. Plot C shows two functions obtained from one observer in two different sessions. The difference between the functions shows that the size of the neural quantum was larger during the second session. As seen in Plot D, averaging the data from the two sessions produces the ogive function. Plot E contains functions for an increment duration of 200 msec (filled points) and 100 msec (unfilled points). The

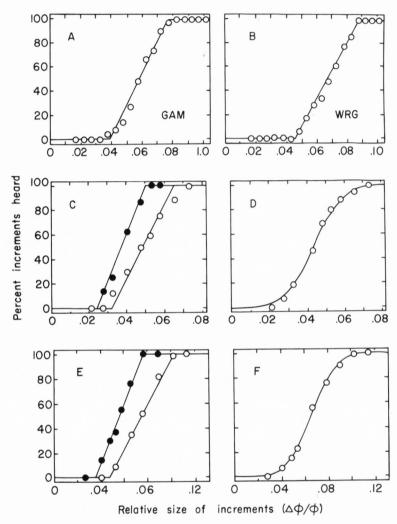

FIGURE 3.5   Plots A and B are psychometric functions of two observers for the detection of an intensity increment in a 1000-Hz tone. Plot C is two psychometric functions for one observer obtained in two different sessions. Plot D is the psychometric function based on the combined data for the two sessions. Plot E contains functions for an increment of 200 msec (filled points) and an increment of 100 msec (open points). Plot F is the function that results from combining the data for the two increment durations. (From Miller & Garner, 1944).

neural quanta for the two conditions appear to be different in size; averaging the data obscures the step functions and produces the ogive seen in Plot F.

4. The transition from the standard to the comparison stimulus must be rapid. If the delay between the two stimuli is long, the observer's sensitivity may not be the same for each stimulus presentation. Under these conditions random changes in

sensitivity will be reflected in an ogive psychometric function. For an adequate test of the neural quantum theory the transition from the standard to the comparison stimulus must be nearly instantaneous.

It is therefore under only the most stringent conditions that we can expect neural quanta, if they exist, to manifest themselves in an observer's performance of a discrimination task. Thus it is not surprising that most psychometric functions have the ogival rather than the linear form. Although Stevens makes a good case for the hypothesis that a well-trained, highly motivated observer under strictly controlled stimulus conditions can make discrimination judgments based on a precise two-quantum criterion, the position of the theory would be made more secure by supporting data from sensory modalities other than vision and audition and by a further delineation of the conditions under which linear psychometric functions are obtained.

Neural quantum theory has been criticized on both methodological and theoretical grounds. Corso (1956, 1973) claims that it is difficult to determine whether the linear psychometric function of neural quantum theory or the classical ogive function is the best-fitting function for a particular set of psychophysical data. The predicted functions do not greatly differ in form; consequently they may fit the same set of data equally well. Furthermore, an adequate statistical test for discrimination between the two hypotheses is lacking. Corso has also been critical of proponents of neural quantum theory for being unable to specify precisely the essential conditions under which the linear psychometric functions predicted from the theory are obtained.

A more serious criticism of neural quantum theory comes from Wright (1974) who has argued that the special procedures employed by neural quantum theorists bias the observer to be very conservative in reporting weak stimuli. He has shown that the results predicted from neural quantum theory can also be predicted from the theory of signal detection when it is assumed that observers adopt conservative judgment strategies in the neural quantum test situation. The theory of signal detection will be extensively discussed later in this chapter. Furthermore, Wright was able to show that as the observer's judgment strategy becomes more conservative the results predicted from the theory of signal detection more closely approach those predicted from neural quantum theory. Under these conditions it is not possible to decide between the two alternative explanations of the data without further experimental investigation. It is unlikely, however, that the neural quantum question will be adequately answered in the near future. Little research has been conducted on the problem during the last ten years, and with the death of S. S. Stevens the theory is left without a major defender. In a 1973 paper Norman pointed out that the rise of the theory of signal detection has led to an almost complete lack of attention to problems of how observers respond in noise-free situations (Norman, 1973). It is unlikely that a satisfactory answer to the question will come as a side effect in the study of detection and discrimination in noisy situations, since such experiments would surely obscure neural quanta if they do exist. What is needed, and will come with a revival of interest in the problem, are experiments specifically designed to test neural quantum theory.

While neural quantum theory was developed to account for discrimination data obtained in a relatively noise-free situation, the theory of signal detection applies to situations in which the observer must detect weak stimuli presented against a noisy background. In psychophysics today perhaps the most powerful arguments that sensation changes on a continuum rather than in discrete steps come from the proponents of the theory of signal detection. Before describing this theory in detail, some evidence will be presented in support of the hypothesis that, in most situations, an observer's judgments of weak stimuli are not determined by the abrupt discontinuity in neural activity implied by the absolute threshold concept, but instead are determined by an adjustable judgment criterion.

EVIDENCE AGAINST THE THRESHOLD CONCEPT

The old concept of the absolute threshold as a boundary or limit below which no sensation can occur is cast in doubt by the results of many recent psychophysical experiments. It is apparent that threshold measurement does not consist of an observer's simply reporting the presence or absence of sensations. Experimenters have therefore directed their attention to the problem of discovering exactly what it is that observers do when they detect stimuli.

Early psychophysicists assumed a close correspondence between the verbal reports of a well-trained observer and concurrent neurological changes in the sensory system caused by stimulation. They worked to obtain results that were pure sensory functions uncontaminated by factors not directly related to the sensory system (e.g., the observer's attitudes and expectations concerning the task). Experimenters assumed that in a well-controlled psychophysical experiment the probability of a "yes" response [p(yes)] for a particular stimulus presentation was entirely a function of the stimulus and the biological state of the sensory system. Since interest was mainly in the sensory system, this assumption simplified matters considerably. The results of recent experiments, however, indicate that many nonsensory variables, even when well-trained observers are used, strongly influence performance in the detection situation.

One nonsensory variable consistently found to affect the p(yes) is the probability of stimulus occurrence [p(S)]. In the early psychophysical experiments, p(S) was always 1.0, for a stimulus was presented on every trial. It seems likely that even for the most conscientious observers the extremely high expectation of stimulus occurrence associated with presenting a stimulus on every trial would itself influence the probability of saying "yes" when a stimulus is presented. In fact, when p(S) is systematically varied, p(yes) is found to increase with p(S). In such an experiment fairly weak stimuli are typically used, and during a session several hundred trials may be administered. The observer's task is to report whether or not

TABLE 3.1
Response Proportions in a Signal Detection Situation in which Stimulus
Probability is a Variable

$p(S)$	Number of stimulus trials	Number of no stimulus trials		Response	
				Yes	No
.90	180	20	Stimulus	.99	.01
			No stimulus	.95	.05
.70	140	60	Stimulus	.91	.09
			No stimulus	.64	.36
.50	100	100	Stimulus	.69	.31
			No stimulus	.31	.69
.30	60	140	Stimulus	.36	.64
			No stimulus	.09	.91
.10	20	180	Stimulus	.05	.95
			No stimulus	.01	.99

a stimulus occurred on a particular trial. A value of $p(S)$ is chosen and the trials on which the stimulus is presented are determined randomly. Several sessions are usually conducted using different values of $p(S)$.

Consider the possible outcomes of a single trial in the detection situation. When the stimulus is present, the observer may report "yes" (a *hit*) or he may report "no" (a *miss*). On trials when the stimulus is absent, a *false alarm* is made if the observer says "yes" but he makes a *correct rejection* if he says "no." A 2 × 2 table containing the experimentally obtained proportions for each of the four possible outcomes summarizes the results of a series of trials for a particular set of stimulus conditions. In an experiment on $p(S)$ we would have a 2 × 2 table for each of the values of $p(S)$. Table 3.1 shows the kind of results the experiment might yield. We need only consider $p(\text{yes})$, since $p(\text{no})$ is equal to 1.0 minus $p(\text{yes})$ and is therefore not an independent measure of performance in a two-choice situation. It is quite clear that the probability of a "yes" response when the stimulus is present increases as the probability of occurrence of the stimulus is made higher. This relationship has been found to exist for weak, moderate, and strong stimuli.

The relationship between the probability of reporting "yes" when the stimulus is present [$p(\text{yes}|\text{stimulus})$] and the probability of reporting "yes" when it is absent [$p(\text{yes}|\text{stimulus})$] can be illustrated by a graph called a *receiver-operating characteristic curve* or *ROC curve* (Figure 3.6). Each point on the ROC curve represents the data obtained under a specific $p(S)$ condition. Each ROC curve represents data obtained for a stimulus of fixed intensity. Thus, the ROC curve is a means of illustrating the often dramatic effects of a nonsensory factor on performance in the detection task. As seen in Figure 3.6, increasing the stimulus intensity influences the function by making it arch higher, and a decrease in

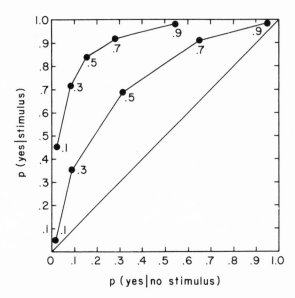

FIGURE 3.6 Receiver-operating characteristic curve. The proportion of "yes" responses when a stimulus is presented is plotted against the proportion of "yes" responses when no stimulus is presented. Each data point corresponds to a different probability of stimulus occurrence. The points on a single curve result from the presentation of a stimulus of a particular intensity.

intensity results in a curve approaching the 45° line. Each individual ROC curve shows the tremendous influence of the observer's expectations about the stimulus.

Since the probability of an observer's "yes" response is affected by his expectancies about the occurrence or nonoccurrence of the stimulus, it is difficult to see how an absolute threshold, if there is one, can be measured using conventional psychophysical methods. For example, psychometric functions are lowered and raised depending on the observer's expectations about the stimulus, and of course the absolute thresholds derived from the functions are different. In other words, the physical value of the stimulus to which the observer says "yes" 50% of the time depends on $p(S)$, a nonsensory variable. Figure 3.7 shows that the psychometric function for the detection of vibration on the fingertip was elevated by increasing $p(S)$ (Gescheider, Wright, Weber, & Barton, 1971). Changing $p(S)$ had a strong biasing effect on the conventional threshold measurement. The threshold was 1.3 μm when $p(S)$ was .7 and 2.3 μm when $p(S)$ was .3. Furthermore, p(yes) when the stimulus is absent is considerably above zero, depending on $p(S)$. According to threshold theory, a well-trained, honest observer should only occasionally report a sensation when a stimulus has not been presented.

When a person is required to indicate the presence or absence of stimuli, whether in the laboratory or in his natural environment, there are always consequences of his response. Consider the person who watches a radar scope for the detection of enemy aircraft. Since the stimulus probability is low, the observer's stimulus expectancy is low and therefore the probability of a correct detection should be low. But since the value of a correct detection and the cost of failing to detect a stimulus are very high, the probability of a hit is kept high and the probability of a miss low. Thus, if the payoff for correct detections and the punishment for misses are made great enough, accurate detection can be maintained even in situations where stimulus occurrence is extremely infrequent. But what happens on occasions when the stimulus is not present? Since the payoff for correctly detecting stimuli is high the radar scope observer will frequently say "yes" in the absence of a stimulus (false alarm). Thus, when response consequences are changed, $p(\text{yes}|\text{stimulus})$ and $p(\text{yes}|\text{no stimulus})$ tend to change together. This principle is also evident when false alarms are punished and correct identifications of stimulus absence are rewarded. In this case the probability of "yes" responding when there is no stimulus is kept low, but likewise the probability of detecting a stimulus by saying "yes" when it is present is low.

If stimulus intensity and stimulus probability are held constant in a psychophysical experiment, an ROC curve can be generated by manipulating the *costs* and *values* in the detection situation. Typically, at the start of an experimental session the observer is told the stimulus probability and payoff conditions. The payoff conditions are specified by a *payoff matrix* such as the one shown in Table 3.2. Money is often used to reward correct responses while loss of money is used to

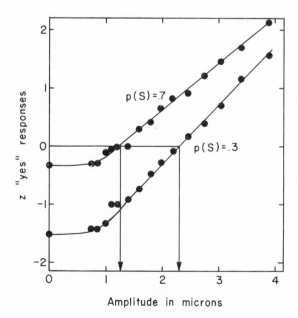

FIGURE 3.7   Psychometric functions for the detection of 60-Hz vibration on the fingertip when $p(S)$ was .3 and when $p(S)$ was .7. It is apparent that $p(S)$ has a large effect on the measured threshold. (From Gescheider, Wright, Weber, & Barton, 1971.)

TABLE 3.2
Payoff Matrix in a Signal Detection Situation

	Response	
	Yes	No
Stimulus	5¢	−2¢
No stimulus	−2¢	5¢

punish incorrect responses. It is the various combinations of costs and values which, by changing the likelihood of reporting a stimulus on a particular trial, result in different data points on an ROC curve. If the value of reporting a stimulus when it is presented is high and the cost of incorrectly reporting it when it is absent is low the observer will exhibit a high probability of reporting stimuli. However, if the cost is high for incorrectly reporting a stimulus and the value is low for correctly reporting it the probability of reporting stimuli will be low. It is signifi- cant that ROC curves that have been generated by changing payoff conditions have exactly the same form as those generated by changing stimulus probability. It seems that the two variables affect the same psychological process. Some inves- tigators have identified this process as *response bias*.

Thus at least two nonsensory factors, stimulus probability and response con- sequences, have been found to have large effects on detection. The evidence for the effects of nonsensory variables on detection performance strongly suggests that the absolute threshold concept does not apply to stimulus detection behavior. If thresholds do in fact exist, it is almost impossible to measure them using classical psychophysical techniques. Human judgments about sensory information are plainly biased by the prevailing conditions of the detection situation.

The early psychophysicists were well aware that response biasing factors such as expectancies and payoff contingencies could contaminate their experimental results. Attempts to control for the effects of biasing factors were made in several ways. Extensive training prior to the experiment which teaches the observer to maintain a consistent approach in making his judgments was one way of obtaining stable data where response bias was held constant, if not eliminated.

Another technique frequently employed to control response bias was the ap- plication of statistical procedures to the data. Early experimenters assumed that detection responses would occur on a certain proportion of trials where the stimulus did not exceed threshold. These detection responses were considered false and were attributed to guessing due to response bias. Such false detection responses were often observed when *catch trials* containing no stimulus were presented. It was assumed that sensory events on catch trials never exceeded threshold and, therefore, that the proportion of false alarms on catch trials would give a good estimation of the guessing rate. The proportion of hits observed in an experiment was thought to be the sum of the proportion of trials where threshold was exceeded by the stimulus and the proportion of trials where the stimulus did not exceed threshold but where the observer guessed anyway and made the detection response. The following equation describes this relationship:

$$p(\text{hits}) = p^*(\text{hits}) + \{p(\text{false alarms})[1 - p^*(\text{hits})]\}. \qquad (3.4)$$

The empirically obtained proportion of hits, $p(\text{hits})$, is equal to the proportion of hits when threshold is exceeded, $p^*(\text{hits})$, plus the proportion of hits when threshold was not exceeded, $p(\text{false alarms})[1 - p^*(\text{hits})]$. The proportion of hits when threshold was not exceeded is the proportion of stimulus trials when threshold was not exceeded, $1 - p^*(\text{hits})$, multiplied by the guessing rate as estimated by the proportion of false alarms on catch trials, $p(\text{false alarms})$. Rearrangement of Equation (3.4) yields a correction for guessing that can be applied to the proportion of hits obtained in an experiment:

$$p^*(\text{hits}) = \frac{p(\text{hits}) - p(\text{false alarms})}{1 - p(\text{false alarms})}. \qquad (3.5)$$

Implicit in the use of this equation to determine the proportion of hits corrected for guessing, $p^*(\text{hits})$, is the assumption of classical psychophysics that a threshold exists. Thus the equation was not merely a statistical tool used by early psychophysicists but was a theoretical statement as well. Fortunately this theoretical statement can easily be tested, since Equation (3.4) states that the

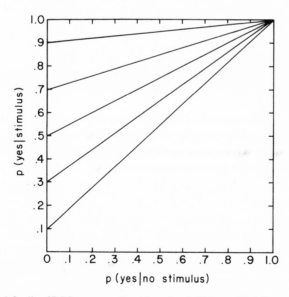

FIGURE 3.8   A family of ROC curves predicted from threshold theory. Each line represents changes in $p(\text{yes} \mid \text{stimulus})$ and $p(\text{yes} \mid \text{no stimulus})$ caused by changes in the guessing rate for the detection of a stimulus of a particular intensity.

relation between the empirically determined proportion of hits and false alarms should be linear. The straight lines start from various values of p(yes|stimulus) when p(yes|no stimulus) is zero. The higher the signal strength, the higher the value of p(yes|stimulus) will be. As the observer increases his guessing rate, p(yes|stimulus) and p(yes|no stimulus) should increase linearly until both become 1.0. A family of ROC curves predicted from threshold theory is seen in Figure 3.8. It is important to note that if Equation (3.5) is applied to the values of p(yes| stimulus) on the ordinate, all of the curves become horizontal lines illustrating the assumed independence of p*(hits) and p(false alarms). It is unfortunate for the proponents of threshold theory that ROC curves have been found to deviate consistently from linearity. The curved shape of empirically obtained ROC curves is thought to constitute powerful evidence for rejection of the threshold concept in favor of a new conception of the observer's behavior in the detection situation (Swets, 1961). We must discard the theory of a threshold that is exceeded only when a stimulus of sufficient strength is presented. But the concept of a lower threshold that is frequently exceeded by spontaneous activity in the nervous system is not in disagreement with the shape of empirical ROC curves. Later in the chapter low threshold theory will be discussed.

THE THEORY OF SIGNAL DETECTION

The discovery that expectancy and payoff have such a dramatic influence upon detection behavior has been incorporated into a new theoretical conception of the detection situation. Tanner and Swets (1954) proposed that statistical decision theory and certain ideas about electronic signal-detecting devices might be used to build a model closely approximating how people actually behave in detection situations. The model is called the *theory of signal detection* (TSD) and is described in detail by Green and Swets (1966).

Signals (stimuli) are always detected—whether by electronic devices or by humans—against a background level of activity. The level of this background activity, called *noise*, is assumed to vary randomly and may be either external to the detecting device or caused by the device itself (e.g., physiological noise caused by spontaneous activity of the nervous system). In the detection situation the observer must therefore first make an *observation* (x) and then make a decision about the observation. On each trial the observer must decide whether x is due to a signal added to the noise background or to the noise alone. When a weak signal is applied, the decision becomes difficult and errors are frequent. One factor contributing to the difficulty of the problem is the random variation of background noise. On some trials the noise level may be so high as to be mistaken for a signal and on other trials it may be so low that the addition of a weak signal is mistaken for noise. This state of affairs can be represented graphically by two probability distributions describing the random variation of noise (N) and the signal plus noise (SN) (Figure 3.9). Since the signal is added to the noise, the average sensory

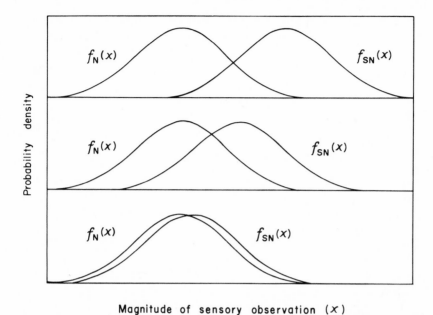

Magnitude of sensory observation (x)

FIGURE 3.9   Theoretical frequency distributions of noise $f_N(x)$, and signal plus noise $f_{SN}(x)$ for three different values of signal strength.

observation magnitude will always be greater for the *signal-plus-noise distribution*, $f_{SN}(x)$, than for the *noise distribution*, $f_N(x)$. However, the difference between the means becomes smaller and smaller as the signal strength is decreased, until the distributions are essentially the same. It is when the two distributions greatly overlap that decision-making becomes difficult.

On a specific trial the observer makes a sensory observation x which consists of a sample from one or the other of the distributions and is required to decide on the correct distribution. The ordinate of $f_N(x)$ gives the *probability density*,[1] or likelihood, of x occurring when only noise is presented. Similarly, the ordinate of $f_{SN}(x)$ gives the likelihood of x occurring when a signal is presented. Each value of x can now be expressed in terms of these two likelihoods or probability densities. For each value of χ there exists a particular *likelihood ratio*, $l(\chi)$, defined as

$$l(x) = \frac{f_{SN}(x)}{f_N(x)} .$$
(3.6)

The likelihood ratio provides the observer with a basis for making a decision since it expresses the likelihood of x in the SN situation relative to the likelihood of x in

---

[1]The term probability density is used because x is continuous rather than discrete. If x had a limited number of discrete values each could be described as having a particular probability of occurrence. In either case the ordinate gives the relative likelihood of a particular value of x.

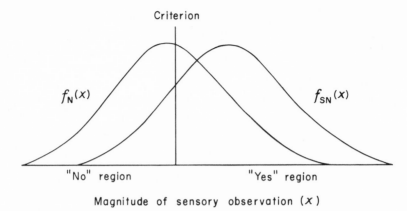

FIGURE 3.10   Theoretical frequency distributions of noise, $f_N(x)$, and signal plus noise, $f_{SN}(x)$. The location of the observer's criterion determines whether a particular sensory observation results in a "no" or a "yes" response.

the N situation. Even though x may vary on several dimensions (e.g., hue, saturation, brightness, shape), each x can be located on a single dimension of likelihood ratio since for each x there exists single values of $f_N(x)$ and $f_{SN}(x)$. Thus, the observer's final decision of whether x is due to N or SN can be based on a single quantity.

One of the assumptions of TSD is that an observer establishes a particular value of $l(x)$ as a cutoff point, or *criterion* (β), and that his decision will be determined by whether or not a particular observation x is above or below the criterion. Proponents of the theory assume that the observer operates by a *decision rule*: when $l(x)$ is equal to or greater than β he should choose SN, and when $l(x)$ is below β he should choose N (Figure 3.10). If the observer properly sets his criterion he will perform optimally in a long series of observations.

Swets, Tanner, and Birdsall (1961) consider the detection situation to be analogous to a game of chance in which three dice are thrown. Two of the dice are ordinary, but the third is a special die with three spots on each of three sides and no spots on the other three sides. When the dice are thrown, the player is told only the total number of spots on all three dice. This information is analogous to the information given for each observation in a detection situation. On the basis of the total number of spots showing, the player must decide whether the unusual die showed a zero or a three. Similarly, in the detection situation the observer must decide whether his observation was a product of noise alone or of signal plus noise. To come out ahead in the long run the player of the dice game would compute the probability of occurrence of each of the possible totals (2 to 12) when the unusual die shows zero and, likewise, the probabilities of each of the totals (5 to 15) when the unusual die shows three. The results could be plotted as two probability distributions and should be thought of as the analogs of the noise and signal-plus-noise distributions (Figure 3.11). Furthermore, as in the detection situation a criterion should be set so that if the total number of spots were greater than some number the player would say "three," and if the total were less than the number he would say "zero." In our example, where the probabilities of a three and a zero are both .50 and the costs and values are the same for the various decision outcomes, the optimal criterion is the point where the two curves cross. In a detection situation, where the stimulus probability is .50 and the costs and values are equal for the various decision outcomes, the optimal criterion is also the point on the observation magnitude dimension where the two distributions cross.

It can be demonstrated mathematically that in the dice game the optimal cutoff point changes when the conditions of the game are changed. For example, if the unusual die were changed to one having three spots on five of the six sides and no spots on only one side, the probability of obtaining three spots would be .83 instead of .50 and the optimal criterion would be lowered. A good player would lower his cutoff point for saying "three." Likewise the optimal criterion would be raised if only one side of the die had three spots and the other five sides had none. In the detection situation, changing the stimulus probability is assumed to have a similar effect on the observer's criterion. In order to perform optimally in a situation where stimulus occurrence is highly probable, an observer will report a signal after a less intense sensory observation than when the stimulus is relatively improbable.

The location of the optimal cutoff point in the dice game is also influenced by changes in the payoff conditions. For example, if the reward is great for correctly saying "three" and the punishment slight for saying "three" when "zero" is correct, the optimal criterion will, of course, be relatively low for saying "three." Rewards and punishments in the detection situation are assumed to have a similar effect on the observer's criterion. A radar scope observer, for instance, maintains a low criterion for reporting signals because of the extreme importance of detecting enemy aircraft and the possible disastrous consequences of failing to do so.

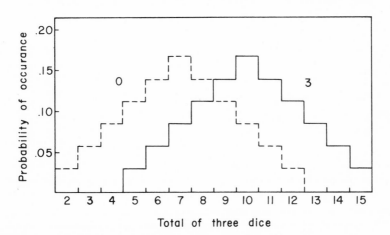

FIGURE 3.11   Probability distributions for the dice game. (From Swets, Tanner, & Birdsall, 1961. Copyright 1961 by the American Psychological Association. Reprinted by permission.)

The criterion set in the dice game will also be influenced by the degree of overlap of the two distributions. If the number of spots on the unusual die is made zero or four instead of zero or three, the distributions will overlap less because the distribution when four is correct will be shifted further up the scale, and the game becomes easier. Since the point where the two distributions cross is also shifted up the scale, the optimal criterion will be higher. This manipulation in the dice game can be translated into an increase in stimulus intensity in the detection situation. When the signal-plus-noise distribution is shifted to a higher point on the observation magnitude dimension, detection becomes easier and the optimal criterion is higher.

In summary, the detection of energy changes in our environment involves, according to TSD, the establishing of a decision rule in the same way as the efficient playing of a game of chance does. The decision rule is the setting of a criterion determining which hypothesis about a given piece of information will be accepted and which rejected. The location of the optimal criterion is a function of (a) the probabilities of the N and SN presentations, and (b) the costs and values for the various decision outcomes.

In the detection situation, where the costs and values of the various decision outcomes and the probability of signal presentation are precisely known, the optimum value of the criterion, β_{opt}, can be calculated by

$$\beta_{opt} = \frac{p(N)}{p(SN)} \times \frac{\text{value(correct rejection)} - \text{cost(false alarm)}}{\text{value(hit)} - \text{cost(miss)}}. \qquad (3.7)$$

β_{opt} is the value of the likelihood ratio, $l(x)$, which, when used as the criterion, will result in the largest possible winnings in the long run; $p(N)$ is the probability of a noise trial; $p(SN)$ is the probability of a signal-plus-noise trial; value is the amount given to the observer for each correct decision; and cost is the amount taken away from the observer for each incorrect observation.

When the value of β, as calculated from the judgments of observers, is compared with β_{opt}, it is generally found that observers do fairly well at optimizing their winnings. An exception to this rule occurs, however, when β_{opt} is very small or very large, in which case β will not be as extreme as β_{opt} and the observer will fail to optimize his winnings. Observers refuse to set extremely low or extremely high criteria even though the conditions of the situation clearly demand such a strategy for optimal performance.

THEORETICAL SIGNIFICANCE OF THE RECEIVER-OPERATING CHARACTERISTIC CURVE

One of the main sources of evidence supporting TSD is the experimental manipulation of variables resulting in data plotted as ROC curves. In fact, shapes of ROC curves for various stimulus intensities can be generated from the postulates of

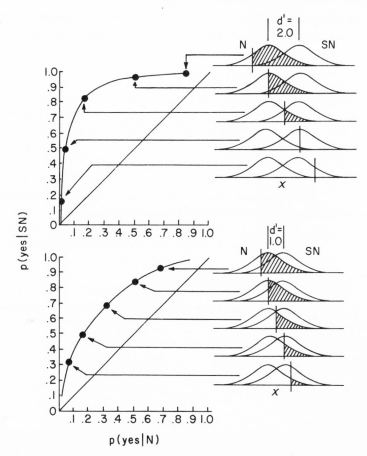

FIGURE 3.12   The relation between ROC curves and theoretical noise and signal plus noise distributions. Variation in the observer's criterion results in different points along the same ROC curve while variation of signal strength produces different ROC curves.

the theory and checked against empirical data. It should be recalled that the high threshold theory was rejected because of its failure to predict empirical ROC curves.

The manner in which ROC curves are predicted from TSD is illustrated in Figure 3.12. The upper ROC curve represents a situation where the signal strength is sufficient to result in only a slight overlap of the N and SN probability distributions. The vertical lines represent the locations of the criterion that might be associated with specific conditions of stimulus probability and payoff. Each point on an ROC curve, according to the theory, is determined by the location of the observer's criterion on the x dimension. If an observation is to the right of the criterion the observer will say ''yes.'' The proportion of the area under the curve to the right of the criterion gives the proportion of "yes" decisions. Therefore, the values of $p(\text{yes/N})$ and $p(\text{yes/SN})$ can be determined by finding the areas under the N and SN distribution curves, respectively, which are located to the right of the criterion. As the criterion is changed from high to low, the values of $p(\text{yes/N})$ and $p(\text{yes/SN})$ change and, when plotted, form an ROC curve. The illustration in the lower half of Figure 3.12 is a predicted ROC curve when the signal strength is so weak as to result in considerable overlap of the N and SN distributions. The finding that the theoretical ROC curves generated in this manner are very similar to those obtained experimentally is strong support for the theory.

In the classical psychophysical experiment the results expressed as thresholds were a function of both stimulus detectability and the location of the observer's criterion. Thus, as a measure of sensitivity to stimuli the threshold may be hopelessly contaminated by changes in the observer's criterion. Such contamination can lead to faulty conclusions about the results of an experiment. For example, there have been cases in which investigators incorrectly attributed large changes in thresholds to changes in the sensitivity of sensory processes. In fact, as revealed by subsequent experimentation, the only thing that had changed was the criterion. TSD and its associated methodology afford a means of independently measuring each of these factors. The theory proposes that d', a measure of detectability, is equal to the difference between the means of the SN and N distributions ($M_{\text{SN}} - M_{\text{N}}$) expressed in standard deviation units of the N distribution (σ_{N}):

$$d' = \frac{M_{\text{SN}} - M_{\text{N}}}{\sigma_{\text{N}}}. \tag{3.8}$$

Because the location of the SN distribution with respect to that of the N distribution is entirely a function of stimulus intensity and properties of the sensory system, d' is a pure index of stimulus detectability which is independent of the location of the observer's criterion.

But how can this theoretical concept of signal detectability be measured? Since different d' values predict different ROC curves, the value of d' in a particular situation can be ascertained by determining on which member of the family of ROC curves an observer's response probabilities fall. A family of ROC curves corresponding to d' values ranging from 0 to 3.0 is seen in Figure 3.13. Because only a limited number of curves are generally presented in such a graph, it is best to use them when only approximate values of d' are needed. Fortunately, simple methods are available for the determination of exact values of d'. The value of d' can be quickly derived from the empirical values of $p(\text{yes/SN})$ and $p(\text{yes/N})$. By the use of a table of the normal distribution found in any textbook on statistics, these proportions are simply converted into z scores. To obtain d', the z score for false alarms is subtracted from the z score for hits. The value of d' can also be determined directly for any combination of false alarm and hit proportions by using a table provided by Elliot (1964).

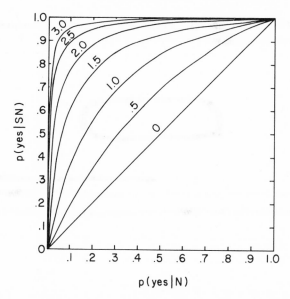

FIGURE 3.13   A family of ROC curves corresponding to d' values ranging from 0 to 3.0.

By reference to a table of the normal distribution, the $p(\text{yes}|\text{SN})$ and $p(\text{yes}|\text{N})$ values of Figure 3.12 can be converted to z scores. If this is done it will be seen that the d' value for each pair of z scores will be 2.0 for the upper graph and 1.0 for the lower graph. Furthermore, it should be clear that for a particular separation of the N and SN distributions the value of d' will remain constant for all possible criterion positions. Thus, an ROC curve is a description of performance changes which are accounted for by a constant d' and a continuously variable criterion.

It has been experimentally demonstrated for both visual stimuli (Swets, Tanner, & Birdsall, 1955) and auditory stimuli (Tanner, Swets, & Green, 1956) that d', as a measure of sensitivity, is not contaminated by the effects of variables which shift an observer's response criterion. Furthermore, d' values, unlike the different threshold values obtained through the use of the various classical psychophysical methods, remain relatively invariant when measured by different experimental procedures. When observers were required to say "yes" or "no" in response to a designated time interval that sometimes contained a signal, d' estimates were found to approximate those obtained when the observer had to choose one of two designated intervals, one of which always contained a signal (Swets, 1959; Tanner & Swets, 1954).

Once the correct ROC curve has been determined, the location of the observer's criterion, β, can be determined by observing exactly where on the ROC curve the point is located. If the point is near the bottom of the ROC curve where the slope is great, the criterion is high; if the point is near the top of the curve where the slope is slight, the criterion is low. The exact value of β is equal to the slope of the ROC curve at a particular point.

To reiterate, β is a value of the likelihood ratio. It is the ratio of the ordinate of the SN distribution at the criterion to the ordinate of the N distribution at the criterion, as follows:

$$\beta = \frac{f_{SN}(x) \text{ at criterion}}{f_N(x) \text{ at criterion}}. \tag{3.9}$$

Figure 3.10 illustrates that moving the criterion to the right increases the value of β and moving it to the left decreases β. A low value of β represents a lax criterion where the observer will be liberal about reporting signals, while a high value of β represents a strict criterion where the observer will be conservative about reporting signals.

The value of β can be calculated from a pair of hit and false alarm rates. The ordinate of the N distribution at criterion can be estimated as the ordinate value given in the table of the normal distribution that corresponds to the false alarm rate. Likewise the ordinate of the SN distribution at criterion is obtained by converting the hit rate into the ordinate value on the normal distribution curve. For example, ordinate values for a false alarm rate of .20 and a hit rate of .85 are .2801 and .2333, respectively:

$$\beta = \frac{.2333}{.2801} = .83.$$

If the investigator wishes to study the effects of a particular variable, he is equipped with a technique for finding out whether the effects of the variable are on detectability or on the location of the criterion. He has only to observe whether systematic changes in the variable result in different points along a single ROC curve or points located on different ROC curves. Also the values of d' and β can be calculated for various experimental conditions. In some experiments manipulation of an independent variable has led to changes in both β and d'.

TESTING THE ASSUMPTIONS OF THE THEORY OF SIGNAL DETECTION

The form of the ROC curve predicted from TSD can be more easily subjected to experimental tests if the values of $p(\text{yes}|\text{SN})$ and $p(\text{yes}|\text{N})$ obtained in an experiment are plotted on the ROC curve as z scores. If the N and SN distributions are normal in form and also have equal variances (σ^2), the ROC curves should be linear with a slope of 1.0 when z scores for hits are plotted against z scores for false alarms. In the normal distribution and equal variance situation, when the criterion is shifted by a particular z score distance on the N distribution, it is also shifted by exactly the same distance on the SN distribution. The linearity prediction follows from the assumption that the N and SN distributions are normal in form. The prediction of a slope of 1.0 follows from the assumption of equal N and SN variances. The prediction from TSD is that ROC curves plotted as z scores should be linear with a slope of 1.0, as in Figure 3.14. The points on the two functions were obtained by converting to z scores the p values plotted in the two ROC curves of Figure 3.12. It is not difficult to determine whether or not experimental results confirm the theory. The standard procedure is to determine the best-fitting straight line for the data plotted as z scores. The use of the method of least squares will provide the best estimate of the intercept and slope of the function. If the data points do not significantly deviate from the function, the assumption of normal distribution is supported. If the slope of the function does not significantly deviate from 1.0, the equal variance assumption is supported.

Empirical ROC curves plotted as z scores are almost always linear and therefore there is rather general acceptance of the hypothesis that the N and SN distributions are normal distributions. This kind of analysis of detection data, however, has also revealed that certain details of the original version of TSD were not correct. For example, the assumption that the N and SN distributions have equal variances is

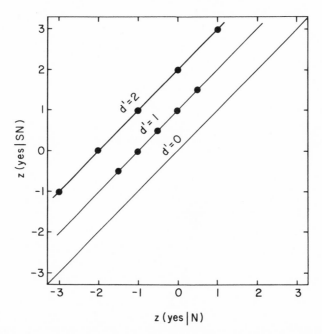

FIGURE 3.14   Receiver-operating characteristic curves plotted in z-score units. The linearity of the functions follows from the assumption that the noise and signal plus noise distributions are normal distributions. If the variances are equal for the noise and signal plus noise distributions the slope of the function should be 1.0.

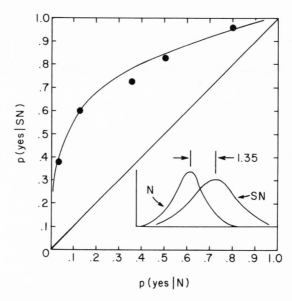

FIGURE 3.15 Receiver-operating characteristic curve for an observer in an experiment on the detection of auditory signals. The asymmetrical ROC curve is consistent with the hypothesis that the noise and signal plus noise distributions are normal in form but have unequal variances. (From Tanner, Swets, & Green, 1956.)

not supported in most experiments. The slope of the ROC curve is frequently found to be less than 1.0. This result is usually explained by assuming that the variance is greater for the SN than for the N distribution. A more general statement of this assumption is that the variance of the SN distribution increases as the mean of the distribution increases.

Figure 3.15 is an ROC curve for an observer in an experiment on the detection of auditory signals (Tanner, Swets, & Green, 1956). Because the ROC curve was asymmetrical, the assumption was made that the standard deviation of the SN distribution (σ_{SN}) was greater than the standard deviation of the N distribution (σ_N). The deviation of the results of this experiment from the equal variance of N and SN distributions can better be seen when the data are plotted as z scores (Figure 3.16). If it is assumed that both N and SN distributions are of normal form, then the reciprocal of the slope of the ROC curve is equal to σ_{SN}/σ_N. The slope of the ROC curve for observer 1 is 1.0, and therefore the N and SN distributions have the same variance since $\sigma_{SN}/\sigma_N = 1.0$. The slope of the ROC curve for observer 2 is .75 and σ_{SN} is greater than σ_N since the reciprocal of .75, the value of σ_{SN}/σ_N, is 1.33.

In cases when the variance of the SN distribution is greater than that of the N distribution the symbol Δm, rather than d', is sometimes used to denote the difference between the means of normal N and SN distributions. Thus, the quantities d' and Δm are symbols for the same measures of signal detectability applied to the cases of equal and unequal variances, respectively.

Note, however, that for observer 2 the value of d', conventionally determined as the value of the difference between $z(\text{yes}|\text{N})$ and $z(\text{yes}|\text{SN})$, is not constant along the ROC curve. In cases where the ROC curve slope is less than 1.0, Δm may be used as the measure of detectability. The value of Δm is equal to the absolute difference between $z(\text{yes}|\text{N})$ and $z(\text{yes}|\text{SN})$ at a point where $z(\text{yes}|\text{SN})$ is equal to 0. Since we start with the mean of the SN distribution [$z(\text{yes}|\text{SN}) = 0$ and $p(\text{yes}|\text{SN}) = .5$] and determine the corresponding z score for yes|N, the value of Δm is expressed in the standard deviation units of the N distribution (σ_N). In the Tanner *et al.* (1956) experiment, Δm for observer 2 was 1.35. Notice that for observer 1 the value of d' is .85 at all points on the ROC curve.

A measure of signal detectability that is sometimes used instead of Δm is d_e'. The value of d_e' is the absolute difference between $z(\text{yes}|\text{N})$ and $z(\text{yes}|\text{SN})$ at a point on the ROC curve where it crosses the negative diagonal. The primary benefit of using this measure is that it gives equal weight to σ_N and σ_SN. In the present example the value of d_e' for observer 2 is 1.23.

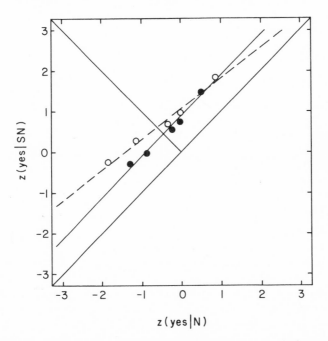

FIGURE 3.16 Receiver-operating characteristic curves plotted in z-score units from an experiment on the detection of auditory signals. The open points are for the observer whose data are plotted in Figure 3.15. The filled points are for another observer. (From Tanner, Swets, & Green, 1956.)

Theodor (1972) has pointed out that the correct equation for calculating d' from the proportion of hits and false alarms is

$$d' = [\sigma_{SN}/\sigma_N] [z(\text{hits})] - z(\text{false alarms}). \qquad (3.10)$$

In cases where the equal variance assumption is made the z score for the proportion of false alarms is simply subtracted from the z score for the proportion of hits. It should be recalled that, as indicated in Equation (3.8), d' is the difference between the means of the N and SN distributions expressed in terms of the standard deviation units of the N distribution (σ_N). In Equation (3.10), σ_{SN}/σ_N represents the scaling factor necessary to convert z(hits) into σ_N units. The value of σ_{SN}/σ_N is obtained by calculating the reciprocal of the slope of the ROC curve plotted in z-score units. The practical significance of Equation (3.10) is that d' can be calculated for any pair of hit and false alarm proportions as readily when $\sigma_{SN} > \sigma_N$ as when $\sigma_{SN} = \sigma_N$. Since the slope of the ROC curve plotted in z units must be known it is necessary to determine the ROC curve during each experiment. This requirement would be very time consuming if an entire experiment on the effects of signal probability or payoff had to be conducted in order to obtain data points for the ROC curve. Fortunately, the confidence rating procedure discussed later in this chapter provides an exceptionally economical method for obtaining the data needed to determine the ROC curve.

One virtue of TSD made apparent by the above discussion of the ROC curve is that the theory is experimentally testable. Precise, quantitative predictions of what should happen in the detection situation under a variety of conditions can be made from the theory. Experimental results that do not correspond to predicted results have served as a basis for modifying the quantitative statements of the theory. Furthermore, the range of predictions from TSD is comprehensive and extends far beyond the limited confines of earlier psychophysical theories which dealt exclusively with sensory processes. Experimental data continue to accumulate rapidly in support of TSD. The use of detectability measures such as d', Δm, and d_e', and of criterion measures such as β to separate the observer's sensitivity from the location of his decision criterion therefore becomes increasingly justifiable.

LOW THRESHOLD THEORY

We have seen that high threshold theory predicts ROC curves which are not consistent with experimental data. The theory of signal detection, an alternative theory consistent with empirically determined ROC curves, was then discussed. In TSD the concept of sensory threshold, so central to classical psychophysics, is rejected in favor of an adjustable decision criterion. In fairness to threshold theory, however, it should be pointed out that one version of the threshold concept predicts ROC curves which fit the data about as well as the predictions from TSD. In this theory the threshold is assumed to be much lower, located slightly above the mean

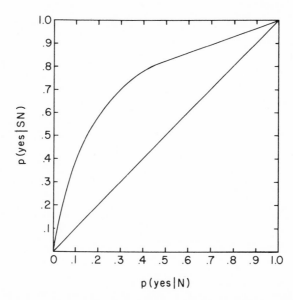

FIGURE 3.17   Receiver-operating characteristic curve predicted from low threshold theory.

of the N distribution, than that of classical threshold theory. The theory was originally described by Swets, Tanner, and Birdsall (1955, 1961). In *low threshold theory* some of the false alarms on catch trials are due to an observation being above threshold while others are due to guessing when the observation is below threshold. It should be recalled that all false alarms on catch trials were attributed to guessing in classical theory. The shape of the ROC curve predicted from low threshold theory is seen in Figure 3.17. The curved shape of the ROC curve up to $p(\text{yes}|N)$ of about .50 is assumed to be due, as it would be in TSD, to a progressive lowering of the observer's decision criterion and would result in an increase in the proportion of hits and false alarms. Beyond this point the function is linear because the criterion is lower than the threshold, which at this point would begin to determine the observer's decisions. For observations below threshold response bias changes the guessing rate and, therefore, this upper branch of the ROC curve must be linear. Thus, the linear segment of the curve and the linear curve of classical threshold theory are both attributed to change in guessing rate.

Luce (1963) proposed another version of low threshold theory. In Luce's theory the threshold is assumed to exist somewhere between the middle and the upper end of the noise distribution. During a sensory observation an observer is in a *detect state* if the observation exceeds threshold and in the *nondetect state* if the observation is below threshold. As in other threshold theories, observations below threshold are assumed to be indiscriminable. But observations above threshold are also assumed to be indiscriminable from one another. Thus for the purpose of detecting signals the observer can discriminate between two kinds of sensory

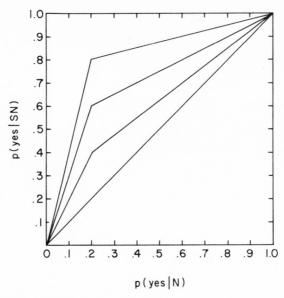

FIGURE 3.18   Receiver-operating characteristic curves predicted from two-state theory.

events—those that put him into the detect state and those that put him into the nondetect state. The response he makes in either state may be biased by nonsensory factors. He may say "yes" when he is in the nondetect state or he may say "no" when he is in the detect state. Manipulating variables such as payoff and signal probability changes the observer's response bias when he is in either one or the other of the two possible detection states. The ROC curve predicted from Luce's theory is two straight lines (Figure 3.18) for several different signal strengths. This ROC curve is often found to fit detection data as well as the ROC curves predicted from signal detection theory.

Krantz (1969) has reviewed the problem of obtaining experimental data that provide an adequate test of low threshold theory. Although low threshold theory is consistent with available experimental data, the threshold that is postulated cannot be measured by classical psychophysical methods. Furthermore, signal detection theory without a threshold concept has accounted for a great deal of the psychophysical data on detection behavior. These data provide compelling evidence that if thresholds do exist they are almost always lower than the observer's decision criterion and consequently seldom influence detection behavior.

It is important to realize that the threshold concept, at least as it is used in threshold theory, represents a barrier separating sensory states inside the observer. These *observer thresholds,* which are inferred from the analysis of detection judgments, are not to be confused with psychophysical *energy thresholds* measured by various psychophysical methods. Krantz (1969) made a sharp distinction betweeen observer thresholds and energy thresholds. He stated that it is possible that both observer and energy thresholds exist, that neither type of threshold exists, or that only one of the two types of threshold exists. We have seen that the evidence for observer thresholds is equivocal. What can be said about energy thresholds?

Even if observer thresholds do not exist, the psychophysical threshold as an experimentally determined energy value necessary for some specified detection performance level can be used to measure sensitivity. In fact, our present understanding of sensory systems would be impossible if it were not for the thousands of experimental studies on energy thresholds conducted since Fechner outlined the psychophysical methods in 1860. The chief limitation of psychophysical energy thresholds as measures of sensitivity is that they may be affected by the observer's decision criterion. If care is taken to control for the effects of criterion shifting, the use of energy thresholds as measures of sensitivity is highly recommended.

The best evidence for energy thresholds comes from studies which illustrate that an observer's performance is the same when a weak stimulus is presented as when no stimulus is presented, unless the weak stimulus is above some critical value. Data from an experiment by Gescheider, Wright, Weber, and Barton (1971) illustrate an energy threshold for the detection of a 60-Hz vibration on the fingertip. Data plotted in Figure 3.19 illustrate that d' was near zero for all stimulus strengths less than 1 μm peak-to-peak displacement of the vibrator contactor. These data, though indicative of an energy threshold, are not inconsistent with TSD. They do not necessarily imply the existence of an observer threshold. Unlike the observer threshold concept, the energy threshold is not tied to the assumption that there is a boundary on the continuum of sensory magnitude below which events cannot be discriminated and above which events can be discriminated. In

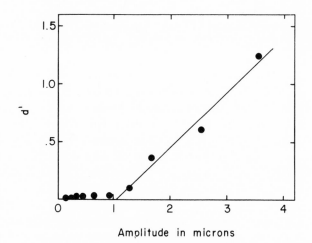

Amplitude in microns

FIGURE 3.19   The relation between d' and signal amplitude for detecting 60-Hz vibration on the fingertip. The data indicate an energy threshold corresponding to a signal amplitude of 1.0-μm peak-to-peak displacement of the stimulator. (From Gescheider, Wright, Weber, & Barton, 1971.)

the context of TSD, an energy threshold simply implies that as stimulus intensity is increased above zero a critical intensity value must be exceeded before the mean of the SN distribution becomes greater than the mean of the N distribution. The use of d' as a performance measure for determining energy thresholds is an advisable procedure. Under such conditions the value of the threshold will not be contaminated by variations in the observer's judgment criterion. The threshold is defined as the point on the stimulus scale where the observer's d' first becomes greater than zero.

Vendrik and Eijkman (1968) found that the probability of detecting mechanical and electrical stimuli on the skin does not change until a certain stimulus strength is exceeded. The perception of warmth and cold, on the other hand, showed a linear increasing function throughout the entire range of stimulus intensities. Vendrik and Eijkman concluded that the temperature sensory system does not have a measurable threshold while both the tactile system and the system stimulated by electrical current do have energy thresholds.

In conclusion, a few definite statements can be made about the present status of the threshold concept. It can be said with confidence that if there is an observer threshold it is not the high threshold of classical theory but a much lower threshold located somewhere near the mean of the noise distribution. Since the observer's criterion would usually be higher than this threshold his judgments of signals would be based on whether a sensory observation is above or below criterion rather than above or below threshold. The results of hundreds of experiments have indicated that TSD is basically correct as a model of detection behavior. Further experimentation is needed, however, to determine whether TSD with a low threshold will be needed to account for all the data of detection experiments. Regardless of the outcome of this particular research problem, it can be said that the usefulness of the energy threshold concept is not in question. Energy thresholds can be measured if care is taken to control for the effects of changes in the observer's criterion. Criterion problems can be dealt with by using well-trained observers who can maintain a constant criterion for all experimental conditions or by using TSD measures which are insensitive to changes in the observer's criterion. When properly measured, energy thresholds provide very useful indices of the sensitivity of sensory systems.

THE THREE BASIC PSYCHOPHYSICAL PROCEDURES OF THE THEORY OF SIGNAL DETECTION

The procedures of TSD are designed to provide the psychophysicist with data in the form of response proportions that can be readily converted into the theoretical constructs of sensitivity, criterion, distribution variance, and distribution shape. TSD can be tested by comparing the values of the constructs predicted from the theory with those that are derived from response proportion data. In those circumstances where the data support the applicability of TSD, the theory can be used to solve many empirical problems. The situation in which a variable is found to have a large effect on response proportions is illustrative. By converting response proportion data into theoretical terms such as d' and β, an investigator can determine whether the effect was due to changes in the observer's sensitivity, his criterion, or both his sensitivity and his criterion. Today there are three basic procedures of TSD used to solve such problems in psychophysics.

The Yes–No Procedure

With the *yes–no procedure* observers are given a long series of trials, usually more than 300 in a session, in which they must judge the presence or absence of a signal. Some proportion of the trials is SN and the remaining proportion is N. At the start of a session the observer is usually told what the proportion of SN trials will be and what the costs and values associated with the various decision outcomes will be. In many experiments an observation interval is designated on each trial by the presentation of a light, a sound, or some other cue during which SN or N alone is presented in the sensory modality under consideration. In a study on auditory detection, for example, a light one second in duration might be presented every five seconds. The observer must judge as quickly as possible whether or not a tone was presented during the period of time when the light was on. Knowledge of results is usually given after each judgment.

An ROC curve for a single signal strength can be plotted if the proportions of hits and false alarms are obtained for several criterion locations. Generally, payoff contingencies and signal probability are kept constant for an experimental session so that the observer's criterion will remain stable for the session. Data for different criterion levels are often obtained by changing signal probability or payoff contingencies for different sessions. The ROC curve in Figure 3.20 was obtained by Tanner, Swets, and Green (1956) in an experiment on the detection of tones against a background of white noise. Signal probability was either .10, .30, .50, .70, or .90. Each data point on the ROC curve was obtained by using one of these values for a block of 600 trials. As expected the data points ordered themselves on the ROC curve according to signal probability. The ROC curve fitted to the data is the theoretical curve for normal N and SN distributions of equal variance. The theoretical N and SN distributions are shown as an insert in the figure. The value of d' was .85 and dashed lines in the insert indicate the location of the five criteria that the observer employed for the five signal probabilities.

In the second part of the experiment the same observer was again induced by variation of payoff conditions to vary his criterion for detecting the same stimulus. Signal probability was .50 and the payoff varied from being relatively high for correct responses on N trials to being relatively high for correct responses on SN

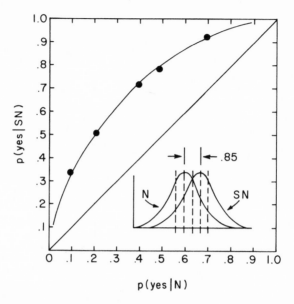

FIGURE 3.20 Receiver-operating characteristic curve from an experiment on the detection of auditory signals. Data points were obtained by varying the probability of signal occurrence. The theoretical noise and signal plus noise distributions with five criterion locations are shown in the insert. (From Tanner, Swets, & Green, 1956.)

trials. The data points on the ROC curve (Figure 3.21) ordered themselves as expected. When the payoff for being correct on N trials was relatively high the values of p(yes|N) and p(yes|SN) were low, and when the payoff for being correct on SN trials was relatively high p(yes|N) and p(yes|SN) were high. It is significant that the same ROC curve fits the data from both parts of the experiments. Because the physical stimulus was the same in both parts of the experiment the shape and locations of the N and SN distributions did not change. Thus, in spite of the fact that large variations in the observer's criterion were produced by two distinct procedures, measurements of sensitivity remained stable under all conditions.

When a single session has been conducted and the proportions of hits and false alarms are available for only a single criterion location, the value of d' and β can be estimated from the data, though an ROC curve cannot be plotted. The difference between the z scores for hits and false alarms will yield an estimate of d'. The value of β can be obtained by dividing the ordinate value on the normal curve corresponding to the z score for hits by the ordinate value corresponding to the false alarms. If the proportion of hits is .84 and the proportion of false alarms .50, the value of d' would be 1.0 and the value of β would be .243/.399 = .61.

The procedure outlined above was used in an experiment to determine the effects of an auditory stimulus on the detection of a tactile signal applied to the fingertip (Gescheider, Barton, Bruce, Goldberg, & Greenspan, 1969). An attempt was made to measure both the detectability of a tactile stimulus and the location of the observer's criterion when the auditory stimulus was set at various intensity levels. The observer was required to decide whether or not a stimulus had been presented in an observation interval. Over a series of such trials a random half of the observation intervals contained a tactile signal while the other half contained no signal. Both the value of d' and the value of β were estimated from the proportions of "yes" responses made on signal and on the nonsignal trials. At two different tactile signal intensities d' was found to decrease slightly while β increased as a function of the auditory stimulus intensity (Figure 3.22). Thus, the disruptive effect of intense auditory stimulation on tactile signal detection performance is primarily due to the observer setting a relatively high criterion.

When ROC curves are not available to check the validity of the normal distribution and equal variance assumptions, measures of sensitivity not requiring these assumptions should be used whenever possible. Such a nonparametric

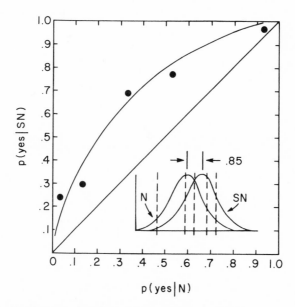

FIGURE 3.21   Receiver-operating characteristic curve from an experiment on the detection of auditory signals. Data points were obtained by varying payoff conditions. The theoretical noise and signal plus noise distributions with five criterion locations are shown in the insert. (From Green & Swets, 1966. Reprinted from D. M. Green and J. A. Swets, *Signal Detection Theory and Psychophysics*. Copyright © 1966 by John Wiley & Sons, Inc.)

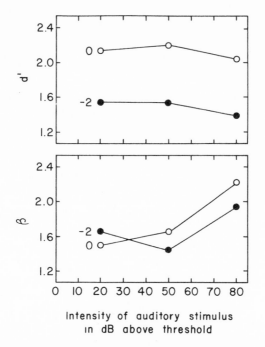

FIGURE 3.22 The values of d' and β for the detection of a tactile signal change as a function of the intensity of a simultaneous auditory stimulus. The results are shown for two tactile signal intensities. (From Gescheider, Barton, Bruce, Goldberg, & Greenspan, 1969. Copyright 1969 by the American Psychological Association. Reprinted by permission.)

measure of sensitivity, termed A', has been proposed by Pollack and Norman (1964). The formula for calculating A' is

$$A' = \tfrac{1}{2} + \frac{[p(\text{hits}) - p(\text{false alarms})]\,[1 + p(\text{hits}) - p(\text{false alarms})]}{[4p(\text{hits})]\,[1 - p(\text{false alarms})]}. \quad (3.11)$$

In the example above where p(hits) was .84 and p(false alarms) was .50

$$A' = \tfrac{1}{2} + \frac{(.84 - .50)\,(1 - .84 - .50)}{(4 \times .84)\,(1 - .50)} = .77.$$

The Forced Choice Procedure

An excellent technique for obtaining a measure of the observer's sensitivity which is uncontaminated by fluctuations in his criterion is the *forced choice procedure*. On a particular trial two or more observation intervals are presented and it is the observer's task to report which observation interval contained a signal. The assumption is made that in the absence of response bias toward one or more of the observation intervals the observer chooses the observation interval containing the largest sensory observation. Since the observer's criterion is not a factor in such a judgment the proportion of correct responses, $p(c)$, can be used as a measure of sensitivity. The value of $p(c)$ will be underestimated when response bias toward one of the observation intervals exists. Procedures for correcting the $p(c)$ obtained when response bias exists are found in Green and Swets (1966).

Confidence Rating Procedure

Often it is desirable to obtain an ROC curve from data in a single session within which signal probability and payoff contingencies are fixed. The *confidence rating method* is very economical since data for several points on an ROC curve can be obtained for a single experimental condition by having the observer make a confidence rating for each of his yes–no judgments. For example, the observer might be instructed to say "five" if he is sure a signal was presented, "four" if he is fairly sure a signal was presented, "three" if he is not sure, "two" if he is fairly sure a signal was not presented, and "one" if he is sure a signal was not presented. It is assumed that to make his ratings the observer sets up n minus 1 criteria along the sensory continuum to delineate his rating categories (Figure 3.23). The number of criteria in Figure 3.23 is one less than the number of categories. In this particular example, "five" is given to observations that are equal to or greater than C_4, "four" to observations that are equal to or greater than C_3 but less than C_4, "three" to observations equal to or greater than C_2 but less than C_3, "two" to observations equal to or greater than C_1 but less than C_2, and "one" to observations that are less than C_1.

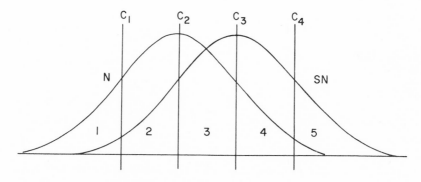

Magnitude of sensory observation

FIGURE 3.23   A representation of how an observer might set up four criteria along the sensory magnitude dimension for the purpose of using the confidence rating method for detecting signals.

TABLE 3.3
Determination of an ROC Curve by the Confidence Rating Procedure

	1	2	3	4	5
SN	.01	.08	.28	.36	.27
N	.10	.23	.47	.17	.03
	C_1	C_2	C_3	C_4	
SN	1.00	.99	.91	.63	.27
N	1.00	.90	.67	.20	.03

During the experiment the proportion of responses for each of the rating categories for the SN trials and for the N trials are determined. Sample data from an experiment on the detection of a 2.78-μm amplitude vibration on the fingertip (Gescheider, Wright, & Polak, 1971) are shown in Table 3.3. The bottom part of the table lists the calculated hit and false alarm rates that would occur if the observer were induced to set his yes–no decision criterion at each of the four criterion points defined by the five rating categories. For the C_4 criterion the estimated hit rate of .27 corresponds to the proportion of "five" responses given on SN trials and the estimated false alarm rate of .03 corresponds to the proportion of "five" responses on N trials. For the C_3 criterion the estimated hit rate of .63 is the proportion of "four" responses plus the proportion of "five" responses for the SN trials since this would include all of the SN observations above C_3. For the same reason the estimated false alarm rate of .20 for C_3 is the proportion of "four" responses plus the proportion of "five" responses for the N trials. The estimated hit rate of .91 for C_2 is the proportion of "three" responses plus the proportion of "four" responses plus the proportion of "five" responses on SN trials while the estimated false alarm rate of .67 for C_2 is the proportion of "three" responses plus the proportion of "four" responses plus the proportion of "five" responses on N trials. Finally, the estimated hit rate of .99 for C_1 is the summation of proportions of "five," "four," "three," and "two" responses for SN trials and the estimated false alarm rate of .90 for C_1 is the summation of proportions of "five," "four," "three," and "two" responses for N trials. Each of the four pairs of hit and false alarm proportions that result for this procedure provides a point for an ROC curve.

In Figure 3.24 the open points of the ROC curve for a 2.78-μm signal amplitude are the values found in Table 3.3. The open points were obtained when the observer was expecting weak signals, while the filled points were obtained when he was expecting strong signals. Signal detectability was apparently not affected by changes in signal strength expectancy since the data for both conditions could be fitted by a single ROC curve. However, it is also evident that when the observer is expecting weak signals he sets a lower criterion than when he is expecting strong ones. Notice that this finding held for all values of stimulus amplitude. Changing

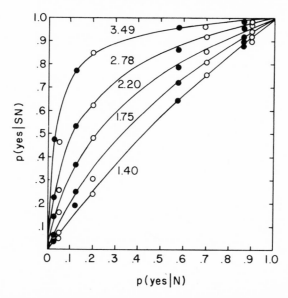

FIGURE 3.24 Receiver-operating characteristic curves for the detection of 60-Hz vibration of the fingertip when observers were expecting weak signals (open points) and when they were expecting strong signals (filled points). Each ROC curve represents data obtained for a particular value of stimulus intensity (peak-to-peak amplitude in microns of the tactile stimulator). (From Gescheider, Wright, & Polak, 1971.)

stimulus amplitude did, however, have a large effect on d', as can be seen from the family of ROC curves.

Because sufficient data can be quickly obtained for constructing an ROC curve by the confidence rating procedure, its use can provide a convenient means of testing the hypotheses of normality of N and SN distributions and equal variance of N and SN distributions. When z(hits) is plotted against z(false alarms), a linear ROC curve is consistent with the normality of distributions assumption and a slope of 1.0 is consistent with the equal variance assumption. When the ROC curve is linear but the slope is not 1.0, the value of σ_{SN}/σ_N can be obtained by calculating the reciprocal of the slope of the function.

The validity of confidence rating data is supplied by the finding that the yes–no procedure and the rating procedure generally yield very similar values of signal detectability (Green & Swets, 1966; Markowitz & Swets, 1967). The values of d' obtained from the yes–no procedure and the rating procedure in the study of vibrotactile sensitivity by Gescheider *et al.* (1971) were plotted against signal amplitude (Figure 3.25). The open and filled points represent d' values obtained from the yes–no procedure when the observer's criterion was low and high, respectively. The squares are d' values from the rating procedure. The correspondence of values obtained with the two methods is remarkable. An important

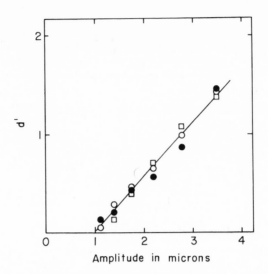

FIGURE 3.25   The relation between d' and vibration amplitude. The open and filled points repre-sent d' values obtained from the yes-no procedure when the observer's criterion was low and high, respectively. The squares are d' values from the rating procedure. (From Gescheider, Wright, & Polak, 1971.)

aspect of this study was the finding of an energy threshold of approximately 1 μm. This threshold was independent of the method of measurement and was not contaminated by the effects of the observer's criterion as determined by his expectations of strong or weak signals. Thus, it appears that TSD methodology provides a powerful technique for determining energy thresholds which are valid measures of sensitivity.

APPLICATION OF THE THEORY OF
SIGNAL DETECTION TO RECOGNITION MEMORY

The continuity–noncontinuity issue has a long history in several areas of psychol-ogy besides the study of sensory processes. The essential form of the issue, however, is always the same: do psychological processes change on a continuum or do they change in discrete steps? For years psychologists have been concerned with the problem of whether learning is an all-or-none or continuous process. Does the learning curve represent a number of small discrete increments in learning or does it represent a gradual and continuous change in the amount learned? A closely related problem arises in the study of recognition memory. To be recognized must a stimulus exceed some threshold below which memory strength is zero or must the stimulus exceed a criterion on a memory–strength continuum?

In a recognition–memory test an observer is first exposed to a series of stimulus items such as words, nonsense syllables, or visual nonsense forms which he attempts to remember. Subsequently the observer is exposed to a series of stimulus items, some of which are old items from the earlier series and some of which are new items. The observer is required to report "old" or "new" for each presentation of an item. Reporting "old" for an old stimulus is a hit, while a false alarm is reporting "old" for a new stimulus.

In the TSD model of recognition memory, each item, whether old or new, is assumed to be located on a continuum of memory strength. Variability in memory strength for different items is assumed to form two overlapping normal distributions on the memory-strength continuum (Figure 3.26). The distributions for new and old items are analogous to the N and SN distributions of the detection situation. According to the TSD analysis the observer will report "new" if the memory strength of the item is below a criterion but will report "old" if the memory strength is above the criterion. The experiment might be repeated several times with different sets of items. By inducing the observer to change the location of his criterion for each new experiment several pairs of hit and false alarm proportions can be obtained and plotted as an ROC curve. If the TSD analysis is correct and memory strength varies on a continuum, the ROC curve, called a memory operating characteristic (MOC) curve, should be curvilinear when plotted as proportions and linear when plotted as z scores.

In the noncontinuity model of recognition memory it is postulated that an item either has a suprathreshold memory strength which always results in a recognition response or is below the recognition threshold and results in a recognition response only when the observer guesses. This model of recognition memory is exactly

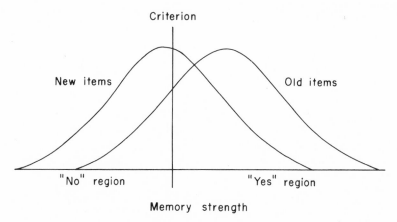

FIGURE 3.26 Distributions of memory strength for new and old items. The criterion indicates the memory strength below which the observer will report "new" and above which he will report "old."

analogous to the high threshold theory of detection. The threshold is assumed to be unaffected by changes in the observer's expectations and motivation. From the threshold model the MOC curve is predicted to be linear when plotted as proportions. The prediction that the proportion of hits will be a linear function of the proportion of false alarms follows from the assumption that all old items above threshold will be recognized while the new items will never be above threshold and therefore will never be recognized. The false alarm proportion is therefore the rate at which the observer will guess ''old'' when an item is below threshold and he is in the nonrecognition state. The hit rate is equal to the proportion of old items of threshold plus the proportion of old items below threshold multiplied by the false alarm rate. When something is done to the observer to induce him to change his rate of guessing old items, the proportion of false alarms and hits will increase. A review of the discussion of Equation (3.4) will reveal that the logic behind the prediction of a linear ROC curve for detection and a linear MOC curve for recognition memory is exactly the same.

The general finding has been that MOC curves are curvilinear rather than linear when plotted as proportions (see Banks, 1970; Lockhart & Murdock, 1970, for reviews of the experimental findings). Thus a model with a high recognition threshold located above the mean of the new item distribution appears to be untenable, while the data are consistent with the TSD model. A mathematically precise statement of a TSD model of memory, in which old and new items are assumed to vary in memory strength along a continuum, has been developed by Wickelgren and Norman (1966).

CONCLUDING STATEMENT ON THE THEORY OF SIGNAL DETECTION

The theory of signal detection has been a major advancement in experimental psychology. Along with the work of S. S. Stevens on psychophysical scaling it has been responsible for recent intense interest in psychophysics. The discovery that human observers behave in ways closely paralleling statistical decision theory when detecting signals immersed in noisy backgrounds is not evidence that observer thresholds do not exist, however. Experimental data clearly indicate that when the observer is placed in a situation in which there is an N distribution and an SN distribution, he behaves as if he were testing a statistical hypothesis. When he is presented with a sensory observation he tries to decide from which distribution it came. An observer will tend to choose one distribution over the other depending on such circumstances as costs and values of decision outcomes and signal probability. Behavior in such noisy situations does not appear to be governed by an all-or-none threshold: instead decisions appear to be determined by the location of the adjustable decision criterion.

But what can we say of the observer's behavior in situations where noise is absent or greatly reduced? Stevens (1961b) suggested that TSD applies to noisy situations where the threshold is obscured. He claimed that when noise is absent the all-or-none step function of the threshold will emerge. Accordingly, Stevens (1961b) suggests that

> We should continue to explore the fertile and heuristic domain of detection theory (because signals often do in fact occur in noise), and we should study methods for reducing the noise in our experiments on differential sensitivity in order to see how the nervous system operates on pure signals, unobscured by noise. A complete suppression of noise may not be possible, of course, but a sufficient reduction may be achieved to allow a quantal step function to manifest itself in the action of the sensory system [p. 808].

Stevens compared this basic problem in psychophysics to the problem of the nature of electricity:

> When, after years of effort, R. A. Millikan finally succeeded in suppressing enough sources of noise in his oil drop experiment, he was able to show that the charge on the electron is not normally distributed, as some evidence had suggested, but has a fixed, all-or-none value [p. 808].

We have seen that a theory of a high threshold near the upper end of the N distribution is not consistent with experimental data. We have also seen that there are no definite experiments which prove that thresholds do not exist at some point relatively low in the N distribution. Furthermore, there are no clear-cut data that disprove the neural quantum theory of the difference threshold. Perhaps further experimentation will reveal that some combination of the postulates of TSD and low threshold theory will best account for the facts of signal detection behavior. Or perhaps the prediction by Urban (1930) of a new psychophysics without the threshold concept as its cornerstone will be confirmed.

4

The Measurement
of Sensory Attributes

Most of the early work in psychophysics was concerned with the problem of measuring absolute and differential sensitivity for the various sense modalities under a variety of stimulus conditions. Little attempt was made to measure directly such sensory attributes as loudness, brightness, pain, warmth, pressure, pitch, hue, and perceived duration.

Although the investigation of sensitivity by measuring absolute and difference thresholds provides valuable information about the senses it does not in itself give a complete picture of a sensory system. If the input to a sensory system is the physical stimulus and the output is sensation, then all measurements in classical psychophysics were made on the input side of the system. Absolute and difference thresholds are not stated in sensation units but in units of stimulus energy at points where output can just be detected or where changes in outputs are just discriminable. An analogous situation is an engineer testing the sensitivity of a photo cell or sound level meter where certain changes in the output of the device are measured as a function of input changes. The absolute sensitivity of the device might be measured by determining the smallest amount of energy that will yield a meter reading. Differential sensitivity could be measured by determining the smallest changes in energy producing a change in the meter reading. Such measurements on the electronic device are useful but obviously incomplete until the output of the device has also been measured and related to the input. If the device were a photo cell we would complete the set of measurements by determining the output in voltage or current as a function of energy input.

Psychophysical scaling of sensory attributes is a necessary part of sensory psychology because sensation changes do not usually stand in a one-to-one relationship with changes in the stimulus. The exact relationships between sensations and stimuli must therefore be determined experimentally. If the intensity of a sound is doubled, its loudness is increased by a barely perceptible amount. To discover how loudness increases with stimulus intensity we must be able to measure both stimulus intensity and psychological loudness. Techniques of physics are employed to measure the energy in the stimulus, and psychophysical procedures have been refined in the past 30 years for measuring such sensory attributes as loudness, pitch, brightness, hue, pain, touch, warmth, cold, taste, and smell. Through the use of these procedures, numbers can be assigned to sensation magnitudes. A psychophysical relationship called a *psychophysical magnitude function* is established when the magnitude of a sensory attribute is plotted against corresponding physical values of the stimulus.

The form of the psychophysical magnitude function for a particular sense modality and a particular set of stimulus conditions may tell us something about the transmission of information through the sensory nervous system. For example, if we know how an observer's judgments of the intensity of his sensations change as stimulus intensity changes we may be able to make inferences about how receptor mechanisms transduce stimulus energy into neural impulses, how neural impulses code information about properties of the stimulus, and how judgmental processes in the central nervous system work. Besides their usefulness in understanding the operation of sensory systems, psychophysical magnitude functions have also been used for practical purposes. Knowing that to double loudness requires sound energy to be increased by about ten times rather than by two has been extremely useful to designers of auditory communications systems. With this sort of information various signals can be specified in terms of their psychological loudness as well as their physical intensity. Psychological magnitude functions have also been useful in solving problems in illumination engineering, the measurement of clinical pain, and the quantification of taste and smell in the food industry.

Psychophysical magnitude functions can be determined only when both the stimulus and the sensory response to the stimulus can be measured. As early as 1860 Fechner recognized this problem; his proposal that sensation magnitude increases with the logarithm of stimulus intensity implies measurement of both stimulus and response terms. Fechner believed that sensations could not be directly measured. He derived measures of sensory magnitude from measurement of difference thresholds. Because all jnd's are minimal increments in sensation necessary for discrimination, Fechner assumed that they must be psychologically equal. Having established the jnd as a unit of sensory magnitude it was logical for Fechner to propose that sensation magnitude could be measured by counting the number of jnd's that sensations were above absolute threshold. The psychophysical magnitude function is the number of jnd's above absolute threshold as a function of stimulus intensity.

When it is not possible to measure and control the physical characteristics of the stimulus, psychophysical magnitude functions cannot be obtained. Nevertheless, many of the psychophysical scaling methods have been used to measure psychological responses to stimuli so complex that it is impossible to specify their relevant physical properties. Notable in this regard was the work of L. L.

Thurstone, who was the first psychologist to develop methods of measuring sensory experience where properties of physical stimuli cannot be specified. Like Fechner, Thurstone also proposed that sensation could be measured only indirectly through measurement of stimulus discrimination. In 1927 he proposed the *law of comparative judgment* as a mathematical model for the analysis of paired comparison judgments. From the proportion of times one stimulus is judged to be greater than another stimulus with respect to some attribute, the psychological scale values for the two stimuli can be calculated. Frequently confused stimuli are thus assumed to be psychologically similar and stimuli that are infrequently confused are assumed to be psychologically different. Thurstone's method has been used to quantify numerous psychological qualities, such as the experience of esthetic worth produced by works of art, for which there are no specifiable stimulus properties. His work was a major advance because it was the first attempt to extend the boundaries of psychophysics beyond the investigation of sensory systems. Much of this work is discussed in Thurstone's book, *The Measurement of Values* (1959).

The distinction has been made between *indirect scaling* and *direct scaling* of sensory magnitude. The attempts of Fechner and Thurstone to measure sensation through measurement of discrimination represent indirect scaling: the measurements are derived from data on how well the observer can tell one stimulus from another rather than from his direct judgments of the sensation magnitudes. In using direct scaling, on the other hand, the observer makes judgments of his sensations which are then directly converted into measurements of sensory magnitude. If an observer must tell how much brighter one light is than another he judges the sensory magnitude of the two lights. Furthermore, his responses directly provide the experimenter with a measurement of the two brightnesses. If, for example, the observer reported that light *A* was three times as bright as light *B*, measurement might be achieved by assigning a number to the brightness of light *A* that is three times as large as the number assigned to the brightness of light *B*. An important assumption is made that the observer can follow the instructions of the experiment and make the required quantitative judgments. If the observer is successful the psychological scale follows directly from the observer's judgments. Although there are many techniques for direct scaling of sensory magnitude the direct *ratio scaling* methods have been most useful in facilitating our understanding of sensation. Although ratio scaling was introduced as early as 1888 when Merkel asked observers to adjust a stimulus to produce a sensation twice as great as that of another stimulus, it was not until the early 1950's that investigators began to refine these techniques. It was the persistent efforts of S. S. Stevens and his fellow workers over a period of more than 20 years that resulted in dozens of ratio scales for sensory magnitude. These scales include psychophysical magnitude functions for brightness, loudness, cutaneous sensations, taste, and smell. Stevens' solution to the problem of direct ratio scaling of sensation was simply to present stimuli to an observer and ask him to assign numbers to them which seemed to correspond to his sensations. The use of this method, now known as *magnitude estimation*, resulted in Stevens proposing a new law to replace Fechner's logarithmic law. *Stevens' power law* is based upon the finding that magnitude estimations for a variety of sensory dimensions increase in proportion to the stimulus intensity raised to a power. The size of the power exponent to which stimulus intensity is raised to predict magnitude estimations changes depending on sensory modality and stimulus conditions. The power law has become one of the best established empirical relations in psychology.

Chapter 4 consists of a description of the various indirect and direct psychophysical scaling procedures. In each case the object is to obtain numerical measures of sensory magnitude. In that psychophysical scaling is a part of the more general problem of measurement in science, measurement theory becomes important in evaluating the various scaling procedures. Thus, a brief discussion of measurement theory precedes the description of psychophysical scaling methods.

MEASUREMENT SCALES

The concept of measurement is basic to an understanding of the various methods devised to quantify sensory attributes. Measurement is the assigning of numbers by rules to represent properties of objects or events. The numbers, as symbols of properties in the world of objects and events, can be manipulated in accordance with the rules of mathematics. If the properties of the number system reflect the properties of objects or events, new information about the measured properties may result from such symbolic manipulations.

It is often the case that for a particular measurement scale the properties of the number system only partially reflect the properties of objects or events. In these cases the operations that can be performed legitimately on the numbers and the conclusions that can be drawn about differences among numbers are restricted, and define four basic types of measurement scales: *nominal, ordinal, interval,* and *ratio*. These scales represent different degrees of correspondence between the number system and the proptery systems of objects or events. The essential properties of the number system to be considered when determining which of these types of measurement scale is in use are *identity, order, interval,* and *origin*.

Each symbol in the number system is different and therefore has a unique identity. Like any set of symbols the number system can be used for classification or identification purposes. Thus, different numbers are assigned to different players on an athletic team. The numbers do not imply anthing about the degree of any properties the players may possess. They are simply labels to allow us to identify individuals. Because the number system is not employed quantitatively in the use of *nominal scales*, such scales cannot be considered to be measurement.

In the number system the numbers are arranged in an ordered sequence so that different numbers have a greater than–less than relation between them. An *ordinal scale* is a set of measurements in which the amount of a property of objects or events can be ranked for the amount of some property, and the rank number represents the scale value for each measurement. Some property of athletic performance is measured on an ordinal scale when first, second, third, fourth, and fifth place are awarded to contestants. Only the property of order in the number system can be applied to ordinal scale measurements. Two numbers, one being larger than the other, can *only* signify greater than–less than relations between measured properties. It is obvious that on the basis of rankings we cannot conclude that the difference in performance between Rank 1 and Rank 2 is necessarily the same as the difference in performance between Rank 3 and Rank 4 (interval) or that Rank 4 represents twice as proficient performance as Rank 2 (origin).

Intervals between numbers are ordered in the number system. The difference between any pair of numbers is greater than, equal to, or less than the difference between any other pair of numbers. If an *interval scale* has been achieved, the intervals between the scale values represent differences or distances between amounts of the property measured. The temperature scale is often cited as an instance of an interval scale because the difference between two scale values can be maningfully compared with the difference between two other scale values. For example, the difference between 40° and 60° is equal to the difference between 70° and 90° as measured physically by a thermometer. This 20° difference in temperature is twice as large as the 10° difference between 100° and 110°, but half as large as the 40° difference between 90° and 130°. Thus in an interval scale the size of the differences between numbers, as well as their ordinal relation, has meaning.

The number system has an origin represented by ''zero.'' A particular number can be said to be so many times greater than or less than another number with respect to zero. In the number system, 10 is twice 5 and half of 20. A *ratio scale*, as well as having the properties of order and distance, has a natural origin to represent zero amount of a property. In these scales the ratios of the scale values have meaning. For example, a 50-lb ball and a 25-lb ball stand in a 2-to-1 ratio on the property of weight. This kind of statement cannot be made about scale values on an interval scale, where the zero point is arbitrary and does not represent zero amount of the property. Zero degrees on the centigrade or Fahrenheit temperature scales do not represent zero amounts of temperature, and thus 100° cannot be said to be twice the temperature of 50°. The Kelvin scale of temperature, however, is a ratio scale, since zero degrees Kelvin represents absolute zero where no heat exists. Ratio scales are highly desirable achievements because they have all three basic properties of the number system and therefore afford greatest opportunity to use the number system as a model of the measured property. It is for these reasons that many of the psychological scaling techniques were designed to construct ratio scales of sensory attributes.

The concept of *invariance* is based on the distinction among nominal, ordinal, interval, and ratio scales. The numbers used in a specific situation are a limited set of numbers drawn from an infinitely large set of numbers. The numbers may be altered in certain ways without changing their significance. If the numbers are changed and their significance remains the same, the transformation is said to leave the scale *invariant*. S. S. Stevens (1951) has classified measurement scales in terms of the nature of the numerical transformations that can be performed upon scale values while leaving the structure of the scale undistorted. The more precise the type of measurement scale (nominal scales being the least and ratio scales the most precise), the more restricted are the transformations that can be applied to a scale, leaving it invariant.

In a nominal scale the numbers are merely symbols for distinguishing one thing from another. A nominal scale remains intact when any number is substituted for any other number. As long as the transformation is public no meaning is lost when two athletes exchange numbers. The only property of the number system that is relevant in this case is that each symbol in the number system has a separate identity that can be used to signify different objects or events. Since amounts in a nominal scale are not considered, the size of the number is not important. The scale is invariant to any transformation as long as no two things are assigned the same number.

The construction of an ordinal scale requires the application of the rule that numbers must be arranged so that the rank order of the numbers corresponds to the rank order of the property being measured. This rule permits much freedom in the selection of specific numbers as scale values. In an ordinal scale the only properties of the number system that are important are the identity and order of the numbers. The differences and ratios among numbers are irrelevant. Thus, an ordinal scale is invariant to any transformation which preserves the rank order of the scale values.

Interval scale measurement requires that numbers be assigned to properties in such a way that the differences among numbers reflect the differences among properties in the real world. In an interval scale the relative difference among scale values is unaffected by any linear transformation of the form $Y = a + bX$, where X is the original scale value and Y is the transformed scale value. In other words, if measurement has yielded a set of scale values X, the meaning of the results is not affected by converting to a new scale Y through multiplying each value by the constant b and adding the constant a to each value. The value of the multiplier constant b determines the arbitrary size of the scale unit, and the value of the additive constant a determines the arbitrary location of the zero point on the scale. An example of such a transformation is the conversion of temperature from the centigrade to the Fahrenheit scale by the equation $F = 32 + 1.8C$. When properties are measured on an interval scale, any nonlinear transformation will violate the structure of the scale by destroying the correspondence of the differences among scale values and the differences among properties in the real world. The critical property of an interval scale is that the ratios of differences are invariant across permissible transformations.

If a ratio scale has been achieved, the nature of the invariance transformation is restricted to linear transformations of the form $Y = bX$. The origin is fixed at absolute zero and, therefore, unlike interval scales, a constant cannot be added to scale values. However, the size of the unit of a ratio scale is arbitrary, and scale values may therefore be multiplied by a constant. For example, one can convert

TABLE 4.1
Four Scales of Measurement[a]

Scale	Operations performed	Permissible transformations	Some appropriate statistics
Nominal	Identify and classify	Substituion of any number for any other number	Number of cases Mode Contingency correlation
Ordinal	Rank order	Any change that preserves order	Median Percentiles Rank-order correlation
Interval	Find distances or differences	Multiplication by a constant Addition of a constant	Mean Standard deviation Product–moment correlation
Ratio	Find ratios, fractions, or multiples	Multiplication by a constant	Geometric mean Percent variability

[a]After Stevens (1975). (Reprinted from S. S. Stevens, *Psychophysics: Introduction to Its Perceptual, Neural and Social Prospects.* Copyright © 1975 by John Wiley & Sons, Inc. Reprinted by permission of John Wiley & Sons, Inc.)

from feet to inches as the unit of length by applying the transformation, inches = feet × 12. Only transformations of this form leave invariant the ratios between scale values, and they are therefore the only permissible transformations of ratio scales. The critical property of a ratio scale is that the ratios of scale values are invariant across permissible transformations.

A summary of the characteristics of nominal, ordinal, interval, and ratio scales is found in Table 4.1. It is important for an investigator to know the type of scale his measurements constitute. Without such knowledge serious errors are likely to arise from the use of inappropriate statistical analysis and other inappropriate calculations performed on the numbers. Incorrect conclusions are often made from an experiment in which the scale of measurement is not as high on the hierarchy as had been assumed by the investigator. In psychophysics the various scaling methods were devised to obtain quantitative data on an observer's responses to stimuli. In most cases attempts have been made to construct either interval or ratio scales of sensation from such data. The procedures used to scale sensation should be critically evaluated in relation to the type of measurement scale that is claimed.

PSYCHOPHYSICAL SCALES

The methods of constructing and validating scales of sensory attributes must be considered before dealing with the use of such scales in psychological measurement problems. The loudness scale, for example, has been used to specify the subjective loudness of sounds in a variety of experimental and practical situations, but it is important to ask first how such scales are developed.

According to S. S. Stevens (1960) the methods for constructing psychological scales can be classified into three types. Each is designed to generate a numerical scale of sensory magnitude, although each requires a different kind of perceptual response from the observer. *Confusion scaling* requires an observer to make discriminative responses between stimuli that are slightly different physically. Confusion scales of sensation are based on indirect scaling procedures in that sensory magnitudes of stimuli are inferred from measures of stimulus discriminability. The observer's task is to report whether the sensation produced by one stimulus is greater than or less than the sensation produced by another stimulus. Discriminability is taken as the measure of how different one sensation magnitude is than another. Successful confusion scaling results in an interval measurement scale since discrimination data indicate the differences but not the ratios among sensation magnitudes. Fechner was the first to employ a form of this method in his construction of a psychological scale from difference thresholds. Thurstone later proposed a method for constructing a scale from data obtained by paired comparison procedures where each stimulus is compared with all other stimuli. *Partition scales* are obtained by direct scaling procedures in which the observer must make direct judgments of the psychological differences among stimuli. The resulting scales are interval scales because they measure the differences among sensations. The observer must attend to several stimuli along the physical continuum and partition them into a limited number of categories. He is instructed to do this so that the categories are separated by psychologically equal intervals. For example, before the development of photometry astronomers judged the apparent brightness of stars on a scale from 1 to 6; 1 stood for the brightest star and 6 for the dimmest. Judgments were made so that the psychological difference between category 1 and category 2 was the same as the distance between category 2 and category 3 and the same as the distance between all other successive pairs of categories. *Ratio scaling* of sensations relies on the ability of the observer to make direct judgments of the ratio relationships between the magnitudes of his sensations. The observer might be required to tell when two loudnesses stand in a 2-to-1 ratio. If the observer is able to perform this task, we have a basis for measuring sensations on a ratio scale. Since the observer has indicated that one loudness is twice as great as another, we may assign to the sensations any pair of numbers that stand in a ratio of 2 to 1. The actual units, whether 2 and 1, 4 and 2, 20 and 10, or 2000 and 1000, are arbitrary, as they are in physical measurement. Length, weight, and sensory magnitude, if they are measured on ratio scales, can be specified in units of any size as long as the ratios between scale values are maintained as the size of the unit is changed.

Confusion Scales

Confusion scaling methods are designed to construct interval scales of psychological attributes indirectly from the discrimination responses of the observer.

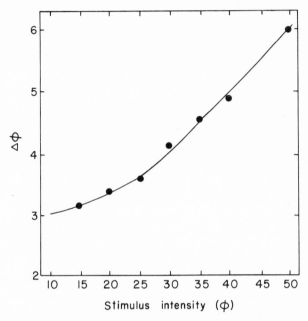

FIGURE 4.1   The results of a hypothetical experiment in which $\Delta\phi$ was determined for seven values of stimulus intensity. The curve is extrapolated down to an absolute threshold of 10 units.

DL Scales

Fechner's law ($\psi = k \log \phi$) requires the assumption that DLs are equal increments in sensation magnitude at all levels of stimulus intensity. This assumption, combined with the assumption of the correctness of Weber's statement that the size of the DL in physical units is proportional to stimulus intensity, permitted the mathematical derivation of Fechner's law. As pointed out previously, the Weber fraction is not constant over the entire range of stimulus intensities. The interesting possibility remains, however, that a valid psychophysical scale might still be established from DLs if the size of the DL as a function of stimulus intensity is obtained experimentally rather than by calculation from Weber's law. If the assumption is made that DLs are equal sensation magnitude increments, a scale is derived by adding up DLs along the stimulus dimension.

Any one of the psychophysical methods outlined previously can be used to determine the DL for each of several values along the stimulus dimension. The results of such an experiment are plotted on a graph such as Figure 4.1, and a smooth curve is fitted to the data points. The absolute threshold in stimulus units is 10 and the size of the first DL above threshold obtained from Figure 4.1 is 3. This value is added to the value of the absolute threshold (10 + 3 = 13) to obtain the stimulus value one jnd above absolute threshold. The stimulus at absolute threshold is considered as the zero point on the scale of sensation and the stimulus intensity of 13, being one jnd above this point, is regarded as capable of producing a sensation magnitude of one unit. The stimulus value producing a sensation magnitude of two units is obtained by discovering the stimulus that is two jnd's above absolute threshold. From Figure 4.1, it is determined that 3.1 is the size of the DL for a stimulus intensity of 13. The DL value of 3.1 is added to 13 to yield a stimulus intensity of 16.1, which represents a stimulus value two jnd's above absolute threshold. This procedure of successively summating jnd's and relating them to corresponding stimulus values results in a psychophysical function such as that shown in Figure 4.2.

An example of a DL scale is the *dol scale* for the perception of pain determined by Hardy, Wolff, and Goodell (1947). Pain was produced by focusing radiant heat from a powerful lamp on the forehead of the observer for a time period of 3 sec. The absolute threshold was determined by increasing the intensity of radiation until a stimulus presentation resulted in a feeling of warmth followed by a sharp pain just before the end of the 3-sec exposure. The time between trials was sufficiently long to allow for the dissipation of heat from the skin. The absolute threshold was 220 mcal (millicalories)/sec/cm² and the most intense stimulus that could be tolerated without damage to the observer was 480 mcal/sec/cm². Between these two values were found 21 jnd's for detecting increments in the sensory magnitude of pain. The dol scale for pain illustrated in Figure 4.3 is based on the

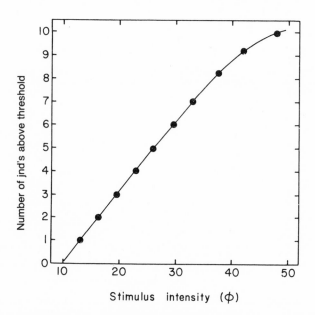

FIGURE 4.2   A psychophysical scale produced by summation of jnd's above absolute threshold. The scale is derived from the $\Delta\phi$ function of Figure 4.1.

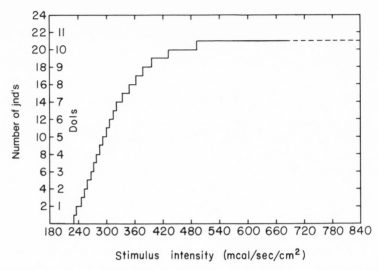

FIGURE 4.3   The dol scale of pain. One dol of pain intensity is equal to two successive jnd's. (From Hardy, Wolff, & Goodell, 1947.)

cumulative number of pain jnd's as a function of stimulus intensity. The *dol* is the unit of measurement for pain, and one dol is equal to two jnd's.

DL scales have been extremely useful to researchers who find it convenient to specify differences among stimuli in terms of the number of discriminable steps rather than in physical units. Often measures of response, for example, those obtained in some conditioning situations and in reaction time experiments, have been found to be meaningfully related to properties of the stimulus only when these properties are expressed in terms of number of jnd's. The limited validity of these scales as measures of attributes of sensation will be considered later. Independent of the outcome of validity testing, however, these scales do appear to measure accurately the important property of discriminable steps.

Paired Comparison Scales

Fechner conceived of the idea that a psychophysical experiment could be conducted in which an observer makes judgments on a psychological dimension having no obvious physical correlate. In his book on the experimental study of esthetics (1876) he suggested that the pleasantness of two objects could be studied by having observers choose the object which was more pleasant. The first experimental study in which this method was employed was an investigation of color preferences by Cohn (1894). A theoretical analysis of the data provided by the method came in 1927, when Thurstone published his paper on the law of comparative judgment as applied to paired comparison judgments.

As in the measurement of DLs, the observer's task in the method of paired comparison is to discriminate between two stimuli, but the logic of scale construction for the method of paired comparison is considerably more elaborate. Both techniques of psychological scaling, however, are based on the notion that the proportion of times stimulus A will be judged greater than stimulus B is determined by the degree to which sensation A and sensation B differ. Fechner simply assumed that DLs along a particular psychological continuum were equal changes in sensation since one DL always represented one stimulus being judged greater than another stimulus 75% of the time. In psychological scaling by the method of paired comparison, the use of p values is not restricted to .75.

If in a large number of comparative judgments the proportion of times an observer judges stimulus B greater than stimulus A is only .55, then the average sensation magnitudes elicited by the two stimuli must be only slightly different with respect to the attribute under study. If, however, the proportion of times stimulus C is judged greater than stimulus A is .95, one can safely assume that the presentation of stimulus C results in a considerably greater average perceptual response than the presentation of stimulus A. Thus, if the average sensation magnitudes produced by two stimuli differ by only a small amount, judgments of the stimuli will be confused and the value of p will be close to .50. But if the average sensation magnitudes are very different the confusion is much less and the value of p approaches 1.00. That this idea might serve as a basis for scaling psychological attributes was recognized by Thorndike (1910), who was interested in developing a scale of excellence of handwriting. Thorndike thought it reasonable to transform the p value associated with comparing two handwriting samples to a z score. The z score was considered as the number of psychological scale units separating the perceptual judgments of excellence elicited by the two stimuli.

The reason for using z scores rather than p values as psychological scale units is clarified by examining the work of Thurstone (1927). He developed fully this method of scaling by providing us with a mathematical model for deriving scale values from comparative judgment proportions. In Thurstone's terms, the application of a stimulus to the organism's sensory receptors results in a *discriminal process* (sensory process) which has some value on the *psychological continuum*. Because of momentary fluctuations of the organism, repeated applications of the same stimulus to sense receptors does not usually result in exactly the same sensation. Thus for Thurstone a stimulus was capable of producing a range of discriminal processes along the psychological continuum. It was assumed that such variation formed a normal distribution on the psychological continuum, the standard deviation of which was called the *discriminal dispersion*. The psychological scale value of the discriminal process associated with the stimulus was taken as the mean on the frequency distribution.

But how can one obtain this distribution on the psychological continuum so that the average discriminal process, that is, the scale value of the discriminal process,

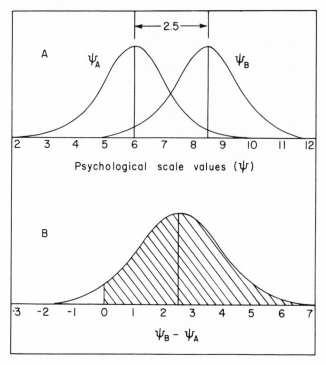

FIGURE 4.4   Two overlapping distributions of discriminal processes on the psychological continuum resulting from the repeated presentation of two different stimuli (A) and the resulting distribution of differences between two discriminal processes produced by repeated presentation of the two stimuli (B).

can be found for a certain stimulus? Thurstone felt that the value of the discriminal process could not be directly reported by the observer but had to be obtained indirectly by consideration of the p values associated with the observer's comparative judgment of pairs of stimuli. For example, if it is known that stimulus A and stimulus B produce pairs of discriminal process distributions with means separated by a certain amount on the psychological continuum (Figure 4.4A), the observer would be expected to judge stimulus B as greater than stimulus A some specific proportion of the time. Therefore in a particular scaling problem the p value is obtained from comparative judgments of stimulus A and stimulus B and, working through the equations of the theory, the separation of the means of the discriminal process distributions on the psychological continuum can be calculated.

Thurstone's logic of psychological scale construction based on discrimination data is somewhat similar to the way TSD has been applied to detection data. In both cases theoretical probability distributions on a psychological continuum are inferred from judgmental response proportions. The differences between the means of the distributions expressed in standard deviation units are used to quantify mental processes in both cases. In TSD the difference between the means of the N and SN distributions specifies stimulus detectability (d'), and in Thurstone's model the difference between the means of two distributions of discriminal processes specifies the difference on the psychological continuum between the sensations for two stimuli. In the language of TSD the problems of TSD are with N and SN distributions while those of Thurstone's model are with many SN distributions.

The symbol ψ will be used to signify the discriminal process (sensory magnitude) elicited by a particular stimulus. The size of ψ, of course, must be measured in psychological units. The scaling problem is to discover the average ψ values corresponding to a number of values of the physical stimulus. Suppose that S_A and S_B are stimuli for overlapping normal distributions of ψ_A and ψ_B on the psychological continuum and that the average ψ_A is 6.0 and the average ψ_B value is 8.5 (Figure 4.4A). An assumption of Thurstone's model is that when S_A and S_B are presented together for comparison the observer will report as greater the stimulus that results in the greater ψ value on that presentation. The size of the difference between the two discriminal processes for a single presentation of S_A and S_B, $\psi - \psi_A$, is called a *discriminal difference*. When a large number of trials is given there will be variation of both ψ_A and ψ_B and, consequently, the discriminal difference will vary from trial to trial. Variation of the discriminal difference can be represented as a normal distribution on the psychological continuum (Figure 4.4B). On trials when $\psi_B - \psi_A$ is greater than zero, S_B will be judged greater than S_A, and on trials when $\psi_B - \psi_A$ is less than zero, S_A will be judged greater than S_B. The mean of this distribution of differences will correspond to the difference between the means of the ψ_A and ψ_B distributions since the difference between the means of two distributions is equal to the mean of a set of differences between randomly selected pairs of scores, one from each distribution.

The formula for computing the standard deviation of differences between pairs of numbers is applied to this problem to determine the standard deviation of the $\psi_B - \psi_A$ values:

$$\sigma_{\psi_B - \psi_A} = \sqrt{ {\sigma_{\psi_A}}^2 + {\sigma_{\psi_B}}^2 - 2r_{\psi_A \psi_B} \sigma_{\psi_A} \sigma_{\psi_B}}, \qquad (4.1)$$

where σ_{ψ_A} and σ_{ψ_B} are the standard deviations of the distributions of ψ_A and ψ_B, respectively, and $r_{\psi_A \psi_B}$ is the correlation between momentary pairs of ψ_A and ψ_B values.

In Figure 4.4B the shaded area to the right of the zero point corresponds to the proportion of times that ψ_B is greater than ψ_A. This zero point can now be converted to a z score by the standard z-score formula:

$$z = \frac{X - \bar{X}}{\sigma}, \qquad (4.2)$$

where X is a particular score, $\bar{X}$ is the mean of the set of scores, and σ is the standard deviation of the set of scores. In this problem $0 - 2.5$ must be divided by $\sigma_{\psi_B - \psi_A}$:

$$z_{BA} = \frac{0 - (\psi_B - \psi_A)}{\sigma_{\psi_B - \psi_A}}. \tag{4.3}$$

Using a conversion table relating z values to p values, this z score could be converted directly to the proportion of times ψ_B should exceed ψ_A.

The easiest way to obtain $\sigma_{\psi_B - \psi_A}$ is to make a few simplifying assumptions about $r_{\psi_A\psi_B}$ and σ_{ψ_A} and σ_{ψ_B}. One assumption often made is that the values of ψ_A and ψ_B are independent; that is, on trials where ψ_A is high there is no systematic tendency for ψ_B also to be high or vice versa. Under these circumstances the term $r_{\psi_A\psi_B}$ in Equation (4.1) becomes zero and may be eliminated. In some experiments, the assumption can also be made that σ_{ψ_A} and σ_{ψ_B} are equal. The value of σ_{ψ_A} and σ_{ψ_B} can then be set at any arbitrary value which will determine the unit of measurement of the psychological scale. For convenience 1.0 is usually employed. The formula for calculating $\sigma_{\psi_B - \psi_A}$ is now simplified to

$$\sigma_{\psi_B - \psi_A} = \sqrt{1 + 1} = 1.41. \tag{4.4}$$

The zero point on the $\psi_B - \psi_A$ distribution therefore corresponds to a z score of $-2.5/1.41 = -1.77$ under these two assumptions. A table of the normal curve reveals that a z score of -1.77 has a proportion of .96 of the normal distribution above it, which in our scaling problem is the proportion of times that ψ_B is greater than ψ_A and is therefore the proportion of times S_B will be judged greater than S_A.

To facilitate understanding of Thurstone's scaling model, our illustration started with knowledge of the scale values $\bar{\psi}_A$ and $\bar{\psi}_B$ (means of ψ_A and ψ_B distributions), and the p values for comparative judgments of S_A and S_B were derived from the model. In actual practice, the p values for comparative judgments of S_A and S_B are determined experimentally, and it is the scale values of $\bar{\psi}_A$ and $\bar{\psi}_B$ that are derived. The difference between $\bar{\psi}_B$ and $\bar{\psi}_A$ can be calculated by converting the proportion of times S_B is judged greater than S_A to a z score and multiplying by $\sigma_{\psi_B - \psi_A}$:

$$\bar{\psi}_B - \bar{\psi}_A = z_{BA}\, \sigma_{\psi_B - \psi_A}. \tag{4.5}$$

In our present example, .96 is converted to a z score of 1.77. The product of 1.77 and 1.41 (the value of $\sigma_{\psi_B - \psi_A}$) is 2.5 (the value of $\bar{\psi}_B - \bar{\psi}_A$).

Since the relation between $\sigma_{\psi_B - \psi_A}$ and the discriminal dispersions and correlation factor for the two stimuli is known from Equation (4.1), Thurstone's complete *law of comparative judgment* can be written as

$$\bar{\psi}_B - \bar{\psi}_A = z_{BA} \sqrt{\sigma_{\psi_A}{}^2 - \sigma_{\psi_B}{}^2 - 2r_{\psi_A\psi_B}\,\sigma_{\psi_A}\,\sigma_{\psi_B}}. \tag{4.6}$$

The separation on the psychological continuum between $\bar{\psi}_B$ and $\bar{\psi}_A$ can be calculated by converting the experimentally obtained proportion $p_{S_B - S_A}$ to a z score, obtaining measures of the terms under the radical, and solving the equation. The terms under the radical cannot be measured experimentally; therefore the values they receive are determined by assumptions or are estimated from experimental data. Thurstone outlined the following five "cases" as different ways of applying the law of comparative judgment:

Case I. The law is applied in its complete form as stated in Equation (4.5) and the unknown terms must be estimated from the data. In Case I repeated judgments are made by a single observer.

Case II. As in Case I, the law is applied in its complete form, but many observers make single judgments of the pair of stimuli.

Case III. An assumption is made that there is no correlation between ψ_A and ψ_B over a large number of judgments. The term $r_{\psi_A \psi_B}$ is assigned a value of zero and therefore dropped from the equation. The law becomes

$$\bar{\psi}_B - \bar{\psi}_A = z_{BA} \sqrt{\sigma_{\psi_A}^2 + \sigma_{\psi_B}^2}. \qquad (4.7)$$

The discriminal dispersions are estimated from experimental data.

Case IV. The discriminal dispersions are assumed to be approximately equal but their values still must be estimated.

Case V. The simplest solution of all is provided by making the additional assumption that the discriminal dispersions are equal. If we arbitrarily give each discriminal dispersion a value of one, the law reduces to

$$\bar{\psi}_B - \bar{\psi}_A = z_{BA}\sqrt{2}. \qquad (4.8)$$

It was this form of the law that was used above in illustrating the major details of Thurstone's model.

The particular solution of the law used in deriving scale values is completely dependent upon the circumstances of each particular scaling problem. Fortunately there are ways of evaluating the adequacy of the assumptions and estimations made when using one of Thurstone's cases (Guilford, 1954; Torgerson, 1958).

When the law of comparative judgment is applied to an actual scaling problem, scale values must be determined for the discriminal processes associated with several values of the stimulus. For example, one might be interested in finding the psychological scale values for S_A, S_B, S_C, S_D, and S_E. The simplest procedure might be to use one of the stimuli, such as S_C, as a standard stimulus for comparison with the four other stimuli. The hypothetical outcome of such an experiment is presented in Table 4.2. From the results of several comparative judgments of each stimulus pair ($S_C - S_A$, $S_C - S_B$, $S_C - S_D$, $S_C - S_E$), p values were calculated and subsequently converted to z scores. Using Thurstone's Case V, the scale value separations between each stimulus and the standard stimulus S_C were computed by Equation (4.8). The scale value of $\bar{\psi}_C$ is arbitrary, and Table 4.3 shows the results when ψ_C was given a value of zero. If one wishes to convert all scale values to positive numbers, the number which yields a value of zero when

TABLE 4.2

Derivation of Differences Among Scale Values by Applying the Law of
Comparative Judgment to Paired Comparison Data

Comparisons	p Values for standard stimulus judged greater than comparison stimulus	z	$\psi_C - \psi$ $= z \sqrt{2}$
$S_C - S_A$	.90	1.28	1.80
$S_C - S_B$	.65	.39	.55
$S_C - S_D$	.30	−.53	−.75
$S_C - S_E$	.15	−1.04	−1.47

added to the lowest negative number is added to all scale values. In our example, a
constant of 1.80 was added to all $\bar{\psi}$ values. Since the placement of the zero point is
completely arbitrary the method results in an interval scale of measurement.

The *method of paired comparison* is the method most frequently employed to
collect data for constructing psychological scales based upon comparative
judgments. It represents an elaboration of the method discussed above, where one
stimulus in a series serves as a standard for comparison with the other stimuli in the
series. In the method of paired comparison, however, the observer is required to
make comparative judgments for all possible pairs of stimuli. This situation can be
regarded as one in which each stimulus serves as the standard in a series of
comparative judgments with the other stimuli. The treatment of the results is
basically the same as that used when only one of the stimuli serves as the standard
stimulus. The p values are first computed for each pair of stimuli and placed in a
proportion matrix such as Table 4.4. Each row of the table gives the p values for
comparative judgments when each of the stimuli served as the standard. In this
example, five separate sets of psychological scale values can be generated by
converting the p values to z scores and applying the appropriate version of the law
of comparative judgment. In other words, for each of five stimuli five independent
estimates of the distances between $\bar{\psi}$ values can be computed (Table 4.5). The final
$\bar{\psi}$ values assigned to the stimulus is the average of these five distances between $\bar{\psi}$
values.

TABLE 4.3

Final Scale Values Derived from the Law of Comparative Judgment

	Scale values				
	$\bar{\psi}_A$	$\bar{\psi}_B$	$\bar{\psi}_C$	$\bar{\psi}_D$	$\bar{\psi}_E$
$\psi_C = 0$	−1.80	−.55	.00	.75	1.47
$\psi_A = 0$	.00	1.25	1.80	2.55	3.27

TABLE 4.4
Proportions Obtained by Using the Method of Paired Comparison

	S_A	S_B	S_C	S_D	S_E
S_A	–	$p_{A>B}$	$p_{A>C}$	$p_{A>D}$	$p_{A>E}$
S_B	$p_{B>A}$	–	$p_{B>C}$	$p_{B>D}$	$p_{B>E}$
S_C	$p_{C>A}$	$p_{C>B}$	–	$p_{C>D}$	$p_{C>E}$
S_D	$p_{D>A}$	$p_{D>B}$	$p_{D>C}$	–	$p_{D>E}$
S_E	$p_{E>A}$	$p_{E>B}$	$p_{E>C}$	$p_{E>D}$	–

Since the law of comparative judgment provides a model for converting observed proportions of a paired comparison experiment into scale values, it should be possible to reverse the procedure and calculate proportions from the scale values. The proportions calculated from the final scale value obtained by paired comparison can be compared with those originally obtained in the experiment. If there is a close correspondence between the proportions predicted from the model for a particular set of final scale values and the proportions obtained experimentally, the applicability of the model is supported. For example, $p_{A>B}$ can be predicted from the difference between the final scale values of $\overline{\psi}_A$ and $\overline{\psi}_B$. Using the law of comparative judgment we can solve for z_{AB} which is then converted to the predicted $p_{A>B}$ by referring to the table of the normal distribution. For example, if Thurstone's Case V had been assumed in deriving the scale values then z_{AB} would be calculated from Equation (4.8). This procedure would be repeated for all possible p values, and a table similar to that of Table 4.4 would be filled in.

The model can be tested by determining how well the predicted proportions correspond to those obtained experimentally. A procedure used frequently is to calculate the average absolute deviation between the predicted and obtained proportions. If the average absolute deviation is small we can conclude that the model fits the data. The overall differences between the predicted and the observed proportions can be tested for statistical significance by using a goodness-of-fit test such as chi square. A statistically significant chi square would indicate that the

TABLE 4.5
Scale Value Differences Obtained by Using the Method of Paired
Comparison

	S_A	S_B	S_C	S_D	S_E	Mean
S_A	—	$\overline{\psi}_A-\overline{\psi}_B$	$\overline{\psi}_A-\overline{\psi}_C$	$\overline{\psi}_A-\overline{\psi}_D$	$\overline{\psi}_A-\overline{\psi}_E$	$\overline{\psi}_A$
S_B	$\overline{\psi}_B-\overline{\psi}_A$	—	$\overline{\psi}_B-\overline{\psi}_C$	$\overline{\psi}_B-\overline{\psi}_D$	$\overline{\psi}_B-\overline{\psi}_E$	$\overline{\psi}_B$
S_C	$\overline{\psi}_C-\overline{\psi}_A$	$\overline{\psi}_C-\overline{\psi}_B$	—	$\overline{\psi}_C-\overline{\psi}_D$	$\overline{\psi}_C-\overline{\psi}_E$	$\overline{\psi}_C$
S_D	$\overline{\psi}_D-\overline{\psi}_A$	$\overline{\psi}_D-\overline{\psi}_B$	$\overline{\psi}_D-\overline{\psi}_C$	—	$\overline{\psi}_D-\overline{\psi}_E$	$\overline{\psi}_D$
S_E	$\overline{\psi}_E-\overline{\psi}_A$	$\overline{\psi}_E-\overline{\psi}_B$	$\overline{\psi}_E-\overline{\psi}_C$	$\overline{\psi}_E-\overline{\psi}_D$	—	$\overline{\psi}_E$

predicted and obtained proportions differed by more than would reasonably be expected by chance and thus that one or more of the assumptions of the model must be incorrect (see Torgerson, 1958).

Partition Scales

Partition scaling methods are designed to construct interval scales of psychological attributes directly from the judgments of the observers. In these methods the observer is required to partition the psychological continuum into equal sensory intervals. To accomplish this objective, two main kinds of method, *equisection scaling* and *category scaling,* have been developed.

Equisection Scales

Equisection is a method which, as its name implies, requires observers to section the psychological continuum into equal *sense distances*. The psychological difference between two brightnesses, two loudnesses, or two sweetnesses are examples of sense distances. The observer's task is to report whether the sense distance between sensations A and B is less than, greater than, or equal to the sense distance between sensations C and D. The experimental problem is to discover the stimuli corresponding to a series of sensations separated by equal sense distances.

The earliest version of the equisection approach to psychological scaling, called *bisection,* was used by Plateau in the 1850's (Plateau, 1872). In this method two stimuli are presented to the observer for inspection; he is then asked to choose a third stimulus of intermediate value so that the sense distance between the two end stimuli is exactly divided in half—thus resulting in two sense distances of equal size defined by three stimulus values. Plateau, for example, had artists paint a gray that was midway between black and white. The term equisection is generally reserved for the extension of this procedure to situations where the observer sections off not just two but several equal intervals on the psychological continuum. Typically the procedure is one in which the observer is asked to choose a limited number of stimuli (e.g., five from a large stimulus assortment) that produce sensations equidistant on the psychological continuum. The ends of the continuum are defined to the observer by the presentation of the lowest and highest stimulus values. The lightness of grays has been scaled by Munsell, Sloan, and Godlove (1933) using such a procedure. Observers chose a series of gray surfaces so that the psychological continuum of lightness, starting with black and ending with white, was divided into eight psychologically equal steps.

There are two somewhat different techniques for extracting estimations of a series of equal sense distances from an observer. The observer may be presented with the two end stimuli and asked to choose n minus 1 stimuli to create n equal sense distances. This procedure is called a *simultaneous solution* because all of the scale values are estimated at once by the observer. Alternatively, a *progressive solution* requires that an observer on a particular trial choose only one stimulus bisecting a sensory distance. By progressively bisecting sense distances into smaller and smaller sense distances the desired number of successive equal sense intervals is obtained. If four equal intervals were desired, for example, the interval between the two end stimuli would be bisected first and the two resulting equal intervals would be subsequently bisected, first one and then the other. The simultaneous solution and the progressive solution are illustrated schematically in Figure 4.5.

The assigning of numbers to the sensory continuum to form an interval scale of the attribute is relatively simple. Since the equisection experiment yields a series of stimulus values corresponding to a series of sensations that change in equal psychological increments, any number series increasing in equal steps $(1, 2, 3, \ldots, n$, etc.) can be assigned as scale values to the sensations. A psychophysical magnitude function may be constructed by plotting psychological scale values against stimulus values.

Stevens and Volkmann (1940) have constructed a psychological scale of auditory pitch by the method of equisection. The basic procedures of their experiment provide a meaningful illustration of the application of this method. The purpose of the investigation was to determine the relationship between psychological pitch and pure tone frequency from 40 to 12,000 Hz. On different occasions observers were required to section into four psychologically equal intervals each of three overlapping frequency ranges (40–1000 Hz, 200–6500 Hz, and 3000–12,000 Hz). For each of these three frequency ranges the end stimuli were of fixed frequency and the observer had to adjust the frequency of three variable stimuli to create four

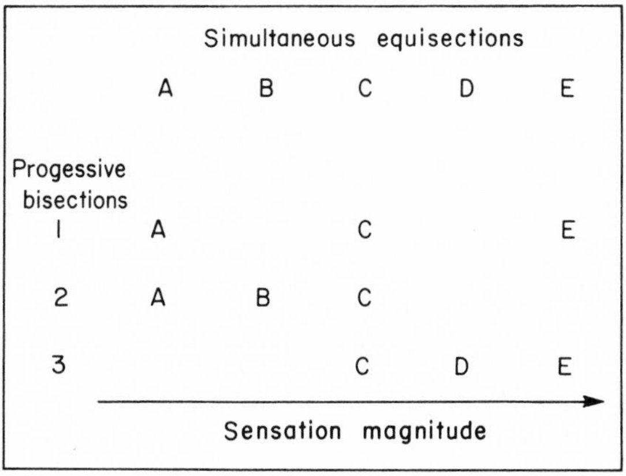

FIGURE 4.5   Sensations that are separated by equal sense distances as determined by simultaneous and progressive solutions.

TABLE 4.6
Results Obtained by Observers Who Equisectioned Each of Three
Frequency Ranges into Four Equal Intervals of Psychological Pitch

Frequency ranges (Hz)	Stimulus frequency defining intervals				
40-1000	40	161	404	693	1000
200-6500	200	867	2022	3393	6500
3000-12,000	3000	4109	5526	7743	12,000

psychologically equal increments in pitch. Ten observers made each of these three equisection judgments five times. Table 4.6 shows the average frequency settings made by the observers for the three frequency ranges.

For each of the frequency ranges a series of numbers representing amounts of pitch was assigned to the five frequencies judged equidistant with respect to pitch. The only requirement for an interval scale of pitch is that equal increments in pitch are designated by equal increments in the number system. Therefore, the five successive frequencies obtained by equisection of a particular frequency range are assigned five successive numbers increasing by steps of one to represent five equal increments in pitch. Pitch values plotted against stimulus frequency for each of the three frequency ranges are seen in Figure 4.6. Smooth curves fitted to the data points yield the three psychological magnitude functions.

The objective of the experiment, however, was to construct not three but one psychophysical function covering the entire stimulus frequency range of 40–12,000 Hz. The three psychophysical functions for the overlapping frequency

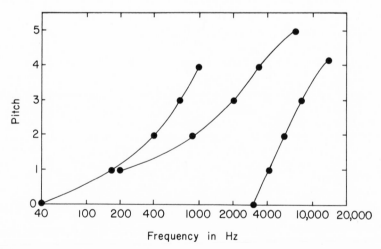

FIGURE 4.6   Three equisection scales of the psychological pitch of pure tones for three overlapping frequency ranges. (From Stevens & Volkmann, 1940.)

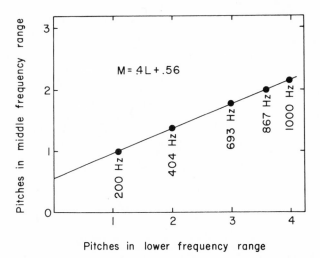

FIGURE 4.7   Psychological pitch for stimuli presented in the context of the middle frequency range plotted against the psychological pitch of the same stimuli presented in the context of the lower frequency range. The linearity of the function indicates that the observers' judgments were internally consistent. The equation is used to convert the scale values of stimuli in the lower range into the units of the scale for the middle frequency range. (From Torgerson, 1958. Reprinted from W. S. Torgerson, *Theory and Methods of Scaling.* Copyright © 1958 by John Wiley & Sons, Inc.)

ranges had to be combined to form a single psychophysical function covering the entire frequency range. To solve this problem, Stevens and Volkmann employed graphical methods that involved much trial and error. The same result is achieved by a more systematic procedure suggested by Torgerson (1958). The procedure converts the scale values of stimuli in the lower and upper frequency ranges into scale units of the middle frequency range, resulting in one homogeneous scale and a single psychophysical function. In Figure 4.7 the scale values assigned the frequencies 200, 404, 693, 867, and 1000 Hz in the middle (M) range are plotted against the scale values for these frequencies in the lower (L) range. The scale values of these stimuli for the middle and lower frequency ranges were read from the psychophysical magnitude of Figure 4.6. A straight line fitted to the data points gave the equation

$$M = 0.4L + 0.56. \tag{4.9}$$

The scale values for *any* frequency in the lower range can be converted to the units of the middle range by this equation. The same procedure was applied to the scale values of frequencies common to the middle and upper (U) frequency ranges (3000, 3393, 4109, 5526, and 6500 Hz) and the equation

$$M = 0.5U + 3.8 \tag{4.10}$$

was determined from Figure 4.8. From this equation the scale values for *any*

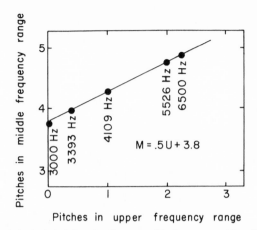

FIGURE 4.8   Psychological pitch for stimuli presented in the context of the middle frequency range plotted against the psychological pitch of the same stimuli presented in the context of the upper frequency range. The linearity of the function indicates that the observers' judgments were internally consistent. The equation is used to convert the scale values of stimuli in the upper range into the units of the scale for the middle frequency range. (From Torgerson, 1958. Reprinted from W. S. Torgerson, *Theory and Methods of Scaling.* Copyright © 1958 by John Wiley & Sons, Inc.)

frequency in the upper range can be converted to units of the middle frequency range.

In the Stevens and Volkmann study (1940) the conversion of all scale values to a common unit resulted in a single scale of psychological pitch for all 15 stimulus frequencies in Table 4.6. The final psychophysical function covering the entire stimulus frequency range is presented in Figure 4.9. The squares, circles, and triangles on the function represent average scale values for stimuli in the lower, middle, and upper frequency ranges, respectively.

Application of the method of equisection, however, does not demand the use of overlapping stimulus ranges requiring separate scalings. In many experiments, observers have simply been asked to section into *n* equal sense distances the entire stimulus range. When the stimulus range is extensive, as it is for the frequency of auditory stimuli, however, judgments may be more accurate when the number of equal sense distances estimated is small, covering a limited stimulus range. Furthermore, the independent scaling of stimuli in different situations or stimulus contexts provides a valuable opportunity to validate scale values. If the observer's judgments of stimuli produce a valid psychological scale they must be independent of the particular stimulus context within which they are made. When this is the case, scale values of stimuli obtained in one stimulus context will be linearly related to the scale values of these stimuli obtained in some other stimulus context. As described earlier, a valid interval scale of measurement is invariant to linear transformations. Figures 4.7 and 4.8 show that the pitch scale meets this particular requirement for validity. Scale values of stimuli in the lower frequency range that

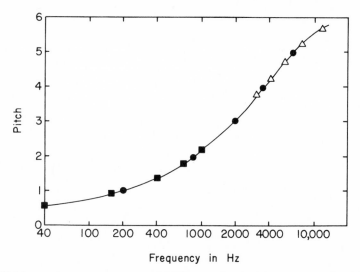

FIGURE 4.9   The final pitch scale for frequencies from 40 to 12,000 Hz. The squares, circles, and triangles represent data obtained from the lower, middle, and upper frequency ranges, respectively. (From Torgerson, 1958; based on the data of Stevens & Volkmann, 1940.) (Reprinted from W. S. Torgerson, *Theory and Methods of Scaling.* Copyright © 1958 by John Wiley & Sons, Inc.)

were also in the middle range were linearly related, as were scale values of stimuli that were common to upper and middle ranges.

Category Scales

Methods of category scaling, like those of equisection scaling, are designed to measure sensory attributes on an equal interval scale. If the scaling is successful, the end product in both cases is a partitioning of the perceptual continuum into several psychologically equal intervals—the boundaries of which are identified by specific stimuli. Category and equisection scaling techniques, though similar in rationale, require the observer to perform somewhat different tasks. The observer's task under the equisection method is to choose from a large stimulus sample the stimuli that result in a specified number of perceptually equal sense distances. In category scaling the observer is presented with a large number of stimuli and told to assign all of them to a specified number of categories. The number of categories is usually somewhere between 3 and 11. Categories are usually specified to the observer either as numbers such as 1, 2, and 3, or as adjectives such as low, medium, and high.

The method of *equal-appearing intervals* is the simplest version of category scaling. In the use of this method it is assumed that the observer is capable of keeping the intervals between category boundaries psychologically equal as he assigns stimuli to the various categories. Under this assumption the experimenter treats the category values assigned to a particular stimulus as interval-scale values.

Accurate estimations of psychological scale values require a fairly large number of judgments of a particular stimulus. Replication of judgments can be achieved by having many observers judge each stimulus once or by having one observer judge each stimulus many times. In the most powerful form of replication, several observers judge each stimulus several times.

For a particular stimulus the psychological scale value of the sensory attribute under investigation is taken as the average (mean or median) category value assigned to the stimulus. The form of the psychophysical magnitude function is revealed when the average category value is plotted against values of the stimulus. Table 4.7 contains hypothetical data for an experiment using five categories and ten stimulus values. The cells of the table contain the numerical frequency with which observers assigned a particular stimulus to a particular category. The median scale values computed for each stimulus value are presented in the far left column. The psychophysical magnitude function is seen in Figure 4.10. The form of this curve is typical of psychophysical magnitude functions obtained by category scaling techniques.

Category scales constructed by the method of equal appearing intervals have frequently been found to have a serious defect. If the category judgment of the observer is determined solely by the sensation magnitude on the psychological continuum produced by some stimulus, the judgment should be completely independent of the values of other stimuli presented on other trials. The scale values for a particular stimulus, however, are often found to be dependent on the values of other stimuli used in the experiment. This results from a strong tendency for observers to assign the stimuli to categories in such a way that all categories are used about equally often. Thus, the particular spacing of the stimuli on the physical

TABLE 4.7
Frequency with Which Each Stimulus Is Judged in Each Category in a
Hypothetical Experiment

	Categories					
Stimuli	1	2	3	4	5	Median scale value
10	38	46	16	0	0	1.76
15	12	42	32	14	0	2.40
20	4	28	38	22	8	2.97
25	0	18	36	32	14	3.39
30	0	12	30	35	23	3.73
35	0	6	24	38	32	4.03
40	0	0	22	40	38	4.20
45	0	0	18	32	50	4.50
50	0	0	12	31	57	4.62
55	0	0	9	29	62	4.69

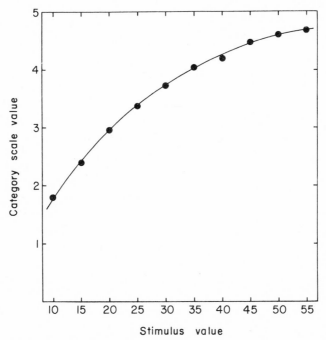

FIGURE 4.10   Category scale based on the hypothetical data of Table 4.7. The median category rating is plotted for each stimulus value.

continuum may greatly influence the shape of the psychophysical function. The typical negatively accelerated curvature of the function obtained by the method tends to be exaggerated when a cluster of low intensity stimuli with a few high intensity stimuli are used. The stimuli at the low end of the physical continuum are distributed over all but a few of the highest categories and the intense stimuli are assigned to the remaining one or two categories. The psychological scale value separation is exaggerated between low intensity stimuli and the separation between high intensity stimuli is minimized—the psychophysical function becomes very negatively accelerated. Likewise, because of the tendency to distribute the stimuli evenly over categories, the curvature of the function is reduced when a cluster of stimuli near the high end of the stimulus continuum with only a few low intensity stimuli is used. Thus, category scales of the same stimuli scaled in the context of different stimulus distributions are not linearly related. Since a valid interval scale is invariant to linear transformations and distorted by any nonlinear transformation, the nonlinearity between category scales of the same stimuli suggests that their usefulness is very limited. Unless distortion due to stimulus distribution effects is eliminated, category scales must be regarded as ordinal scales at best.

Stevens and Galanter (1957) proposed that an iterative procedure could be used to obtain category scales free of the distorting influences of the observer's tendency to use all of the categories equally often. The assumption is made that the observer expects the series of stimuli to be arranged so that categories appear equally often. At the onset of an experiment the stimulus spacing is arbitrary and a scale is constructed based on the category judgments of a group of observers. This scale is the first approximation to the uncontaminated scale. On the basis of this scaling, a new series of stimuli is chosen with the stimuli separated by equal distances on the first psychological scale. This stimulus spacing is used in the construction of a second scale (second approximation to the uncontaminated scale) using a new group of observers. From the second scale a new stimulus spacing, with stimuli separated by equal distances on the second psychological scale, is derived, and a third group of observers is used in the construction of a third approximation to the uncontaminated scale. This procedure is repeated until successive scales do not differ, indicating that an uncontaminated scale has been achieved by neutralizing the effects of the observer's expectations about the stimulus spacing.

Perhaps the oldest category scale of sensation is the scale of stellar magnitude invented by the Greek astronomer Hipparchus over 2000 years ago. The purpose of the scale was to quantify the brightness of stars. The numbers 1 through 6 were used to indicate various perceived brightnesses. The number 1 was assigned to those stars that looked brightest and 6 to the faintest. Between the extremes the numbers 2, 3, 4, and 5 were assigned to stars of decreasing brightness. Until the invention of photometers for measuring the physical intensity of stellar light, the psychological scale of stellar magnitude was used extensively by astronomers. To the delight of Fechner the relationship between category judgments of stellar

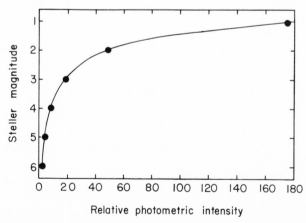

FIGURE 4.11   Category scale of stellar magnitude. The scale indicates how the judgments of early astronomers are related to the photometric intensity of starlight. The relationship is approximately logarithmic. (From Stevens, 1975; based on data from Jastrow, 1887.) (Reprinted from S. S. Stevens, *Psychophysics: Introduction to Its Perceptual, Neural and Social Prospects.* Copyright © 1975 by John Wiley & Sons, Inc.)

magnitude and the physical intensity of light from the stars was found to be approximately logarithmic. The psychophysical magnitude function of Figure 4.11 represents the average relative light intensity values for stars that were assigned to each of the six categories. The light intensity values were derived by Stevens (1975) from the data provided by Jastrow in 1887.

Astronomers no longer depend on visual estimations of stellar magnitude. However, photometric measurements are now converted to the stellar magnitude scale which has been corrected to be a perfect logarithmic function of light intensity. Thus, the astronomer's scale of star brightness came to be in perfect agreement with Fechner's incorrect law. The logarithmic decibel scale of sound pressure has also been misinterpreted as an equal interval scale of sensory magnitude. It has only been in the last 15 or 20 years that research on ratio scales of sensation has convincingly demonstrated the inadequacy of Fechner's law.

Ratio Scales

Measurement of physical properties on ratio scales has always been a highly desirable achievement since these scales containing the characteristics of order, distance, and origin have maximal correspondence with the number system. Methods for constructing ratio scales of sensation have been used extensively only in the past 20 years. However, as far back as 1888 Merkel was interested in finding the stimulus that doubled sensation. Merkel had observers adjust a variable stimulus so that its sensation was twice as great as the sensation produced by a fixed stimulus. A similar procedure used by Fullerton and Cattell (1892) required observers to adjust a stimulus to produce a sensation that was some fraction or multiple of the sensation produced by a standard stimulus. These procedures result in ratio scales of sensation when the observer's judgments allow one to specify the ratio of one sensation magnitude to another. It was not until the 1930's, when acoustical engineers became concerned with the problem of numerically specifying psychological loudness, that psychologists became interested in ratio measurements of sensation.

The practical problem of measuring loudness arose out of an obvious failure of Fechner's law. Acoustical engineers had assumed the validity of Fechner's law and adopted the decibel scale, which is a logarithmic scale of sound energy. It was hoped that with this new scale sounds could be specified in numbers reflecting the magnitude of the sensations they produced. It soon became apparent, however, that a sound of 60 dB was much more than twice as loud as a sound of 30 dB. It was through the development of special techniques for measuring loudness that psychophysics was supplied with the several ratio scaling methods subsequently used with success in the construction of scales of literally dozens of perceptual dimensions.

The methods of *ratio production, ratio estimation, magnitude estimation,* and *magnitude production* require observers to make judgments of the ratio between the magnitudes of two sensations. The observer's proficiency in performing this task determines the validity of a sensory scale constructed by any one of these methods. Fortunately there are tests of internal consistency for evaluating an observer's performance on such a task. The construction of a psychophysical scale for a particular sensory attribute requires knowledge of the ratios between sensations at several points along the sensory dimension. If an experiment has provided this information and has withstood tests of internal consistency, one has a basis for assigning to sensations numbers that have true numerical significance.

Ratio Production

In the use of the method of *ratio production,* often called fractionation, the observer is required to adjust a variable stimulus while observing a standard stimulus. The two sensations are adjusted to a prescribed ratio, e.g., $1/4$, $1/3$, $1/2$. This method was used in several studies of psychological loudness that were summarized by Churcher (1935) for the purpose of developing measures of the sensation magnitude of industrial noise. Based on Churcher's work, Stevens (1936) produced the original loudness scale called the *sone* scale. Several procedures were employed to find stimulus values that resulted in sensation loudnesses standing in a 2-to-1 ratio. In one procedure, observers listened to a tone of a certain fixed intensity level and were required to adjust the intensity of another tone until it was exactly half as loud as the stimulus of fixed intensity. The intensity levels in physical units for the two stimuli were recorded and the procedure was repeated for several stimulus intensities.

A second procedure was based on the assumption that a tone will be perceived as exactly twice as loud when presented to both equally sensitive ears (binaural stimulation) as when presented to only one ear (monaural stimulation). To find stimulus intensities that produce loudnesses in a 2-to-1 ratio, the observers were required to adjust the intensity of a monaural tone to match the loudness of a binaural tone of fixed intensity. If this monaural stimulus were applied binaurally, it should have a loudness exactly twice that of the binaural stimulus of fixed intensity. The results obtained using this method, being in close agreement with those obtained by the half-judgment method, lend support to the validity of both methods.

To construct a measurement scale of the attribute loudness, a unit of measurement called the sone was established by defining one sone as the loudness of a 1000-Hz tone at 40 dB above absolute threshold (Stevens, 1936). A scale value of 2 sones of loudness was assigned to a stimulus intensity of 47 dB, since this stimulus produced a sound judged twice as loud as the sound of the 40-dB tone. Likewise, a stimulus intensity of 55 dB was given a loudness of 4 sones because it was judged to be exactly twice as loud as the 47-dB tone. In this stepwise fashion loudness values were assigned to intensities from 40 dB to 120 dB. For loudnesses less than 1 sone the stimulus judged exactly half as loud as the 40-dB stimulus was determined (34 dB) and given a loudness value of .50 sones, and the stimulus judged half as loud as 34 dB was found to be 28 dB and was given a loudness of .25 sones, and so on down the scale.

Figure 4.12 represents the psychophysical magnitude function for loudness where loudness in sones is plotted against stimulus intensity in decibels. Fechner's theoretical statement that sensation intensity is proportional to the logarithm of stimulus intensity is not supported by the shape of this empirically determined loudness function. A straight-line relationship between loudness and decibels (a logarithmic scale of sound energy) is predicted from Fechner's law. The psychophysical function is positively accelerated, rather than linear, when loudness is plotted against decibels.

Many scales of sensation intensity have been constructed by the method of ratio production. There are, for example, scales of brightness, loudness, weight, taste, smell, apparent duration, pain, touch, and vibration, to name only a few. The forms of the various psychophysical functions relating values of the scaled sensation to values of the stimulus are often quite different. For example, apparent duration has been found to be linearly related to actual time (Gescheider, 1967; Gregg, 1951; Ross & Katchmer, 1951), apparent weight increases as a positively accelerated function of physical weight (Harper & Stevens, 1948), and loudness and brightness increase as negatively accelerated functions of sound energy and

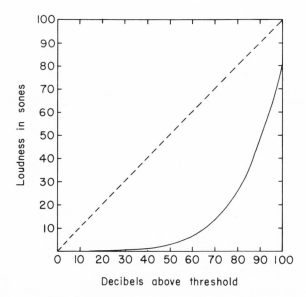

FIGURE 4.12   Loudness of a 1000-Hz tone in sones as a function of stimulus intensity in decibels above absolute threshold. The relationship deviates greatly from the straight-line predicted from Fechner's law. (From Stevens, 1936. Copyright by the American Psychological Association. Reprinted by permission.)

light energy, respectively (Hanes, 1949a, b; Stevens, 1936). One form of the psychophysical function conspicuously absent from the large compilation of scales constructed by this method is the logarithmic relationship predicted from Fechner's law.

The application of the ratio production method requires that a stimulus be continuously variable over the range of stimuli used in the experiment. Stimulus variation in small steps may be sufficient to fulfill this requirement, for under such conditions the stimulus can be manipulated with respect to a fixed standard stimulus until the observer is satisfied that the two sensations stand in exactly the ratio prescribed by the experimenter.

One of the psychophysical methods described in Chapter 2 is usually employed to obtain an estimation of the stimulus which, when paired with a standard stimulus, results in the prescribed sensation ratio. If the method of average error is used, the observer or experimenter may manipulate the variable stimulus until the observer is satisfied that it is psychologically set at some prescribed fraction of the standard stimulus. When the method of constant stimuli is used, the observer is required to indicate whether a particular setting of the comparison stimulus is psychologically greater or less than some prescribed fraction of the standard stimulus. If the method of limits is used, the variable stimulus is changed progressively in steps until the observer indicates that the sensation is just noticeably greater than the prescribed fraction of the standard stimulus, or until he indicates that the sensation is just noticeably smaller than the prescribed fraction. With both the method of constant stimuli and the method of limits, the stimulus value analogous to the point of subjective equality is taken as the estimation of the stimulus value corresponding to the prescribed sensory ratio.

The prescribed ratio most frequently employed in experiments has been 1/2, presumably because halving judgments seems to be easier than making judgments of larger ratios. Many investigators, however, have used more than one ratio within the same experiment to evaluate the validity of scale values. For example, from a scale based on halving judgment data, one should be able to predict with reasonable accuracy the values of pairs of stimuli judged to result in sensation ratios of 1/3, 1/4, 1/10, and so on. It seems advisable at least to use both the ratio and its complement for the construction of any scale using the ratio production method. In using a 2-to-1 ratio observers would be required to make both halving judgments and doubling judgments. Using such a balanced procedure provides a validity check on the observer's judgments. Furthermore, when the scale obtained with a particular fraction differs from that obtained with the complement fraction, averaging the two scales often eliminates the biasing effects due to the use of the two fractions chosen for the experiment.

No set rule can be stated for deciding on the number of standard stimulus values to be used in a given experiment. Torgerson (1958) has, however, suggested that at least seven standard stimuli distributed over the range of the attribute to be scaled should be employed. It is important that enough values be used so that a smooth

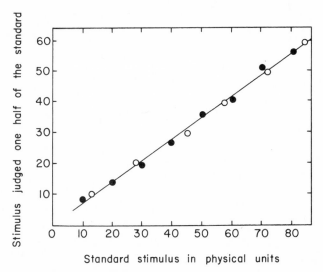

FIGURE 4.13   Stimulus intensity judged to be one half of the standard stimulus as a function of the value of the standard stimulus. The filled points are based on halving judgments and the open circles are based on doubling judgments. In order to make the data from the two kinds of judgment directly comparable, the observer's half judgments are plotted on the ordinate but his doubling judgments are plotted on the abscissa. Hypothetical data.

curve can accurately be fitted to the ratio judgments plotted against standard stimulus values. An example of such a curve is shown in Figure 4.13, where the value of the stimulus judged half as intense as a standard stimulus is plotted against eight values of the standard stimulus. Each point on the curve represents an average (such as the arithmetic mean, geometric mean, or median) of several judgments either of the same observer or of different observers.

As a test of the validity of the results, data from both halving and doubling judgment procedures have been included in this graph, and it can be seen that judgments made by the two procedures are in close agreement. Fitting a smooth curve to these data points provides a means of estimating the stimulus that would be judged half as great as any stimulus value within the range of values used in the experiment.

To generate the psychophysical magnitude function, a scale unit must first be established. The unit is specified when any positive number is assigned to any one of the stimulus values. The particular number and stimulus value used to establish the unit may be completely arbitrary, but in some cases they have been determined by considerations such as making a scale comparable to some other scale. In our example using hypothetical data, 800 is arbitrarily assigned to the sensation produced by a stimulus value of 40, and the first point is entered on the psychophysical function of Figure 4.14. From the half-judgment function (Figure 4.13) it is seen that a stimulus of 28.5 is judged to be psychologically half that of

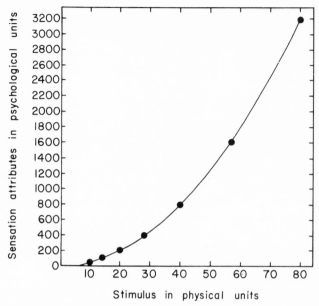

FIGURE 4.14   Psychophysical magnitude function based on the half-judgment function of Figure 4.13.

the stimulus of 40. Since a stimulus of 40 has a psychological scale value of 800, a psychological scale value of 400 must be assigned to the 28.5 stimulus, establishing the second point on the psychophysical magnitude function. The half-judgment function is again examined to determine the stimulus value judged to produce a sensation magnitude half as great as that produced by the 28.5 stimulus. This is seen to be a stimulus value of 20.0, which is assigned a psychological scale value of 200 since the stimulus value of 28.5 has been given a psychological scale value of 400. Thus a third point on the psychophysical magnitude function is established. Working further down the scale, a stimulus of 14.0 is assigned a psychological scale value of 100 since the half-judgment function revealed that this stimulus was judged as psychologically half as great as the stimulus of 20. The fourth point of the psychophysical function is plotted. Finally, by the same procedure the lowest point on the psychophysical function is established at a stimulus value of 10 and a psychological scale value of 50.

In our hypothetical example, psychological scale values for stimuli above 40 may also be obtained by referring to the half-judgment function. However, the procedure is slightly different than that used for stimuli smaller than 40. If we locate 40 on the ordinate of the half-judgment graph in Figure 4.13 we find the stimulus judged as having a sensation magnitude twice that of the 40 stimulus by referring to the half-judgment curve and locating the corresponding stimulus value on the abscissa, which is seen to be 57. Since a stimulus value of 40 has a psychological scale value of 800, the stimulus value of 57 is given a scale value of 1600 and another point is plotted on the psychophysical magnitude function. Similarly, the half-judgment function reveals that a stimulus value of 80 results in a sensory magnitude twice that of the 57 stimulus. The stimulus of 80 is therefore given a scale value of 3200. The points on the psychophysical magnitude function are connected by a smooth curve. From this graph the sensation magnitude for any stimulus within the range used in the experiment can be estimated.

Ratio Estimation

The method of *ratio estimation* is closely related to the method of ratio production. Instead of adjusting two stimuli so that sensations are in a prescribed ratio, however, the observer's task in ratio estimation is to respond to two stimuli by estimating the apparent ratio between them. This method has proved very useful as one means of testing the validity of scales constructed by ratio production. For example, a reexamination of the ratio production in Figure 4.14 reveals that many predictions could be made about an observer's estimations of the apparent ratios between pairs of stimuli. Stimuli of 20 and 40 units produce sensations of 200 and 800, respectively; therefore the prediction can be made that an observer will estimate the apparent ratio of these two stimuli to be 1/4. If the observer were then asked to repeat the procedure for stimuli of 20 and 80 units, his predicted response would be 1/16. When observers are required to make estimations of the apparent ratios for several pairs of stimuli along the stimulus dimension, the degree of correspondence between results predicted from the ratio production scale and the obtained results serves as a check on the validity of both methods. In general, psychophysical scales constructed by ratio estimation and ratio production methods are in close agreement.

Today, ratio production and ratio estimation methods are not frequently used because they have been found to be particularly sensitive to stimulus context effects. Garner (1954) demonstrated that changing such factors as the stimulus range from which the observer had to choose greatly influenced the observer's fractionation judgments. However, such errors can be minimized in a carefully controlled experiment. For example, Engen and Tulunay (1956) found that practiced observers are much less affected by context effects than are inexperienced ones.

Magnitude Estimation

The method of psychophysical ratio scaling most frequently used in current investigations is the method of *magnitude estimation*. The observer in a magnitude estimation experiment is required to make direct numerical estimations of the sensory magnitudes produced by various stimuli. S. S. Stevens, whose name is most closely associated with this method, conducted early experiments using magnitude estimation to study brightness and loudness (1953, 1955). According to

Stevens: "It all started from a friendly argument with a colleague who said 'You seem to maintain that each loudness has a number and that if someone sounded a tone I should be able to tell him the number.' I replied, 'That's an interesting idea. Let's try it' '' (Stevens, 1956, p. 2).

Stevens (1958) described two main ways of applying the magnitude estimation technique to a scaling problem. In one, the observer is presented with a standard stimulus and told that the sensation it produces has a certain numerical value (modulus) such as 10. On subsequent trials other stimuli are presented and the observer assigns numbers to his sensations relative to the value of the modulus. The observer is instructed to make his judgments reflect how many times greater one sensation is than another (the ratio between the two sensations). If a stimulus seemed to have twice the apparent magnitude of the modulus the observer would say 20, but if it had half the apparent magnitude he would say 5. The data from several observers may be combined by calculating the median or geometric mean of the judgments for each stimulus value. The arithmetic mean is seldom used because its value may be greatly affected by a few unrepresentative high judgments.

In the other version of the method the modulus is not defined by the experimenter. The stimuli are randomly presented to the observer, who assigns numbers to his sensations in proportion to their magnitudes. Since the observer is readily able to establish his own modulus, psychophysical scales with or without an experimenter-defined modulus are in close agreement. Instructions to the observer may be modeled after the following example provided by Stevens (1975):

> You will be presented with a series of stimuli in irregular order. Your task is to tell how intense they seem by assigning numbers to them. Call the first stimulus any number that seems appropriate to you. Then assign successive numbers in such a way that they reflect your subjective impression. There is no limit to the range of numbers that you may use. You may use whole numbers, decimals, or fractions. Try to make each number match the intensity as you perceive it [p. 30].

Most investigators feel it is better to permit the observer to choose his own modulus than to designate one for him. In either variation of the method the average of the numbers assigned to a particular stimulus is the psychological scale value for that stimulus. The psychophysical magnitude function, then, is simply the average magnitude estimation plotted as a function of some proptery of the stimulus. It has been recommended that when no modulus is designated the data of the different observers can be combined by computing the geometric mean for each stimulus value (see Stevens, 1971a).

During an experimental session, between 10 and 20 stimuli should be presented in irregular order. The order of stimulus values should be different for each observer. Stevens (1971a) suggests that one or two judgments should be obtained from each observer. No extensive training on the task is necessary and therefore all the data for a single observer can be obtained in one or two sessions. Because in most circumstances judgments can be obtained relatively rapidly, magnitude estimation provides a valuable method for use in extensive experiments where several parameters of the stimulus are varied.

Such an experiment was conducted by J. C. Stevens and Marks (1971). A description of their experiment will serve as an illustration of how the method of magnitude estimation has been used to investigate complex problems of sensory information processing. Stevens and Marks were primarily interested in spatial summation in the perception of warmth. Before they conducted their experiment it was known that spatial summation extends over several hundred square centimeters of skin surface for the detection of warmth at absolute threshold. In determining absolute thresholds for warmth Kenshalo, Decker, and Hamilton (1967), for example, found a near-perfect trading relationship between stimulus intensity and the areal extent of the stimulus. As the area of the stimulus was made smaller the required increase in temperature needed to barely detect a sensation of warmth increased. In fact, to arouse a threshold sensation a constant value of stimulation equal to the product of intensity and area was sufficient. Thus, the critical factor which determines whether or not warmth is felt is not just intensity (energy per unit area), but the total heat input to the skin. This experiment demonstrated that the sensory system for warmth is capable of integrating stimulation over large areas of the skin.

Stevens and Marks were interested in the relationship between intensity and area for warmth sensations above threshold. The method of magnitude estimation provided a means of quantifying warmth sensations for stimuli of various intensities above threshold and various areal extents. Stimuli were applied to the skin of the back or the forehead by the heat from a 1000-watt (W) projector lamp. Radiant intensity was varied by regulating the voltage of the lamp. By means of a timer that operated a shutter located between the lamp and the skin, the experimenter applied the radiation to the skin for precisely 3 sec. The areal extent of radiation was varied by placing aluminum masks of various sizes between the lamp and the skin. During a session a stimulus was presented to the observer once every 30 sec. Each of 18 observers made two magnitude estimations of each stimulus. Observers were instructed to judge how warm each stimulus felt by assigning numbers to stand for the amount of apparent warmth. No fixed standard stimulus or modulus were used.

The data in Figure 4.15 are the geometric means of the magnitude estimations of the 18 observers for stimuli applied to the forehead. The family of curves plotted on double logarithmic axes are psychophysical magnitude functions for stimuli of various sizes. Spatial summation is indicated by the higher magnitude estimation for larger areas of stimulation for any particular stimulus intensity. The amount of summation, however, is not constant for all levels of stimulus intensity. The amount of spatial summation is relatively small at high stimulus intensities. It can be seen in Figure 4.15 that the area of the stimulus has a diminishing effect on the judgments of warmth as stimulus intensity increases. In fact extrapolation of the functions for different areas of stimulation indicates that at an irradiance of 800 mW/cm² the amount of spatial summation should become zero. It is significant

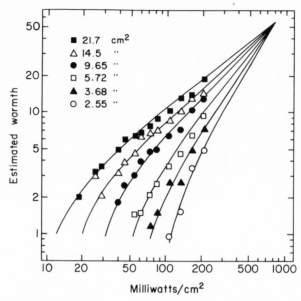

FIGURE 4.15   Magnitude estimation as a function of stimulus irradiance on the forehead. The parameter is areal extent of stimulation. (From J. C. Stevens & Marks, 1971.)

that at approximately 800 mW/cm² the sensation changes from warmth to pricking pain, and pain has been found lacking in spatial summation (Greene & Hardy, 1958). In a subsequent experiment Marks and J. C. Stevens (1973), using a wider range of stimulus intensity values, were able to obtain magnitude estimation data for different areas of stimulation that converged on the pain threshold as stimulus intensity increased.

In order to further evaluate the amount of spatial summation of warmth at different stimulus intensities Stevens and Marks determined from Figure 4.15 the combinations of intensity and area necessary to keep warmth at some particular level. The results are plotted in Figure 4.16 as equal warmth contours for seven levels of apparent warmth. It can be seen from Figure 4.15 that when judged warmth was 55 the stimulus intensity was 800 mW/cm² for all areas of the stimulus. This relationship is indicated in Figure 4.16 as a horizontal line at 55 for intensity as a function of area. In order to keep the sensation of warmth constant at a value of 55 no compensating reduction in intensity is necessary as area is increased. Thus the sensory system, when operating at this high level, is unable to take advantage of increases in stimulus area. On the other hand at the lowest warmth levels there is nearly perfect spatial summation as indicated by the nearly complete trading relation between intensity and area. Each of the parallel dashed lines in Figure 4.16 represents the predicted slope for complete spatial summation. For all points along one of these lines the products of intensity and area are constant. By reducing irradiance as area is increased the total amount of irradiance is kept constant. It can be seen from the psychophysical data that there ia a gradual progression from nearly complete summation to no summation as the intensity of the warmth sensation approaches the threshold for pain.

If the pain threshold determines the point of convergence of the psychophysical functions, changing the pain threshold should change the convergence point. The pain threshold is increased by reducing the duration of the radiant stimulus. When Marks and Stevens (1973) used a .5-sec stimulus rather than the 3.0-sec stimulus used in the earlier study they found that the psychophysical magnitude functions converged at the higher value of 2300 mW/cm². The new convergence point is in reasonable agreement with the higher pain threshold. Thus, the appearance of pain seems to correspond to the complete loss of spatial summation in the warmth sense.

Marks (1974a) has pointed out that spatial summation of warmth is important for the regulation of body temperature. Since body temperature is determined by the total irradiance over large body areas it is to the advantage of the organism to also

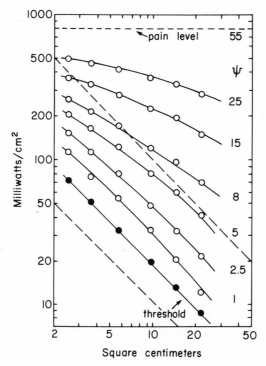

FIGURE 4.16   Contours of equal warmth for different levels of sensation magnitude. Each contour gives the combinations of stimulus intensity and area needed to keep warmth at some particular level. The predicted values for perfect spatial summation are the dashed lines or any line parallel to them. (From J. C. Stevens & Marks, 1971.)

sense warmth in this way. On the other hand, tissue damage due to burning is more dependent on the absolute temperature of the skin than on the size of the heated area. In this case it is to the organism's advantage to feel pain at critical intensity levels that are independent of the areal extent of stimulation.

The discussion of experiments on the sense of warmth and pain serves as an example of how the magnitude estimation procedure has been used to investigate the complex problems of how a sensory system functions. The method has become one of our most valuable tools for the study of sensory processes. The use of the technique has not been restricted to the study of the senses, however. In fact, the simplicity of the method makes it applicable to the scaling of any psychological attribute. Attributes as different as the brightness of a light and the psychological worth of money have yielded to measurement through the use of magnitude estimation.

Magnitude Production

Magnitude production is the inverse of magnitude estimation. The experimenter tells the observer the numerical value of some sensory magnitude and then requires him to adjust a stimulus to produce it. It is essential in the use of this method for the stimulus to be continuosly variable over the stimulus range used in the experiment. The psychophysical magnitude function is constructed by plotting the prescribed sensation magnitude values against the average setting of the stimulus. Magnitude production can also be put to use as a valuable method of testing the validity of scales constructed by magnitude estimation. Close agreement between magnitude production and magnitude estimation scale values constitutes one source of evidence supporting the validity of the scale.

S. S. Stevens (1958) has suggested that the use of magnitude production and magnitude estimation procedures in the same scaling experiment might be a way to offset any systematic errors inherent in either method. This idea is based on the assumption that systematic errors inherent in magnitude estimation and magnitude production are on the average equal in size but opposite in sign. One systematic error which tends to affect psychophysical judgments is a regression of the observer's judgments toward the mean of his judgments. In other words, the observer is reluctant to make extremely low or extremely high judgments even though they may be correct in terms of his perceptions. Consequently his magnitude estimations may not be low enough for the weak stimuli or high enough for the strong stimuli. Likewise, in magnitude production he may fail to adjust the stimulus to a low enough value when he is asked to produce a particular weak sensation magnitude or to a high enough value when he must produce a particular strong sensation. In the case of magnitude estimation the effect is to reduce the slope of the psychophysical function, while in magnitude production the effect is to increase its slope.

The results of an experiment by Stevens and Guirao (1962) shown in Figure 4.17 illustrate the regression effect in magnitude estimation and magnitude production for judgments of the loudness of a 1000-Hz tone. Each data point is the geometric mean of two magnitude estimations or two magnitude productions by each of ten observers. Because of the regression effect, magnitude production resulted in a steeper function than magnitude estimation. It is generally assumed that the unbiased function lies somewhere between the two functions; therefore it is considered advisable to combine them by some procedure. The resulting function should be a better estimate of the unbiased function than either the magnitude estimation function or the magnitude production function.

A procedure for combining the functions for magnitude estimation and magnitude production has been described by Hellman and Zwislocki (1963), who were interested in establishing an unbiased psychophysical magnitude function for the loudness of a 1000-Hz tone. Essentially it consists of geometrically averaging the two psychophysical functions. The procedure has been called the *method of numerical magnitude balance*.

Loudness functions were obtained by Hellman and Zwislocki (1968) for three pure tone frequencies. Each loudness function seen in Figure 4.18 was obtained by the method of numerical magnitude balance. It is significant that the growth of loudness with intensity is more rapid for the low frequency tones than for the 1000-Hz tone. At low intensity levels the frequency of the stimulus has a relatively large effect on loudness, but the effect of frequency diminishes as intensity increases. These results are in agreement with the way the equal loudness contours reported by Robinson and Dadson (1956) change shape at different intensity levels

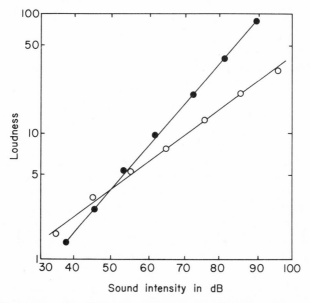

FIGURE 4.17   Loudness of a 1000-Hz tone as determined by magnitude estimation (open circles) and magnitude production (filled circles). (From Stevens & Guirao, 1962.)

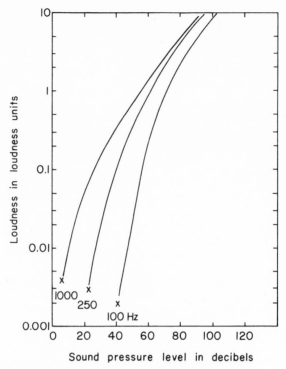

FIGURE 4.18   Loudness scales for three pure tone frequencies determined by the method of numerical magnitude balance. (From Hellman & Zwislocki, 1968.)

(Figure 2.9). The relatively flat contours at high intensity levels indicate that loudness can be kept constant with only slight adjustment of intensity as frequency is changed. In contrast, at low intensity levels intensity must be greatly increased for low frequencies if loudness is to be kept the same for all frequencies. Each equal loudness contour was obtained by having observers adjust the intensity of a tone of some frequency so that its loudness was the same as that of a 1000-Hz tone of fixed intensity.

Although the procedures of numerical magnitude balance and sensation magnitude matching represent two extremely different tasks for the observer, the results from the two procedures are essentially the same. Such agreement between measurements obtained by diverse methods constitutes strong support for their validity. For this reason it is advisable to design experiments whenever possible that will yield one set of measurements with one method that predict the outcome of a second set of measurements made with a different method.

5

The Psychophysical Law

One of the fundamental issues in psychophysics concerns the form of the psychophysical law. The problem is that of discovering a simple equation which describes how the intensity of stimuli and our impressions of them are related. The solution of the problem would have far-reaching implications for scholars in a variety of fields. Certainly the philosopher's concepts of epistemology and the psychologist's theories and research on information processing would be influenced by a psychophysical law. No doubt the neurophysiologist's search for the mechanisms by which the nervous system encodes environmental stimuli would be facilitated. Perhaps even some of the difficult problems confronting social scientists in their attempts to understand man in his social environment would become somewhat simplified by a psychophysical law. The law probably would even have a variety of practical applications in fields such as architectural design, communication systems design, the arts, medicine, and law.

One of the first efforts to formulate precisely a psychophysical law was that of Daniel Bernoulli (1738). Bernoulli, a mathematician, was interested in the psychological worth of money. He proposed that people do not act on the basis of the actual value of money but on some psychological transformation of the actual value. It seemed to Bernoulli that the *utility* of money increases at a decreasing rate as the actual amount increases. A gain of one dollar is psychologically greater if you have only two dollars than if you have one hundred dollars. The economist would say that money exhibits a decreasing marginal utility. Bernoulli's specific proposal was that the utility of money increases as a function of the logarithm of the amount of money. Over one hundred years later Fechner proposed a logarithmic function for sensations and stimuli.

It is interesting that in a footnote to Bernoulli's paper he mentioned that a young mathematician named Gabriel Cramer had suggested in a letter a few years earlier that a power function may describe the relation between utility and the amount of money (see Stevens, 1975). Both Cramer and Bernoulli thought that the utility of money increases at a diminishing rate as the amount of money increases, but their equations were different. Specifically, Cramer stated that utility grows with the square root of money; that is, utility is proportional to money raised to the power of .5.

According to Stevens (1975) Bernoulli's logarithmic function, which has had a large influence on those who theorize about utility, is incorrect, while Cramer's little-noticed power function is correct. Recent experiments in which people made various kinds of judgments on the value of money show that utility increases as a function of the amount of money raised to a power of approximately .45.

The first psychophysical law in psychology was that of G. T. Fechner. Fechner, like Bernoulli, proposed a logarithmic function. While in bed on the morning of October 22, 1850, Fechner was attempting to solve the problem of how the inner world of sensation is related to the outer world of stimuli when it became clear to him that increasing a stimulus by a constant ratio should cause sensation to increase by a constant amount. For example, a temporal sequence of stimuli with intensities of 1, 2, 4, 8, and 16 should cause the sensation to increase in equal amounts with each successive presentation. Doubling the stimulus should always cause the same increment in sensation. The details of how Fechner derived his law are described in Chapter 1. The point to be made here is that for over one hundred years Fechner's law went relatively unchallenged. In fact, during this time the logarithmic law dominated psychophysics. It was so widely accepted that investigators using confusion and partition scaling methods incorrectly identified logarithmic functions in their data, some neurophysiologists found logarithmic functions in data recorded electrically from receptors, and engineers developed the decibel scale with the belief that loudness increased with the logarithm of sound pressure level.

It was not until the mid 1950's that scientists began seriously to question the validity of Fechner's law. It started when S. S. Stevens, using ratio scaling methods, obtained psychophysical magnitude functions for brightness and loudness that did not even slightly resemble logarithmic functions (Stevens, 1953). Psychophysical judgments of both brightness and loudness were instead found to be proportional to the cube root of the energy in the stimulus. Stevens' discovery marked the start of what some scientists have called the "new psychophysics." The new psychophysics is characterized by the extensive use of methods for directly measuring sensation. Chief among these methods have been magnitude estimation and magnitude production.

STEVENS' POWER LAW

As a result of literally dozens of experiments on direct psychophysical scaling conducted in American and European laboratories, a new psychophysical law has emerged to take the place of Fechner's logarithmic law. S. S. Stevens (1957) proposed that the form of the relationship between sensation magnitude and stimulus intensity is a power function. This power law is stated as

$$\psi = k\phi^a, \tag{5.1}$$

where ψ is sensation magnitude, ϕ is stimulus intensity, k is an arbitrary constant determining the scale unit, and a is the power exponent which depends on the sensory modality and stimulus conditions. The value of the power function exponent determines the shape of the curve on a graph where ψ is plotted as a function of ϕ. For example, if the exponent is 1.0, the relationship is a straight line because the equation reduces to a statement that sensory magnitude is proportional to stimulus intensity. The relationship is positively accelerated when the exponent is greater than 1.0 and negatively accelerated when the exponent is less than 1.0. Recall that for Fechner's logarithmic law the predicted psychophysical function was always negatively accelerated.

If the power law is correct, the scaling problem becomes the experimental determination of the exponent of the power function. The power function has a convenient feature of becoming a linear function with a slope equal to the value of the power exponent when a logarithmic transformation is performed on each side of the equation:

$$\log \psi = \log k + a \log \phi. \tag{5.2}$$

The exponent a of the power law for a particular set of experimental results can be found by plotting the logarithm of the psychological scale values ψ against the logarithm of the corresponding stimulus values ϕ and finding the slope of the straight line fitted to the points. This technique has also proved very useful in evaluating the closeness of fit of the power law to experimental data. Any systematic deviation of the data points from a straight line on a log–log graph is an indication that the psychophysical magnitude function is not a power function. If the psychophysical function of a particular experiment turns out to be a power function, the method of least squares can be used to determine the constants $\log k$ and a in the power equation which best fit the data. In this application of the method of least squares, $\log \psi$ would be Y and $\log \phi$ would be X [Equations (2.1) and (2.2)].

Support for the power law comes from experiments on a large number of perceptual continua. The exponents of the power functions describing the relationship between sensation magnitude and stimulus magnitude are as small as .33 for brightness (Stevens & Stevens, 1963) and loudness (S. S. Stevens, 1955) and as large as 3.5 for electric shock on the fingertip (S. S. Stevens, Carton, & Shickman, 1958). Figures 5.1 and 5.2 show the psychophysical magnitude functions on log–log axes and on linear axes, respectively, for the brightness of a 5° target, the apparent length of lines, and electric shock of the fingertips. It can be seen that the sensation of electric current through the fingertips increases very rapidly with stimulus intensity, whereas brightness grows very slowly as stimulus

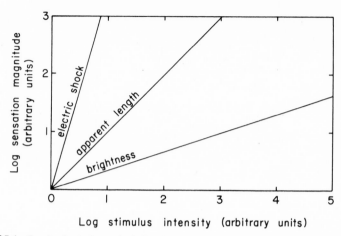

FIGURE 5.1   Psychophysical magnitude functions for three perceptual continua. The linearity of the functions on double logarithmic coordinates indicates that sensation magnitude is a power function of stimulus intensity. The slope of the line corresponds to the exponent of the power function. The exponents for electric shock to the fingertips, line length, and the brightness of relatively large stimuli lasting about 1 sec are 3.5, 1.0, and .33, respectively.

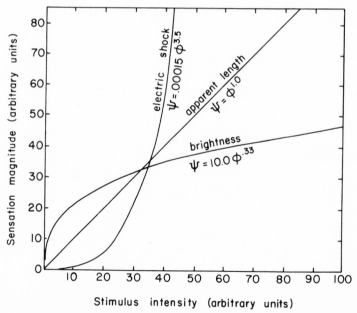

FIGURE 5.2   Psychophysical magnitude functions for three perceptual continua plotted on linear coordinates. Each function is a power function. The form of the function is greatly influenced by the size of the exponent. An exponent of 1.0 corresponds to a linear function. An exponent less than 1.0 corresponds to a concave downward function and an exponent greater than 1.0 corresponds to a concave upward function.

energy is increased. The apparent length of lines is directly proportional to actual length. Exponents of power functions of some representative perceptual continua are found in Table 5.1.

The values of exponents obtained for various sensory modalities are usually very dependent on stimulus conditions. For example, it can be seen in Table 5.1

TABLE 5.1

Representative Exponents for Power Functions Relating Sensory Magnitude to Stimulus Intensity[a]

Continuum	Measured exponent	Stimulus condition
Loudness	0.67	Sound pressure of 3000-Hz tone
Vibration	0.95	Amplitude of 60 Hz on finger
Vibration	0.6	Amplitude of 250 Hz on finger
Brightness	0.33	5° Target in dark
Brightness	0.5	Point source
Brightness	0.5	Brief flash
Brightness	1.0	Point source briefly flashed
Lightness	1.2	Reflectance of gray papers
Visual length	1.0	Projected line
Visual area	0.7	Projected square
Redness (saturation)	1.7	Red–gray mixture
Taste	1.3	Sucrose
Taste	1.4	Salt
Taste	0.8	Saccharine
Smell	0.6	Heptane
Cold	1.0	Metal contact on arm
Warmth	1.6	Metal contact on arm
Warmth	1.3	Irradiation of skin, small area
Warmth	0.7	Irradiation of skin, large area
Discomfort, cold	1.7	Whole body irradiation
Discomfort, Warm	0.7	Whole body irradiation
Thermal pain	1.0	Radiant heat on skin
Tactual roughness	1.5	Rubbing emery cloths
Tactual hardness	0.8	Squeezing rubber
Finger span	1.3	Thickness of blocks
Pressure on palm	1.1	Static force on skin
Muscle force	1.7	Static contractions
Heaviness	1.45	Lifted weights
Viscosity	0.42	Stirring silicone fluids
Electric shock	3.5	Current through fingers
Vocal effort	1.1	Vocal sound pressure
Angular acceleration	1.4	5-Sec rotation
Duration	1.1	White noise stimuli

that the exponent for brightness is .33 for a 5° target, .5 for a point source or a brief flash, and 1.0 for a point source briefly flashed. The exponent for the loudness of pure tones is slightly higher for the low frequencies than for midrange and high frequencies. The observer's state of sensory adaptation and the presence of masking stimuli have been found to alter the exponents for vision, audition, the cutaneous senses, and the chemical senses. In addition to the sensory modality and stimulus conditions, exponents are sometimes found to depend on specific experimental procedures. The exponents for taste, for example, are considerably higher when the substance is sipped in the mouth than when it is flowed over the tongue.

Much can be learned about a sensory system by studying the changes in the power function exponents as stimulus conditions are changed. In fact, in many scaling experiments today, stimulus variables in addition to intensity are systematically varied. For example, in the study of warmth by J. C. Stevens and Marks (1971) described in Chapter 4, a great deal was learned about spatial summation of warmth sensations by studying how the power function exponents changed as the areal extent of a radiant stimulus changed.

Let us examine some of the actual data of some of the first experiments on magnitude estimation and the power law. In Figure 5.3 the results of experiments reported by Stevens (1961a) on loudness and brightness scaling are plotted. In the loudness experiment each of 32 observers made two magnitude estimations of a 1000-Hz tone at each of several intensity levels. In the brightness experiment each of 28 dark-adapted observers made two magnitude estimations at each stimulus level. The visual stimulus subtended an angle of about 5° and lasted about 3 sec. The magnitude estimation data in Figure 5.3 constitute compelling evidence that both loudness and brightness grow as a power function of stimulus energy. Furthermore, the exponents, as estimated from the slope of the curves, are approximately .33 in both cases. The loudness and brightness functions are directly comparable on the same graph since in both cases stimulus energy is specified on the logarithmic scale of decibels. Increasing energy by 10 dB is equivalent to increasing it by a factor of 10 (i.e., 1 log unit):

$$N_{dB} = 10 \log \frac{E_1}{E_0}. \tag{5.3}$$

The number of decibels (N_{dB}) is equal to 10 times the logarithm of the ratio of a particular energy level (E_1) to an arbitrary reference energy level (E_0). Since it is advisable to specify stimulus energy on a common scale when psychophysical data on different sense modalities are compared, the decibel scale should be used whenever possible. Furthermore, in testing the psychophysical power law a straight line is always predicted when log magnitude estimation is plotted against the logarithmic decibel scale.

Almost all of the psychophysical magnitude functions reported in support of the power law have been constructed by plotting the average magnitude estimation

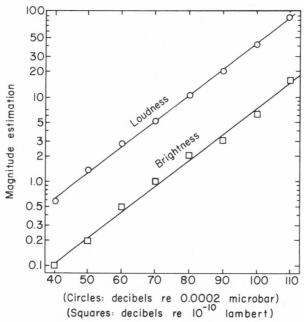

(Circles: decibels re 0.0002 microbar)
(Squares: decibels re 10^{-10} lambert)

FIGURE 5.3   Median magnitude estimations for loudness and brightness. (From Stevens, 1961a. Reprinted from *Sensory Communication*, W. A. Rosenblith, Editor, by permission of the M.I.T. Press, Cambridge, Massachusetts. Copyright © 1961 by the Massachusetts Institute of Technology.)

for a number of observers as a function of stimulus intensity. Psychologists for some years have been aware of the general problem of making inferences concerning the behavior of individuals from curves based on group data (e.g., Estes, 1956). Pradhan and Hoffman (1963) have suggested that the psychophysical power function is an artifact of the averaging of data from a number of observers. Based on an experiment in which observers made judgments of the apparent heaviness of weights, Pradhan and Hoffman proposed that individual observers seldom produce power functions but that when their data are combined by averaging, the power function inevitably emerges. Contrary to the results of Pradhan and Hoffman, J. C. Stevens and Guirao (1964) reported clear evidence that the power law applies to individual observers and that the psychophysical power function is in no way an artifact of averaging procedures. Magnitude production and estimation were combined by permitting the observer to adjust the intensity of an auditory stimulus to whatever level he liked and requiring him to report its apparent loudness. The observer was instructed to set the tone to different levels of loudness and to assign numbers to each of the loudnesses. He was told that he should make as many settings as he wanted and to cover a wide range of loudness. Eleven observers gave the results seen in Figure 5.4. The results indicate that power functions were obtained without averaging data from individual observers.

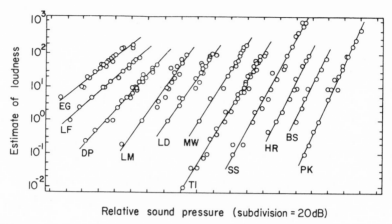

FIGURE 5.4   Individual psychophysical magnitude functions obtained for each of 11 observers. Each data point represents a single judgment. (From J. C. Stevens & Guirao, 1964.)

In fact, power functions were obtained without even averaging the repeated judgments by individual observers. All judgments are plotted on the graph. Essentially the same results were obtained for the perception of brightness by Marks and J. C. Stevens (1966), who repeated the procedure in an investigation of brightness psychophysical functions for individual observers.

The power law seems to apply without exception to any perceptual continuum which involves variations in sensory magnitude. Perceptual continua of sensory magnitude where observers are required to make judgments of "how much" (heaviness, brightness, loudness, etc.) have been termed *prothetic* by S. S. Stevens and Galanter (1957). Another class of perceptual continua in which sensations vary in quality and spatial location and observers make judgments of "what kind" and "where" (pitch, lateral position, etc.) has been labeled *metathetic* by Stevens and Galanter. Psychophysical scales of metathetic continua generally do not obey the power law.

Stevens and Galanter (1957) proposed that the two continua are mediated by different sorts of physiological processes. Prothetic continua are thought to be associated with additive neural processes, whereas metathetic continua are associated with substitutive neural processes. When sensations change in magnitude, an addition or subtraction of neural excitation occurs, but when sensations change in quality or spatial location, frequently one sort of neural excitation is substituted for another. For example, as pressure on the fingertip is made greater and sensations of pressure increase, the frequency of neural firing and the number of neural elements excited will increase. When the stimulus is moved to another finger, the location of the sensation and the mediating neural elements are changed. In light of this difference in underlying physiology of prothetic and metathetic continua it is not surprising that they should yield different kinds of psychophysical magnitude functions.

During the last twenty years dozens of investigators from laboratories in various parts of the world have confirmed the power law for prothetic continua. The power law has become one of the best established empirical relations in psychology. If the experiment is conducted with care, magnitude estimation will inevitably be found to increase as a power function of stimulus intensity. Because of the consistency of this experimental outcome the psychophysical power function has, for most psychophysicists, attained the status of an empirical law.

In science the significance of an empirical law is greatly enhanced if it can be derived from general principles. Mathematically the power law has the simplicity of many of our basic natural laws. But are there any fundamental reasons why in nature sensation should increase with the power of the stimulus? The significance of the power law may lie in its implication that equal stimulus ratios produce equal sensation ratios. This principle is clearly suggested from psychophysical magnitude functions in which log magnitude estimation is linearly related to log stimulus intensity. If it is assumed that magnitude estimation data provide direct measurements of sensation magnitude then it can be seen from a graph such as Figure 5.1 that changing the stimulus by some constant ratio (constant number of log units) will always change the sensation by some constant ratio (constant number of log units). For example, the power function for judgments of brightness with its exponent of .33 implies that brightness can always be doubled by increasing the intensity of light by 8 times. This relation is independent of the starting light intensity. Because the exponent is 3.5 for electric shock to the fingertips only a 22% increase in a stimulus of any intensity is sufficient to double sensation magnitude. Between the extremes of brightness and electric shock we find that it is possible to double apparent length with its exponent of 1.0 by simply doubling the actual length of the stimulus. These examples illustrate the principle that when stimuli are changed by a constant ratio the corresponding sensations also change by a constant ratio although the ratios in the two domains may be quite different.

It follows from this principle that if the intensity of all stimuli in a particular environment are increased or decreased by some percentage the ratios among the sensations will remain constant. Yilmaz (1967) has made a strong case that it is exactly this capacity which permits the organism to respond to constant relationships among stimuli in a changing environment. The phenomenon of brightness constancy illustrates how the sensory system is able to preserve the relationships among the stimulus intensities of various objects as the overall level of illumination changes. Since each object reflects a constant percentage of incident light the ratios of stimulus intensities among the various objects remain constant as overall illumination changes. For example, if object A and object B reflect 50% and 20% of the incident light, respectively, the ratio of the light reflected from the objects would be 5 to 2 for all illumination levels. If the relationship between brightness and light intensity is a power function then the ratio of the perceptual brightness of object A and object B must also be constant for all levels of incident illumination of the objects. In this particular example the brightness of object A would always be 35% greater than that of object B.

Thus, Yilmaz (1967) was able to mathematically derive the power law from the assumptions that perceptual relations tend to model the relations among stimuli in the environment and that perceptual relations are invariant under multiplicative transformations of the stimuli. These assumptions appear to be justified by repeated demonstrations that perception depends on the ratio relations among stimuli as well as on the absolute levels of stimuli. S. S. Stevens (1975) pointed out that such a theoretical deduction of the power law does not necessarily prove that the theoretician's model is correct, but he also took obvious delight in the fact that his empirical law did not clash with a mathematical derivation from a pair of reasonable postulates.

CROSS-MODALITY COMPARISONS AND THE POWER LAW

The validity of a psychophysical ratio scale depends upon the observer's ability to detect and report accurately ratios between sensation magnitudes. Thus the validity of the power law depends upon the observer's correct use of the number system in communicating the true magnitude of his sensations. S. S. Stevens (1959a) has devised a technique of confirming the power law which does not require the observer to make numerical judgments. The observer's task is to equate the sensation magnitudes produced in two different modalities. For example, the observer might be asked to adjust the intensity of a vibration on his fingertip so that the sensory impression of vibration matches the loudness of a burst of noise. Such cross-modality matches are obtained at various levels of stimulus intensity. A graph called an *equal sensation function* is constructed showing the stimulus values of one modality plotted against the stimulus values of the other modality that result in judgments of equal sensory magnitude. Figure 5.5 is the equal sensation function for cutaneous vibration and sound.

The form of the equal sensation functions can be predicted from the psychophysical magnitude functions of each modality obtained by conventional ratio scaling techniques. If power functions are the correct equations for the two psychophysical magnitude functions then the equal sensation function should also be a power function. Thus, the function should be linear when stimuli in both modalities are expressed in logarithmic units. If the equal sensation function is not a power function, one has reason to doubt the power law. Furthermore, when the exponents of the power function for the two modalities are known, a precise prediction of the slope of the equal sensation function can be made. The power equations for the two modalities can be stated in the general form

$$\psi_1 = \phi_1{}^a,$$

$$\psi_2 = \phi_2{}^b.$$

(5.4)

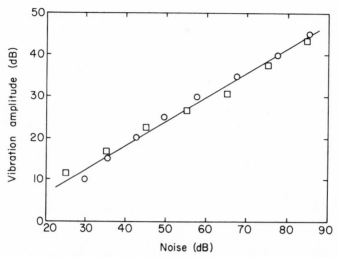

FIGURE 5.5   Equal sensation functions relating 60-Hz vibration on the fingertip to the intensity of a band of noise. The circles represent adjustments of loudness to vibration and the squares represent adjustments of vibration to match loudness. Both coordinates are logarithmic decibel scales. (From Stevens, 1961a. Reprinted from *Sensory Communication*, W. A. Rosenblith, Editor by permission of the M.I.T. Press, Cambridge, Massachusetts. Copyright © 1961 by the Massachusetts Institute of Technology.)

If the observer equates ψ_1 and ψ_2 by cross-modality matching at various intensity levels, the equation for the equal sensation function should be

$$\phi_1{}^a = \phi_2{}^b. \tag{5.5}$$

This is a power function which states that stimuli in one modality, ϕ_1, when raised to the power a will result in the same sensory magnitude, ψ, as will a stimulus in another modality, ϕ_2, when raised to the power b. In logarithmic form this equation becomes

$$a \log \phi_1 = b \log \phi_2 \tag{5.6}$$

or

$$\log \phi_1 = \frac{b}{a} \log \phi_2 , \tag{5.7}$$

which is the formula for a straight line with a slope equal to the ratio of the exponents of the power function of the two modalities (b/a).

It has been proposed by Stevens that cross-modality matching provides a test of the validity of the power law because results obtained using one procedure can be used to predict results obtained by an entirely different procedure. The results of a large number of experiments using cross-modality validation techniques are consistent with the power law (Stevens, 1975). In these experiments, observers made cross-modality comparisons of vibration and loudness, vibration and electric shock, electric shock and loudness, loudness and ten perceptual continua, and force of handgrip and nine perceptual continua. The experiments involving force of handgrip provide a dramatic illustration of the use of this scale validation technique. The sensation of muscle tension has been measured by the methods of magnitude estimation and magnitude production (J. C. Stevens & Mack, 1959). Observers squeezed a device called a hand dynamometer. A force gauge attached to the instrument provided a measure of the physical force exerted by the response. Observers judged the magnitudes of sensations produced by squeezes of varied physical force. When sensation magnitude was plotted against physical force the psychophysical function was a power function with an exponent of 1.7. S. S. Stevens (1975) has summarized the results of a series of experiments in which observers squeezed a hand dynamometer to produce sensations of tension that were equal in magnitude to sensations of varied magnitudes on nine other perceptual continua (J. C. Stevens, Mack, & Stevens, 1960; J. C. Stevens & Stevens, 1960). The equal sensation functions obtained in these experiments are shown in Figure 5.6. The slope of each function is in accordance with the prediction based on the magnitude functions for force of hand grip and the other continuum involved (Table 5.2). In another study (S. S. Stevens, 1966a) the loudness of a sound was matched to the intensities of sensations on ten other perceptual continua. In all cases the slopes of the equal sensation functions were accurately predicted from the magnitude estimation functions of the two modalities. The results of an experiment

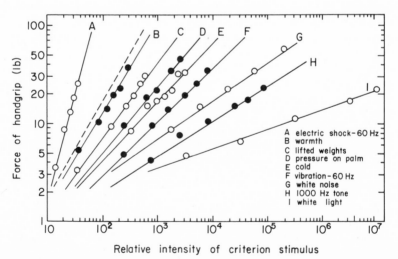

Relative   intensity   of   criterion   stimulus

FIGURE 5.6   Equal sensation functions obtained by matching force of handgrip to various stimuli in other modalities. Each point is based on the median judgments of 10 or more observers. The dashed line has a slope of 1.0. (From Stevens, 1961a. Reprinted from *Sensory Communication*, W. A. Rosenblith, Editor, by permission of the M.I.T. Press, Cambridge, Massachusetts. Copyright © 1961 by the Massachusetts Institute of Technology.)

TABLE 5.2
Predicted and Obtained Exponents for Matching Force of Hand Grip to Nine
Other Continua[a]

	Exponent obtained by hand grip	Predicted value
Electric shock	2.13	2.06
Warmth on arm	0.96	0.94
Heaviness of lifted weights	0.79	0.85
Pressure on palm	0.67	0.65
Cold on arm	0.60	0.59
Vibration, 60 Hz	0.56	0.56
Loudness of white noise	0.41	0.39
Loudness of 1000-Hz tone	0.35	0.39
Brightness of white light	0.21	0.20

[a]After Stevens, 1975. (Reprinted from S. S. Stevens, *Psychophysics: Introduction to Its Perceptual, Neural and Social Prospects.* Copyright © 1975 by John Wiley & Sons, Inc. Reprinted by permission of John Wiley & Sons, Inc.)

by Bond and Stevens (1969) in which five-year-olds were used as observers indicate that cross-modality matching probably does not depend on prior experience with scales of physical stimuli or on the ability to translate sensations into numbers. The observers adjusted the intensity of a light to match the loudness of a 500-Hz tone of variable intensity. The results were essentially identical for five children between the ages of 4 years, 2 months and 5 years, 8 months and a group of five adults. The authors concluded that hypotheses concerning prior learning fail to account for cross-modality matching data. It seems more reasonable to assume that judgments of sensation magnitude depend primarily on the operation of sense organs and that the sense organs of children function like those of adults.

Once it is accepted that cross-modality matching is a valid procedure for measuring sensation then the procedure can be used for a variety of scaling problems where it is not practical to have observers assign numbers to their sensations. An example of such a problem is the measurement of clinical pain. Instead of only asking patients how they feel, some physicians have adopted the procedure of asking them to adjust the loudness of a noise presented through earphones to match the intensity of their discomfort. The intensity of the patient's pain is calculated by converting his noise adjustment into psychophysical loudness units. This procedure has been used to quantify the effectiveness of medications for relieving a patient's distress (Peck, 1966). The success of the procedure has warranted the commercial production of a device called a thymometer that can be used to quantify pain from loudness matches.

Cross-modality matching has also been used to study clinical patients with hearing defects. Thalmann (1965) examined a group of ten patients who had

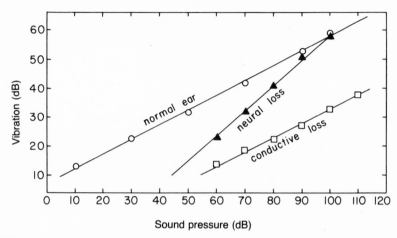

FIGURE 5.7   Cross-modality matches of patients with normal hearing in one ear and a hearing loss in the other. Each patient adjusted vibration to match loudness in the normal ear and in the abnormal ear. The circles represent the results for the normal ear. The triangles and squares show matches when the stimuli were presented to ears with neural hearing loss and to ears with conductive hearing loss, respectively. (From Stevens, 1975; after Thalmann, 1965.) (Reprinted from S. S. Stevens, *Psychophysics: Introduction to its Perceptual, Neural and Social Prospects.* Copyright © 1975 by John Wiley & Sons, Inc.)

hearing thresholds about 50 dB higher than normal in one ear but had normal hearing in the other ear. Five of the patients had been diagnosed as having conductive hearing loss whereby sound is not effectively transmitted through the mechanical elements of the auditory system to the receptors. The hearing loss of the other five patients was attributable to problems in the auditory nervous system. In the experiment patients adjusted the intensity of a 150-Hz vibration on the fingertip to match the loudness of a 1000-Hz tone delivered to the defective ear on some trials and to the normal ear on other trials. The results are seen in Figure 5.7. When the tone was delivered to the normal ear a linear function on log–log axes with the predicted slope was obtained. The matching function for ears with conductive loss had the same slope as the function for normal ears but it was displaced to a position about 50 dB higher up on the intensity scale. It is apparent that a conductive hearing loss has the effect of attenuating sounds at all intensities by a constant number of decibels. A very different picture of the hearing problem emerges from examining the results for the ears with neural loss. The unusually steep function for the ear with neural loss indicates that the exponent for the loudness function is abnormally high. Once the sound intensity exceeds the high threshold, loudness grows at a very rapid rate as intensity is increased. It can be seen from Figure 5.7 that at high intensity levels the loudness of the defective ear eventually catches up with the loudness of the normal ear. This phenomenon, found in neural hearing loss and in masking experiments, has been called recruitment. Since the matching functions are distinctly different for normal ears,

ears with conductive loss, and ears with neural loss, cross-modality matching provides a valuable diagnostic method for identifying various kinds of auditory defects.

MODIFICATIONS OF THE POWER LAW

In most psychophysical experiments $\psi = k\phi^a$ has been found to be a very accurate statement of the relation between sensory magnitude judgments and stimulus magnitude. However, for weak stimuli near absolute threshold this equation becomes highly inaccurate. When log apparent magnitude is plotted against log stimulus magnitude the relationship is linear (a power function) only at the higher stimulus values. At stimulus values near absolute threshold the relationship is concave downward. Fortunately this deviation from the power law can be eliminated by a slight modification of the equation. The power law has been found to hold for the entire range of perceptible stimuli when a constant ϕ_0 is subtracted from the values of ϕ. According to some investigators the constant ϕ_0 represents the absolute threshold. Thus subtraction of ϕ_0 from ϕ may be equivalent to specifying the stimulus in effective units above threshold rather than in units above the zero point on the physical scale. The general form of the power function becomes

$$\psi = k(\phi - \phi_0)^a, \tag{5.8}$$

where ϕ_0 is the value of the absolute threshold. This procedure of correcting the stimulus scale so that its zero point corresponds to the zero point on the psychological scale has been successfully applied to psychophysical scales such as brightness (J. C. Stevens & Stevens, 1963), loudness (Scharf & Stevens, 1961), temperature (S. S. Stevens, 1961a), cutaneous vibration (Gescheider & Wright, 1968; S. S. Stevens, 1959b), cutaneous apparent successiveness (Gescheider, 1967), and the taste of salt (McBurney, 1966).

In an experiment by Gescheider and Wright (1968) the effect of adaptation upon the form of the psychophysical magnitude function for cutaneous vibration of the fingertip was investigated. The family of curves presented in Figure 5.8 represents the relationship between sensation magnitude and amplitude of 60-Hz vibration applied 5, 60, 120, 180, and 360 sec following termination of an intense adapting stimulus of 10 min duration. It is apparent that each of the sensation magnitude functions deviates from linearity by becoming concave downward for the range of stimulus values near the absolute threshold.

To test the applicability of the revised power law to cutaneous vibration following recovery from adaptation, sensation magnitude was plotted as a function of $\phi - \phi_0$, that is, vibration amplitude in microns above absolute threshold (Figure 5.9). To obtain $\phi - \phi_0$ the appropriate empirically determined value of ϕ_0 for each adaptation–recovery time was subtracted from the corresponding values of ϕ for

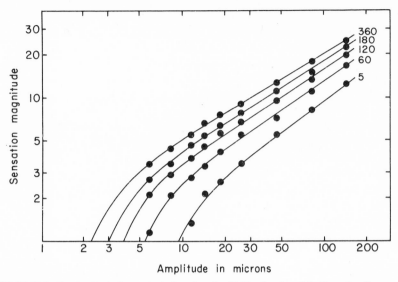

FIGURE 5.8   Psychophysical magnitude functions for 60-Hz vibration of the fingertip after varying durations of recovery time from the effects of a 10-min adaptation period during which the fingertip was continuously stimulated by intense 60-Hz vibration. (From Gescheider & Wright, 1968. Copyright 1968 by the American Psychological Association. Reprinted by permission.)

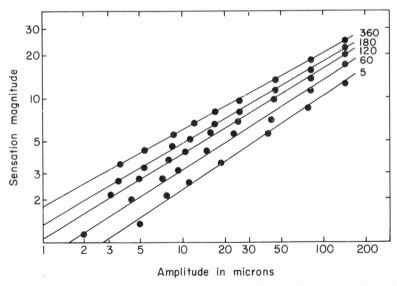

FIGURE 5.9   Psychophysical magnitude functions for 60-Hz vibration of the fingertip after varying durations of recovery time from adaptation. Stimulus intensity was expressed in vibration amplitude above absolute thresholds measured at the various recovery times. (From Gescheider & Wright, 1968. Copyright 1968 by the American Psychological Association. Reprinted by permission.)

that particular adaptation–recovery time. Figure 5.9 illustrates that this transformation of the stimulus scale produced on log–log coordinates a linear growth in sensation magnitude as a function of vibration amplitude over the entire range of stimulus intensities.

In most experiments, however, ϕ_0 is not generally determined experimentally since such factors as the particular psychophysical method employed and the location of the observer's decision criterion would greatly affect its value. Instead it is usually determined indirectly by finding the value of ϕ_0 that will work, that is, one that will produce a power function over the entire range of stimulus values. In describing a mathematical procedure for estimating ϕ_0 Ekman (1959) pointed out that the value of ϕ_0 is sometimes negative. When ϕ_0 is negative the use of Equation (5.8) implies that ψ is greater than zero when $\phi = 0$. Subtraction of a negative value of ϕ_0 from zero yields a positive value of ψ. Ekman identified the positive value of ψ when ϕ was zero as sensory noise resulting from the spontaneous activity of the nervous system and proposed another form of the power law

$$\psi = \psi_0 + \phi^a, \qquad (5.9)$$

where ψ_0 is the basic sensory noise to which the sensory magnitude produced by an external stimulus, ϕ^a, is added to determine the total subjective magnitude, ψ, for a particular stimulus value, ϕ.

It should be understood that Equations (5.8) and (5.9) represent two distinct hypotheses about the growth of sensory magnitude with increases in stimulus intensity. In Equation (5.8), the subtraction of a constant from stimulus intensity implies that sensation magnitude is a power function of effective stimulation above threshold. On the other hand, the concept of sensory noise rather than threshold is implied by the use of Equation (5.9). Equation (5.9) states that sensation magnitude is proportional to stimulus intensity raised to a power plus a constant which has been interpreted to represent sensory noise. There have been several other equations proposed as modified power laws, and the problem has been reviewed by Marks and J. C. Stevens (1968). It is not possible to select a single equation which applies accurately to data obtained under all circumstances. It is likely that different equations will be found to apply in different experimental situations.

The work of Zwislocki (1965) illustrates the application of one particular modified power function to the problem of auditory masking. Hellman and Zwislocki (1964) carefully measured loudness functions for a 1000-Hz tone presented to observers against noise backgrounds of various levels of intensity. Zwislocki's formulation of the power law for loudness may be written in the form

$$L_S = k(E_S + E_N)^\theta - E_N{}^\theta . \qquad (5.10)$$

The loudness of the signal, L_S, is equal to a constant, k, times the sum of the energy of the signal, E_S, and the energy of the noise, E_N, raised to a power, θ, minus the energy of the noise raised to a power. This formulation takes into account analytic properties of the auditory system and permits the calculation of the loudness of the total acoustic event, the random noise alone, or the signal. When we listen to a signal in the presence of relatively loud noise the signal does not sound loud when it is barely audible above the noise background even though it is very intense, yet the noise sounds loud and the overall acoustic event sounds loud. Zwislocki's formula permits us to calculate the loudness of a signal by subtracting the loudness of the noise from the loudness of the signal plus noise.

When the noise is external, its energy can be measured and its value specified in the equation. However, internal noise produced by spontaneous activity in the sensory system must be specified in terms of equivalent stimulus energy. Zwislocki has provided the means for making the necessary calculations. It was assumed that the threshold of audibility for a tone signal presented in the quiet is determined by masking by internal noise. Research in auditory psychophysics has conclusively revealed that when a tone is masked by noise, only the frequencies in the noise close to the frequency of the tone do the masking. The range of frequencies in the noise that bracket the frequency of a tone signal and act as a masker is called the critical band. It has been determined that when a tone is barely audible against a noise background the energy in one critical band is approximately 2.5 times that of the signal (see Scharf, 1961). Zwislocki employed these concepts, which had been developed from experiments in which external noise was used to mask tones, to arrive at a procedure for calculating the equivalent sound energy of internal noise. It was simply proposed that the equivalent sound energy of internal noise is 2.5 times the threshold energy of a barely audible tone presented in quiet.

More complicated computations are required to calculate the equivalent sound energy of internal noise that has a wider frequency spectrum than the critical band for a particular tone. These procedures are fully developed in Zwislocki's paper. The virtues of Zwislocki's formulation are that it integrates certain notions of critical band theory and signal detection theory with psychophysical data on loudness scales, that it makes physiological sense, and that it accurately describes how signals sound in noisy situations.

POWER TRANSFORMATIONS

S. S. Stevens (1966b) has described some situations in which modified or unmodified power function equations fail to correspond to the psychophysical data. In the situations the observer judged a stimulus in the presence of an inhibitory stimulus such as a bright glaring background light in the case of vision or a masking noise in the scaling of auditory stimuli. Psychophysical magnitude functions obtained under these conditions appear to consist of two separate power functions, each with its own exponent. For stimuli more intense than the inhibitory stimulus the exponent is approximately what it would be in the absence of the inhibitory stimulus. But for stimuli weaker than the inhibitory stimulus the exponent is often much larger than normal.

If a white stimulus is viewed against a black background the cube-root brightness function (exponent .33) is generally obtained. If, however, the white target is surrounded by an area of illumination the cube-root function is obtained only for stimuli that are more intense than the surrounding illumination. For stimuli less intense than the surround the data also follow a power function, but instead of the .33 exponent a larger value is found. On log–log coordinates the function abruptly becomes steeper for stimuli below than above the intensity of the surround. Figure 5.10 depicts a family of such functions for different intensities of the surround. The surrounding stimulus seems to have an inhibitory effect on the perception of weaker stimuli but not on the perception of stimuli more intense than the surround. In most studies it is found that the change in the power function exponent is always at the intensity of the inhibiting stimulus. The inhibiting stimulus has the effect of transforming to a higher value the power function exponent for weaker stimuli, while having little, if any, effect on the exponent for stronger stimuli. The degree to which the inhibiting stimulus changes the exponent of weaker stimuli depends on its intensity. It can be seen from Figure 5.10 that as the intensity of the inhibiting surround is increased the transformation of the exponent increases. An intense surround 85 dB above threshold resulted in large amounts of inhibition as indicated by the extremely high exponent for the weaker stimuli. On the other hand, a weaker surround of 60 dB above threshold caused less inhibition and, con-

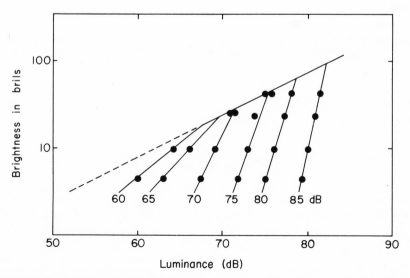

FIGURE 5.10   Brightness functions for a stimulus with a surrounding annulus background of various intensities. (From Horeman, 1965.)

sequently, the difference between the exponents for weaker and stronger stimuli was not so great.

A change in the exponent of a psychophysical magnitude function due to the effects of some particular variable is called a *power transformation*. The investigation of power transformations can be a fruitful approach in the psychophysical study of sensory systems. Stevens (1966b) has extended this approach to the study of inhibition in general. He applied the analysis to the problem of auditory masking and hearing loss due to neural defects as well as to the problem of visual inhibition. For example, Stevens has argued that the loudness function may exhibit a power transformation due to a masking stimulus. The exponent for the loudness function may be considerably higher for stimuli weaker than some masking noise than for stimuli more intense than the masker. Stevens points out the close analogy between the results of visual and auditory experiments in which inhibitory stimuli are presented. In both modalities the inhibiting stimulus increased the exponent for weaker stimuli while having little or no effect on the exponent for stronger stimuli.

INTERPRETATIONS OF THE POWER LAW

There is little doubt that the power function represents the best description of the relationship between an observer's judgments and stimulus intensity. However, there is more than one possible interpretation of this finding.

Sensory Transducer Theory

One interpretation of the power law is that it reflects the operation of sensory mechanisms as they transduce stimulus energy into neural activity. S. S. Stevens (1970, 1971b) has proposed that because the neural output of the sensory system is a power function of stimulus intensity, the observer's judgments will also be a power function of stimulus intensity. Thus, for Stevens the exponent of a psychophysical power function may tell something about the basic transducer properties of sensory receptors.

Since the classic work of Adrian and Matthews (1927) on the eye of the eel, many investigators have assumed that the relationship between the neural output of a receptor and stimulus energy is logarithmic. Adrian and Matthews reported that the frequency of neural impulses increased as a logarithmic function of light intensity, and concluded that the results were consistent with Fechner's general psychophysical law as applied to the perception of brightness in man. Stevens (1970) replotted the data of Adrian and Matthews and found that a better description of the results is that impulse frequency for the eel's visual system grows as a power function with an exponent of .32 of light intensity. The exponent for the psychophysical function for the perception of brightness by human observers is .33 for stimuli that are not point sources or brief flashes.

It is apparent that the way in which Adrian and Matthews interpreted their data was greatly influenced by the general acceptance at the time of Fechner's law. At the time of their experiment Fechner's law was the only psychophysical theory of the perception of stimulus intensity that was under general consideration. Stevens' reevaluation of the Adrian–Matthews data is subject to the same limitations imposed by available theory. Perhaps an even closer approximation to the true input–output relation for the eel will come with subsequent advances in psychophysical theory. However, it does appear that based on Stevens' evaluation of the Adrian–Matthews data we can now say that a power function is better than the logarithmic function as a description of the transducer action of the eel's visual system.

How general is the finding that the neural output of a sensory system increases as a power function of stimulus input? In a review of experimental work on neuroelectric recording in sensory systems, Stevens (1970, 1971b) concluded that the results of a number of studies using different species, including man, indicate that neural activity grows as a power function of stimulus intensity. Furthermore, in many cases the exponent of the power function for neural activity had a similar value to those determined in psychophysical experiments under similar stimulus conditions.

When Stevens replotted the results of Hartline and Graham (1932) on the frequency of action potentials recorded from a single fiber of the compound eye of the horseshoe crab *Limulus,* he found that the frequency of impulses increased as a power function with an exponent of .29 of light intensity. Based on an evaluation of data of a more recent study on *Limulus* by Fuortes and Hodgkin (1964), Stevens proposed that the amplitude of the electrical activity of the receptor increased as a power function with an exponent of .32 of stimulus intensity.

Not all of the experiments reviewed by Stevens (1970, 1971b) revealed that there is such a close correspondence between the exponents of the neural input–output function and the comparable psychophysical functions. Many of the differences might be accounted for in terms of species differences, differences in experimental conditions, and electrophysiological recording methods that are in various stages of refinement. It is Stevens' view, however, that sensory modalities having large psychophysical function exponents have large neural function exponents, and modalities that have small psychophysical function exponents have small neural function exponents.

One of the problems of attempting to correlate neurophysiological and psychophysical data is that the two sets of data are almost always obtained from different species. No doubt much could be learned if a method were developed for training animals to make ratio discriminations of sensory magnitude. In the absence of such methods comparisons of animal neurophysiological data and human psychophysical data will be our main source of information on the problem.

There have, however, been some attempts to directly compare psychophysical and neurophysiological data from humans. In one successful experiment recordings were made from the taste nerve while the observer made magnitude estimations of taste substances such as sucrose, sodium chloride, and citric acid applied in various concentrations to the tongue (Borg, Diamant, Ström, & Zotterman, 1967). The experiment was possible only because the observers were patients having surgery in which a branch of the taste nerve became accessible to a recording electrode. The patients required surgery that involved removal of the eardrum to expose the middle ear. Since a branch of the taste nerve passes through the middle ear on its way from the tongue to the brain, psychophysical and electrophysiological data on the sense of taste could be obtained from the same observer. A very close correspondence was found between the two sets of data. The response of the taste nerve and the judgments of the observer both increased as a power function of the concentration of the substance placed on the tongue. Furthermore, the exponents were the same for the neural and psychophysical responses.

The results of electrophysiological experimentation indicate that we are at the beginning of a period where direct observations will be made of the nonlinear transformations of stimulus energy by neural mechanisms that have been implied for many years by psychophysical data and theory. In his 1969 Nobel address, Delbrück recognized the importance of this problem:

> Sensory physiology in a broad sense contains hidden as its kernel an as yet totally undeveloped but absolutely central science: tranducer physiology, the study of the conversion of the outside signal to its first "interesting" output. I use the word "interesting" advisedly because I wish to exclude . . . the primary photochemical reactions of the visual systesm. . . . Transducer physiology proper comes after this first step, where we are dealing with devices of the cell unparalleled in anything the physicists have produced so far with respect to sensitivity, adaptability, and miniaturization [Delbrück, 1970, p. 1313].

Whether or not research in Delbrück's "central science" will reveal that the power functions observed in psychophysical experiments can be accounted for mainly in terms of the operation of sensory transducers will be seen in the future. The small amount of data existing on this problem seems to indicate that power functions frequently describe the neurophysiological input–output relationship in the receptor, in the peripheral sensory nervous system, and in the brain.

One tentative conclusion based on very limited information has been that a power transformation of the stimulus is made at the receptor and that all subsequent transformations as the information is conducted toward the brain are linear. Stevens (1970) reported that at the 1966 Ciba Symposium Sir John Eccles expressed the opinion that after the sensory transducer has performed its operation on the input, neural information undergoes a series of linear transformations at each succeeding synaptic junction. In the same discussion, Mountcastle expressed the opinion that the nonlinear relationship between stimulus and sensation may be localized at the receptor level. This position is essentially Stevens' sensory transducer theory. Obviously, more work on recording neural activity at various points along the sensory nervous system is needed to give Stevens' transducer theory a firm empirical foundation.

Perhaps as important as measuring more intensity functions in the nervous system is the development of theoretical models for the data already available. In a theoretical analysis of receptor intensity functions, Zwislocki (1973, 1974) pointed out that when intensity characteristics of sensory receptors are recorded over a sufficient range of stimulus intensity they fit neither Fechner's logarithmic function nor Stevens' power function. Intensity functions are instead S shaped. The low end of the function becomes flat when the receptor output can not become lower because of its spontaneous activity level. As stimulus intensity is increased receptor output increases but because the receptor eventually saturates in its ability to respond to further increases in intensity the function again becomes flat at high intensities. Zwislocki was, however, able to show that if spontaneous activity level, the saturation point, and threshold effects were mathematically taken into account the remaining receptor activity was a power function of stimulus intensity. According to Zwislocki's calculations on empirical intensity functions from a variety of different receptors, it is possible that receptors of all sensory modalities have power exponents of either .5 or 1.0. Only taste and temperature receptors had exponents of 1.0; all others were .5. Zwislocki made the additional suggestion that if threshold and neural noise factors are taken into account psychophysical judgments that seem to parallel the peripheral neural output may also obey the rule of increasing as a function of stimulus energy raised to the power of either .5 or 1.0. The obvious exceptions to this generalization are vision and audition, where the psychophysical exponents are often clearly smaller than the receptor exponents. According to Zwislocki the difference between receptor and psychophysical data in these cases may be due to the fact that receptors respond over an energy range of only a few log units while the dynamic range of visual and auditory sensation extends over 12 or more log units of energy. That the psychophysical exponent is lower than the neural exponent may result from the interaction of several receptor processes with sensitivities staggered along the intensity scale.

Zwislocki's formulation is attractive because it represents an attempt to simplify further the relation between stimulus and sensation. The large differences among power exponents for various modalities and stimulus conditions in both the receptor domain and the psychophysical domain may be the result of differences in thresholds, neural noise levels, and saturation points of receptors. With the exception of vision and audition psychophysical and receptor exponents may parallel each other with power function exponents of either .5 or 1.0. The visual and auditory psychophysical exponents of .33 may result from the interaction of different receptor populations, each having the .5 or 1.0 exponent but operating at different stimulus energy levels.

The fate of sensory transducer theory may depend primarily on the success of theoretical analyses such as that of Zwislocki. Marks (1974b) has strongly emphasized the importance of evaluating the validity of a particular psychophysical magnitude function in the context of the study of sensory processes in general. Throughout this book he has clearly demonstrated that power functions generated

by ratio scaling methods are often precisely predictable from our current understanding of sensory processes such as temporal summation, spatial summation,
adaptation, and inhibition. The analyses of Zwislocki and Marks are important
examples of recent attempts to integrate the ratio scaling data into the very
substantial body of psychophysical and physiological facts and theory presently
available on sensory processes.

Criticisms of the Sensory Transducer Theory

A strong argument against the sensory transducer theory has been made by Poulton
(1968). He proposed that variation in the size of the exponents for different
psychophysical magnitude functions reflects changes in experimental conditions
that affect psychological processes involving judgment more than changes in the
behavior of sensory receptors. Poulton has reviewed experimental evidence which
indicates that the observer's judgments of sensation magnitude may be influenced
by a number of situational factors such as (*a*) the range of stimulus values, (*b*) the
distance of the stimulus from the threshold, (*c*) the value of the standard stimulus,
(*d*) the size of the difference between the standard stimulus and the first comparison stimulus presented, (*e*) whether the range of numbers the observer is permitted
to use is infinite or finite, and (*f*) the sensation magnitude value that the observer
is instructed to use for the standard stimulus.

The brightness sensation magnitude function with its exponent of .33 (J. C.
Stevens & Stevens, 1963) and the sensation magnitude function for electric shock
with its exponent of 3.5 (S. S. Stevens, Carton, & Shickman, 1958) have been
thought to reflect differences between the two sensory systems. Poulton (1968)
questioned the validity of this assumption and attempted to account for differences
in exponents of different sensory systems in terms of the experimental conditions
under which they were determined. In Poulton's model the observer's judgment is
determined by sensation magnitude, which is some function of the transducer
properties of the sensory system plus the operation of a number of judgment-
biasing factors such as those listed above. The exponents determined in
psychophysical scaling experiments, rather than giving us information about the
sensory nervous system, may simply reflect situational parameters of the experiment. For example, Poulton proposed that differences in the size of exponents for
different modalities may be more a function of the range of stimuli employed than
of the operation of sensory transducers.

According to Poulton an inverse relationship between stimulus range and power
exponent exists because there is a tendency for the observer's judgments to cover a
constant range of log sensation magnitudes for all sensory modalities. Since the log
of the range of stimulus intensity values used in experiments is not the same for
different modalities, the exponents must be different. The greater the log stimulus
intensity range, the lower the exponent must be if the log range of sensation

magnitude judgments tends to be constant. For example, the stimulus range for electric current applied to the fingertip was less than one log unit and the exponent was 3.5 while the stimulus range for light presented to the eye was six log units and the exponent was .33. The large difference in exponents could simply be an artifact of the tendency for an observer to vary his judgments over a certain range of values for both electric shock and brightness.

Poulton states that there is a highly significant negative correlation ($r = -.60$, $p < .001$) between the exponent values and log stimulus intensity ranges reported in 21 studies conducted by Stevens and his associates. The correlation is not perfect because, presumably, the observers' judgments were also determined by the transducer properties of the sensory systems. However, the differences in exponents may tell us more about the range of stimulus intensities employed than about the sensory system. In psychophysics we would like to be able to learn something about the sensory system from the observer's judgments, but according to Poulton this is not possible using magnitude estimation procedures because of judgmental biases inherent in the method which obscure the very sensory process that we wish to study. Poulton finds these judgmental biases interesting, but for most psychophysicists who are interested in sensory processes they cause only frustration.

Teghtsoonian (1971) has suggested that Poulton underestimated the closeness with which power exponents are related to the stimulus range employed. Based on his own statistical analysis of the same 21 studies Poulton considered, Teghtsoonian concluded that at least 87% of the variance in exponents can be accounted for by variation in stimulus range. Teghtsoonian, however, interpreted the high negative correlation of $-.94$ between stimulus range and exponent as support for Stevens' transducer theory rather than as evidence against it. He hypothesized that the ratio of the strongest to the weakest possible sensory magnitude for a sensory system is approximately constant for all modalities. In this hypothesis the approximate constancy in the range of the observer's judgments is due to the underlying constancy in the range of sensory magnitudes rather than to the judgmental rigidity assumed by Poulton to be inherent in the magnitude estimation procedure. Variances in power exponents are due to variations in the *dynamic range* of stimuli (ratio of the greatest to the smallest stimulus to which the observer is responsive) when the range of sensation magnitude is constant. Thus, according to Teghtsoonian (1971), "in this context, the various receptor systems can be regarded as performing the necessary expansions or compressions required to map the widely varying dynamic ranges into this constant range of subjective magnitudes" [p. 74].

Stevens (1971a) has pointed out an important exception to Teghtsoonian's interesting rule in the case of odor perception. Odors often have a short stimulus range and a low exponent. Stevens (1957) reported an exponent of only .2 for the odor of benzaldehyde. A similar low value has more recently been reported by Berglund, Berglund, Engen, and Ekman (1971). The odor of benzaldehyde has a relatively short range compared with loudness or brightness. Nevertheless, it is an interesting hypothesis that exponents vary in nature, at least to some extent, so that sensory systems can accommodate particular ranges of stimulation. If this hypothesis is correct, the brightness exponent of .33 and the electric shock exponent of 3.5 are not reflections of an artifact in experimental procedure, as suggested by Poulton, but instead reflect real differences in the input–output functions of the two sensory systems.

The Measurement of Sensations

Some behavioristically oriented psychologists have argued that psychophysics is based on the fallacious notion that private events such as sensations can be measured (e.g., Savage, 1966, 1970; Zuriff, 1972). Many critics of psychophysics strongly disagree with the use of subjective terms such as sensation, perception, sensory magnitude, and apparent magnitude because they seem to refer to events that cannot be observed in a scientific experiment. The distinction made frequently by psychophysicists between a physical stimulus continuum and a corresponding psychological continuum is rejected as unnecessary and misleading. To claim that subjective events on a psychological continuum have been measured is considered illogical, since such events are not publicly observable. The distinction between a physical stimulus continuum and a psychological continuum has been very useful to psychophysicists, however, since it separates the stimulus from the effects that the stimulus has on the organism's sensory system. In psychoacoustics, for example, it makes sense to describe the response of the auditory system as varying along continua of loudness and pitch while the stimulus varies in intensity and frequency of vibration. Likewise, in visual research investigators often describe responses of the visual system as varying on continua of brightness, hue, and saturation as the intensity and wavelength characteristics of light are manipulated. It is the fact that the brightness or loudness experienced by an observer cannot be publicly verified that has led the radical behaviorist to reject such subjective concepts as meaningless.

The radical behaviorists appear to fear that the use of subjective-sounding terms to describe the responses of sensory systems, no matter how well they are defined or how much it facilitates the research effort, may cause a regression of psychology to the morass of confusion generated by the mind–body dualism of early experimental psychology. An examination of the writings of such critics of psychophysics will reveal that their arguments are mainly philosophical and, however interesting, have little bearing on the design, analysis, and interpretation of psychophysical experiments. However, a brief discussion of the issue seems in order if for no other reason than to reassure the reader that psychophysicists are not engaged in some kind of futile attempt to solve the mind–body problem.

Is psychophysics based on the fallacious notion that private events can be measured? In a scholarly analysis of the problem, Savage (1966, 1970) proposes that the concept of sensation magnitude be abandoned and suggests that psychophysical scaling procedures be regarded as procedures for measuring perceptual abilities. His argument is based on the assumption that psychophysicists like S. S. Stevens have mistakenly attempted to measure private events. It is true that private events can never be measured since such attempts could never be verified publicly. However, Savage's arguments for the rejection of subjective-sounding concepts, as pointed out by Stevens in a rebuttal at the end of Savage's 1966 article, are mainly over the use of words and have little substance when it comes to the design and conduct of psychophysical experiments. Stevens pointed out that the operations in an experiment, rather than particular words, are important in scientific investigation.

When Stevens said he had measured subjective sensation he was intending to communicate the fact that a certain paradigm of operations had been employed. The specifics of these operations are discussed in detail by Stevens (1966c), and many of them have already been described in Chapters 4 and 5 of this book. The basic operation in the study of sensation magnitude is matching by an observer. For example, in magnitude estimation of loudness the observer is required to match the loudness of various stimuli with various values on the number scale, while in cross-modality matching he may be required to match the loudness of a tone to the brightness of lights of various intensities. According to Stevens the focal issue centers on the use of the observer as a comparator. Sensory magnitude is simply measured by a systematic investigation of the observer's behavior as he performs as a matching comparator. This is essentially all that is meant by the term sensory magnitude. It should be evident that the term refers rather specifically to a class of publicly observable experimental operations. The experimental results produced by such operations can be easily replicated by several investigators. The reliability of the results can be established and their usefulness can be evaluated in terms of how they relate to other experimental data and to psychophysical theories.

If the problem is only with the use of words, one might argue that psychophysicists should drop the use of subjective-sounding terms such as subjective magnitude so that they would not be misinterpreted. In the appended comments to Savage's article Stevens' explanation for his use of subjective-sounding terms is that they refer to a configuration of defining operations rather than to scientifically unmanageable private entities. We should therefore think of subjective magnitude, sensory magnitude, or whatever it is called, as a scientific construct. It appears to be advantageous to use words such as subjective, sensory, perceptual, or apparent to identify the construct, since these words refer to a specific kind of judgment an observer will make in a psychophysical experiment. Stevens (1966a) explained that:

> From an experienced photographer you can get two estimates of the light level, depending on whether you ask him to judge the physical or apparent level. And for the apparent or subjective value he will give widely different estimates if you vary the states of adaptation of his eyes. Similarly, a sound engineer can estimate the decibel level of a noisy factory, or, under a different *Aufgabe,* he can judge apparent loudness [pp. 36–37].

Stevens' point is well illustrated by an experiment of Teghtsoonian's (1965). She found the exponent for the power function of apparent size to be .76, but when she asked the observers to judge the physical area, they changed their basis of judgment and the exponent became 1.03. The exponent of nearly 1.00 indicates that when the observers tried to judge physical area they were, on the average, almost perfectly accurate. Obviously, different psychological processes were being investigated in the two parts of the experiment. Telling the observer to give his judgment of the apparent or subjective magnitude of a stimulus rather than to estimate its physical value appears to encourage him to make a direct response to the stimulus which is unaffected by mediating thoughts concerning physical measurement scales. Since the use of subjective terms as part of the instructions to the observer makes a large difference in the experimental data, such subjective concepts should be retained. The important point is that for purposes of scientific communication, these concepts are not references to vague, mentalistic, inaccessible private events, but rather are operationally defined scientific concepts.

The Physical Correlate Theory

Warren is another investigator who has questioned the validity of the assumption that sensation can be quantified (Warren, 1958, 1969; Warren & Warren, 1963). He claimed that instead of making judgments of sensory magnitude observers make judgments of some physical attribute associated with the stimulus. According to his physical correlate theory, it is through past experience that an observer learns to attend to a particular physical attribute when he is required in a psychophysics experiment to make sensation magnitude judgments of stimuli. The varying power function exponents found for different sense modalities do not reflect the operating characteristics of different biological transducers but instead are thought to be determined by the observer's responding to particular physical attributes of different stimuli.

A psychophysical power function with an exponent of approximately 1.0 for the judgment of duration may simply indicate that observers, through years of experience, have become capable of making judgments of duration that are linearly related to stimulus duration. A sound that is twice as long as another sound will be judged to be twice as long in apparent duration. According to the physical correlate theory the observer does not call one stimulus twice as long as another because this is how their apparent durations are perceived. Instead he makes this judgment because through experience he has learned the physical cues that correspond to a doubling of duration. In instrumental conditioning language, the observer has learned through years of reinforcement and extinction to make the correct response to a stimulus of a particular duration. Consequently the observer's judgments on the psychophysical task are determined by physical attributes of the stimulus rather than by the duration of the sensation. Contrary to sensory transducer theory, apparent duration, if it exists, is certainly not measured by the observer's judgments of the stimulus. What is measured, according to the physical correlate theory, is the observer's ability to discriminate among stimuli of various durations. The present example does not offer a test of the two theories but instead illustrates how they can account for the same data. Some basis for evaluation of the two theories is provided by examining the results of experiments on loudness and brightness scaling.

Unless a person is an acoustical engineer he would probably not have the opportunity to learn to make accurate judgments of the energy level of sound. Most people do, however, learn to make fairly accurate judgments of the distance of a sound. Warren has proposed that the distance between the observer and a sound source is the physical attribute to which the observer responds when he makes judgments of loudness in a laboratory situation. For example, if sound A is twice as far from the observer as sound B, then sound A should be judged to be half as loud as sound B. Because of the inverse square law, however, the sound energy at the observer's ears would not be half as great for A as for B, but only 25% as great. Thus, if the Warren theory is correct, loudness judgments should be proportional to the square root of sound energy, that is, the loudness function should be $L = kI^{.5}$ when L is loudness, k is a constant, and I is sound energy. S. S. Stevens (1972b), in a review of the many experiments on loudness scales, concluded that the best estimate of the exponent for loudness is .33. Warren, Sersen, and Pores (1958), in an article on the applicability of the physical correlate theory to loudness judgments, claimed that when pure tones are presented through earphones under conditions that eliminate reflections, the highly unusual quality of the stimulus prevents the observer from accurately using distance information. According to the authors it is only under these artificial conditions that the exponent for the loudness function is .33. When auditory stimuli were generated through a loudspeaker in a room which produced reverberations within the range normally encountered, the loudness function $L = kI^{.5}$, which is predicted from physical correlate theory, was obtained. Further evidence in support of the physical correlate theory of loudness was presented by Warren (1963).

It is possible that the biological transducer theory and the physical correlate theory are both correct. It may be that under conditions in which the observer hears sounds in the familiar setting of a reverberating field he finds it most natural to judge their loudness by their apparent distance. Certainly such sounds would be clearly localized as sound sources with relative positions in respect to other objects in the environment. Under these conditions the observer may find it impossible to avoid making what Titchener (1905) called the *stimulus error*.[1] The early psychophysicists throught that the observer made the stimulus error when he failed to judge his sensations and instead made judgments based on what he knew about the stimulus. Perhaps the relatively unfamiliar setting of a reverberation-free environment, such as those employed by the dozens of investigators who found the

---

[1]For an excellent analysis of the stimulus error in psychological experiments see E. G. Boring's article, The stimulus error. *American Journal of Psychology*, 1921, **32**, 449–471.

exponent for loudness to be approximately .33, permitted observers to judge correctly the magnitude of their sensations of loudness. The physical correlate theory may be correct when the observer is encouraged to make judgments about the physical attributes of stimuli, but the sensory transducer theory may apply in situations where the observer has been trained to avoid making the stimulus error of judging objects instead of sensations.

Warren (1969) has reviewed the evidence supporting the physical correlate theory for brightness judgments. Most people having little experience in measuring light are unable to make accurate estimates of light intensity, yet they are constantly making judgments of the brightness of objects. According to Warren, individuals are familiar with the way in which an object's appearance changes as the distance between the object and the source of light that illuminates it changes. It is assumed that when an observer is asked to make brightness judgments in a laboratory situation he bases his responses upon this familiar effect. A judgment of "half as bright" should occur when the stimulus intensity has been reduced by exactly the same amount that would occur when the distance between an object and a light source is doubled. Because of the inverse square law, if object A is twice as far from an illuminating light source as object B, then object A will receive 25% as much illumination. Therefore a perceived brightness ratio of one-half should require a stimulus energy ratio of one-quarter and the brightness function should be $B = kI^{.5}$, where B is judged brightness, k is a constant, and I is light energy.

Warren (1969) has claimed that exponents other than .5 are obtained only under very restricted and unnatural viewing conditions. For example, S. S. Stevens, based on data from experiments by Hanes (1949a,b) and data from his own experiments (Stevens, 1961a; Stevens & Galanter, 1957) has proposed that the exponent for brightness is .33. This value was obtained for a dark-adapted eye when the observer viewed a small luminous disc (about 5°) against a dark background. Warren, in a review of the experimental evidence for a brightness exponent of .5 (1969), reports that the .5 exponent is consistently obtained when stimuli are presented in a fashion closely resembling conditions under which the eyes are normally used (i.e., large stimuli with eyes adapted to the stimulus level). S. S. Stevens (1963), on the other hand, argues that the exponent for brightness may vary over a wide range depending on conditions of adaptation and glare. According to Stevens, .5 is a limited case and therefore does not constitute evidence in support of Warren's theory.

The interpretation of loudness judgment data, in which it was suggested that both the biological transducer theory and the physical correlate theory may be correct, is equally applicable to brightness judgment data. When stimuli are viewed as objects the brightness exponent may be close to .5. Under these conditions the observer may be attending to the stimulus correlate of changing luminance with changes in light source distance. Under conditions where it is difficult to identify the stimulus as an object or when the observer has been trained to avoid viewing the stimulus as an object, the stimulus error is not made and the exponent may vary over a wide range depending on how the viewing conditions affect the operating characteristics of the sensory transducers. Brightness functions obtained in both of these two different ways are important, for one set of functions applies to sensory transducers while the other applies to object perception. However, since the primary aim of psychophysical research has been to determine the operating characteristics of sensory systems, the work of Warren and his associates has been regarded by many psychophysicists as interesting but irrelevant.

RATIO SCALING OF SOCIAL CONSENSUS

What is the esthetic value of a work of art? What is the social status of a particular occupation? What is the political importance of various heads of government? What is the seriousness of various criminal offenses? These are questions of human judgment and represent only a few of the socially significant problems to which ratio scaling methods have been applied. Advances have not occurred without some resistance, however. Social scientists have been skeptical of the psychophysicists' claim that psychological processes can be measured on a ratio scale while the stimuli that elicit them can only be specified on a nominal scale. Social scientists in resorting to ranking procedures or biased category scales must admit that the most they can say about the psychological values of two stimuli is that one is greater than the other.

The endeavors of psychologists to obtain precise quantitative measurements of social consensus are as old as psychophysics itself. The work of Fechner on experimental esthetics was the first important attempt to scale the psychological value of nominally specifiable stimuli on a quantitative scale. The fundamental concepts of Fechner's sensory psychophysics were extended to the measurement of esthetic judgments. Thus, according to Fechner esthetic stimuli that are equally discriminable are equally different psychologically. In the 1920's Thurstone retained Fechner's basic logic and worked out the law of comparative judgment as a mathematical model for converting measures of discriminability into psychological scale values. Thurstone was particularly interested in applying the method to socially significant problems such as the measurement of preferences for nationalities and judged seriousness of offenses.

It has only been very recently that ratio scaling methods have been extensively applied to the scaling of nonsensory variables. The logic of ratio scaling in these cases is no different than it is for scaling loudness, brightness, or any other sensory process that has a quantifiable stimulus. The only requirements are that stimuli be nominally specified and that observers are able to match numbers or other stimuli to the strength of their psychological impressions. Generally, it is found that if an observer assigns numbers to impressions, or if he adjusts the intensity of a stimulus such as a tone or light to impressions, the same psychological scale emerges from the data. This constitutes strong support for the validity of the procedure.

Beyond the fact that ratio scaling procedures result in the highest level of measurement, a great advantage of their use is in the relative ease of application. Large amounts of data can be obtained quickly and data analysis is not complicated. The category scales that have been so popular among social scientists are also extremely efficient. A person is simply asked to assign each of a number of items to one of a limited number of categories. The category scale, however, yields at best an interval scale of measurement. Often biasing factors render it no better than an ordinal scale. Stevens (1975) noted that it would be possible to generate a ratio scale by a slight rewording of the instructions to the observer. He would simply be told to use any number which seems appropriate rather than to use a restricted set of categories.

The applicability of ratio scaling to problems of social significance has been clearly demonstrated in a study on the measurement of criminality by Sellin and Wolfgang (1964). In part of this extensive project lasting three years, 38 juvenile court judges, 286 police officers, and 245 students made judgments of the seriousness of 21 criminal offenses. Since there was an impressive invariance for the results of such diverse observers as judges, policemen, and students, it seems probable that there is a general consensus in the society on the seriousness of a wide variety of criminal offenses. Furthermore, according to Sellin and Wolfgang (1964), "this agreement transcends simple qualitative concordance; it extends to the estimated degree of seriousness of these offenses" [p. 268]. For example, it is now possible to make quantitative statements about how much more serious armed robbery is than car theft.

That a ratio scale of the seriousness of criminal offenses as judged by members of society was achieved was supported by several checks on the validity of the data. In one of these checks the magnitude estimations were found to meet the ratio measurement requirement of additivity. Crimes that combined two offenses were judged to be equal in seriousness to the sum of the judgments made for the two separate offenses. The mean magnitude estimation for the crime of breaking into a building and stealing $5.00, for example, was approximately equal to the mean magnitude estimation for breaking into a building plus the mean magnitude estimation for stealing $5.00.

Among the 21 crimes ranging from minor offenses to murder there were the crimes of stealing $5.00, $20.00, $50.00, $1000.00, and $5000.00. It is interesting that the judged seriousness of the crime was found to grow as a power function with an exponent of .17 of the amount of money stolen. This finding represents an extension of the power law far beyond the original problems of sensory processes. The exponent of .17 indicates that for a crime to be considered twice as serious as another the amount stolen must be approximately 65 times as great. This result cannot be interpreted as a simple reflection of how the psychological value of money grows with the actual amount of money. The exponent of .17 is much smaller than the .5 value for the utility of money proposed by Cramer in the eighteenth century and recently confirmed experimentally by Galanter (1962) and

Galanter and Pliner (1974). Obviously, factors in addition to the perceived worth of the stolen money determined judgments of the seriousness of the crime.

Sellin and Wolfgang were also interested in the question of whether or not the punishment fits the crime. Are the punishments given by the state consistent with the seriousness of the crimes as judged by members of society? Magnitude estimation of the judged seriousness of crime was found to be a power function with an exponent of .7 of the maximum penalty stated in terms of time in jail prescribed by the Pennsylvania Penal Code. Since the exponent was not 1.0, the penalty expressed by time in jail is not proportional to the seriousness of the offense. However, before being able to conclude that the Pennsylvania Penal Code is a violation of justice we would have to determine the psychophysical magnitude function for the relation between the judged severity of a jail term and the actual time in jail. If the psychological severity of the term in jail increases as a power function with an exponent of .7 of the actual time in jail, then the punishment fits the crime. Both the judged seriousness of the crime and the judged severity of the punishment would be the same function of the duration of the jail term. An exponent of less than 1.0 would indicate that people judge the severity of the punishment to be a decelerating function of actual time in jail. Although this experiment has not been performed, I think most people would judge a term of two years in jail to be less than twice as punishing as a term of one year in jail.

The study by Sellin and Wolfgang illustrates that important social problems can be attacked with the methods originally developed to study sensory processes. The use of the highly efficient ratio scaling methods in such new areas has a promising future.

In many of the studies of social consensus more than one scaling method was employed. The scales derived from ratio scaling have been found to systematically deviate from those obtained by Thurstonian confusion scaling or category scaling. One of the most consistent findings in psychophysics is that the Thurstonian scale is a logarithmic function of the ratio scale. Many experiments have been conducted in which the same stimuli were scaled by both Thurstonian and ratio scaling procedures. When Case V is used, the Thurstonian scale values are almost always a linear function of the logarithm of the corresponding ratio scale values.

Many of the first studies of psychophysical ratio scaling of nonmetric stimuli were done by Gösta Ekman and his associates at the University of Stockholm. The logarithmic relation between ratio and Thurstonian scales was consistently found in these studies. When observers judged the quality of 18 samples of handwriting by the method of paired comparison and by a ratio estimation procedure, two distinct scales were produced. The Thurstonian scale was a logarithmic function of the ratio estimation scale (Ekman & Künnapas, 1962a). The same relation was found between scales derived by the two methods when observers judged 17 drawings of a tree made by sixth grade students (Ekman & Künnapas, 1962b). The logarithmic relation was again found when students judged the political importance of eleven Swedish monarchs who lived between 1550 and 1850 (Ekman &

Künnapas, 1963) and when the prestige of occupations was judged (Künnapas & Wikström, 1963). The systematic difference between the results from the two methods might have caused the investigators to become skeptical about their procedures. Instead the finding has become a basis for understanding why different methods produce different scales under some conditions and the same scale under other conditions. The significance of the logarithmic relation between ratio and Thurstonian scales will be clarified in evaluating the different scaling methods.

EVALUATION OF SCALING METHODS

Agreement among scientific results obtained under different conditions and by different methods is often thought to constitute a type of validation of the particular finding. Therefore, the forms of the psychophysical magnitude functions obtained by the various confusion, partition, and ratio scaling methods should be essentially the same if the scales are valid. When correspondence between the different scales is lacking, the validity of each scaling method is questionable. A careful examination of each method should be made to determine (a) which if any of the methods yield valid results, and (b) the reason for the lack of agreement among the results of the different methods.

On metathetic continua all three kinds of psychophysical scale show remarkable agreement. For example, the form of the mel scale of pitch is the same when constructed by summating jnds, equisectioning pitch intervals, and making ratio judgments (S. S. Stevens, 1954; S. S. Stevens & Galanter, 1957). When the scale values obtained by one method are plotted against the scale values obtained by another method for various stimulus values, the relationship is a straight line. Furthermore, the pitch scale for pure tones corresponds almost exactly to a graph of how the point of maximum vibration on the basilar membrane of the inner ear changes as a function of frequency. Thus, psychological pitch is approximately linearly mapped out on the basilar membrane.

Ratio scaling techniques have been subjected to intensive validation testing. As was pointed out when describing these methods, the scales constructed by fractionation, ratio estimation, magnitude estimation, and magnitude production have consistently been found to be linearly related to each other. The application of validation procedures such as cross-modality matching, comparing fractionation scales based on different fractions, and comparing the results of scaling two overlapping sets of stimuli support the validity of scales based on these techniques. Ratio scales are frequently found to be predictable from data obtained with entirely different psychophysical procedures such as stimulus matching. Furthermore, the scales are often found to be highly consistent with our general understanding of how a particular sensory system functions. Since evidence suggests that ratio scaling techniques commonly yield valid psychological scales, linearly related discrimination or partition scales would also appear to be valid. This happy state of affairs, however, is to be found only for scaling of perceptual attributes on metathetic continua.

On prothetic continua, ratio scales, partition scales, and discrimination scales are nonlinearly related. Stevens (1961a), comparing scales constructed by magnitude estimation, jnd summation, and category rating, states that

> . . . on all prothetic continua the magnitude scale is a power function, the discriminability (jnd) scale approximates a logarithmic function, and the category scale assumes a form intermediate between the other two. Over the different sense modalities, these relations among the three scales are strikingly invariant; they constitute one of the really stable aspects of psychophysics [p. 9].

The results of extensive validation testing of ratio scales have led some investigators to accept the ratio scales as valid and to reject the discrimination and partition scales because of their lack of agreement with the ratio scales.

Why do the three kinds of scaling method result in comparable scales on metathetic continua but not on prothetic continua? Stevens has taken the position that on metathetic continua the three kinds of scaling method measure the same aspect of the sensory response—discriminability. Because metathetic continua are qualitative, relating to the "what" and "where" of sensory experience, the important consideration in scaling would seem to be the measurement of the amount of difference between sensations. Discrimination scales such as summated jnd's give a direct measure of the discriminability of sensations. Partition scales are in agreement with discrimination scales because when the observer is asked to partition the continuum into psychologically equal segments he apparently bases his judgments on the discriminability of sensations and creates a series of segments, each of which contains the same number of jnd's. When a ratio scaling method is used, the observer will judge one sensation to be twice as great as another sensation if the second sensation corresponds to twice the number of summated jnd's as the first. Thus, on metathetic continua all three kinds of scaling method seem to result in valid psychological scales of the discriminability of sensation.

On prothetic continua the relevant aspect of the sensory response is not discriminability but sensation magnitude. However, as on metathetic continua, the discrimination and partition scales measure discriminability when applied to the prothetic continua. Discriminability of sensations is certainly important, but it should not be confused with sensation magnitude. On prothetic continua the discriminability of two sensations does not correspond to the difference in magnitude between the two sensations. Sensation magnitude is assumed to be directly and validly measured only by the ratio scaling methods.

Ekman's Law

At the University of Stockholm, an effort has been made by Ekman to establish a precise theoretical formulation that would account for the difference between psychophysical scales derived by ratio scaling and discrimination scaling. Ekman's principle (1956, 1959), known as *Ekman's law,* states that the psychological size of the jnd is a linear function of sensation magnitude. The formulation states

$$\Delta\psi = k_\psi(\psi + a), \tag{5.11}$$

where $\Delta\psi$ is a change in sensation magnitude that is just noticeable, ψ is the starting value of sensation magnitude, and k_ψ and a are constants. This equation, which applies to the psychological continuum, is exactly analogous to Weber's law, $\Delta\phi = k_\phi(\phi + a)$, which applies to the physical stimulus continuum. The k_ϕ in Weber's law refers to the constant fraction by which all values of ϕ must be changed to produce a just noticeable difference in stimulation; the k_ψ in Ekman's law refers to the constant fraction by which all values of ψ must be changed to produce a just noticeable difference in sensation.

The first empirical evidence for Ekman's law came from an experiment by Harper and Stevens (1948) in which a psychological scale for heaviness, called the veg scale, was constructed. Harper and Stevens determined the weight which was judged to be half as heavy as a standard weight of 20, 40, 70, 100, 300, 500, 1000, and 2000 gm. From the fractionation data a sensation magnitude scale was constructed which turned out to be a power function with an exponent of 1.45. From the data of Oberlin (1936) on the size of $\Delta\phi$ for heaviness for different values of ϕ, it was possible for Harper and Stevens to calculate $\Delta\psi$ values for different values of ψ. This could be done graphically by simply converting ϕ into ψ and $\Delta\phi$ into $\Delta\psi$ for several values of ψ. Figure 5.11 illustrates the procedure for a single value of ϕ. In the experiment by Harper and Stevens a linear relation was found between $\Delta\psi$ and ψ. Also in support of Ekman's law, Ekman (1959) reported that $\Delta\psi$ is proportional to ψ for visual velocity and auditory time.

In essence, Ekman's law is a statement that variability in sensory magnitude is proportional to the average sensory magnitude value. The derivation of Harper and Stevens that $\Delta\psi$ is proportional to ψ is complemented by the finding that the standard deviation is proportional to the mean magnitude estimation over a fairly wide range of stimulus values (Eisler, 1962, 1963). But even if relevant experimental data were absent Ekman's hypothesis would seem very reasonable. Weber's law indicates that the variability of discrimination measured in the physical stimulus domain obeys the proportionality rule. Furthermore, in other sciences the variability of measurements is often proportional to the average value of the measurements. In measuring properties such as distance, duration, and weight, the result is frequently stated as a value in the appropriate units plus or minus some percentage and the standard deviation is proportional to the mean. As early as 1874 Brentano speculated that the relativity of variability applies in the psychological as well as in the physical domain. Had Brentano's idea been seriously considered it would probably have resulted in the derivation of the power function as the psychophysical law. In contrast to Fechner, Brentano proposed that the psychological size of the jnd was not a constant value but rather a constant ratio on the sensory

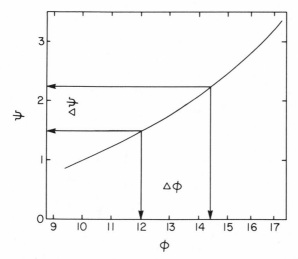

FIGURE 5.11   Hypothetical psychophysical magnitude function. If the value of $\Delta\phi$ is known for a particular stimulus intensity the corresponding value of $\Delta\psi$ can be determined from the psychophysical magnitude function.

continuum. Fechner's law, based on the less reasonable assumption that variability and consequently the jnd are constant all along the sensory magnitude continuum, carried the day and remained dominant for another 80 years.

Stevens' power law implies that both Ekman's law and Weber's law are valid. Since in the power law $\log \psi$ is linearly related to $\log \phi$ as ϕ is increased by some constant ratio (constant number of log units), ψ will also increase by some other constant ratio (constant number of log units). For example, the power function, with its exponent of .33 for loudness, indicates that every time we increase stimulus energy by 8.2 times (.91 log unit) we cause a doubling of loudness (.30 log unit).

In another example we could increase ϕ by a constant ratio, k_ϕ (Weber's law), and cause ψ to increase by the constant ratio k_ψ (Ekman's law). Suppose that k_ϕ is .2 and k_ψ is .5. Successive $\Delta\phi$ values along the ϕ scale could be calculated by using the procedure described in Chapter 1 in the discussion of Fechner's law. Each ϕ value is .2 times greater than the previous value. The ψ values corresponding to the ϕ values can be calculated by determining successive values of $\Delta\psi$ along the ψ scale. For example, the first ψ value is 1.0 and the first $\Delta\psi_1$ is equal to .5 since $\psi_1 \times k_\psi = 1.0 \times .5$. The second ψ value is 1.5 since $\psi_1 + \Delta\psi_1 = 1.0 + .5$. The second $\Delta\psi_2$ is .75 since $\psi_2 \times k_\psi = 1.5 \times .5$ and the third value of ψ is 2.25 since $\psi_2 + \Delta\psi_2 = 1.5 + .75$. After a series of such calculations we end up with a series of ϕ values that increase according to Weber's law and a corresponding series of ψ values that increase according to Ekman's law. A graph of $\log \psi$ as a function of $\log \phi$ yields a linear function with a slope of 2.2 (Figure 5.12). Thus, when Weber's law is true

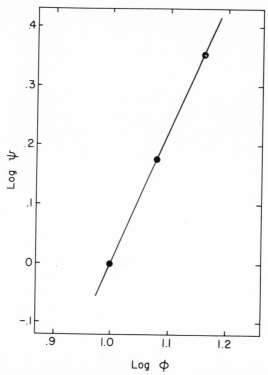

FIGURE 5.12   A power function derived by assuming Weber's law in the stimulus domain and Ekman's law in the senation domain.

for the ϕ dimension and Ekman's law is true for the ψ dimension, the relation between ϕ and ψ is a power function. The exponent of a particular psychophysical power function would be determined by the values of k_ϕ and k_ψ.

As was stated earlier, Teghtsoonian (1971) has hypothesized that the ratio of the weakest to the strongest ψ experienced is the same for all sensory modalities even though the stimulus ranges are different. This hypothesis suggests that there may be only one value of k_ψ that applies to all modalities. Teghtsoonian, using power functions and $k\phi$ values for nine different modalities, found $k\psi$ to be nearly constant at about .03. If further research substantiates this finding, Ekman's law may be more precisely stated as

$$\Delta\psi = .03(\psi + a). \qquad (5.12)$$

The Fechnerian jnd scale, which generally shows the number of empirically determined jnd's above threshold to be a logarithmic function of ϕ, becomes a power function when each successive jnd above threshold is regarded as a constant ratio increment in sensation. Had Fechner assumed Weber's law to be applicable to both ϕ and ψ dimensions he would have proposed a psychophysical power law rather than a logarithmic law.

If Ekman's law bridges a gap between jnd scales and psychophysical ratio scales it should also bridge the gap between other confusion scales and psychophysical ratio scales. For example, there appear to be some interesting relationships between Stevens' power law, Ekman's law, and Thurstone's law of comparative judgment. The finding that $\Delta\psi$ increases linearly with ψ implies that the variance of a distribution of ψ values on the psychological continuum would be proportional to the mean of the distribution. Generally Thurstone's Case V is applied to paired comparison proportions to derive a psychophysical scale. The resulting Thurstonian scale in which ψ is not a power function of ϕ appears to be an artifact of the incorrect assumption that variability in psychological units, $\Delta\psi$ or σ_ψ, is constant along the psychological continuum. Recall that when Ekman and his fellow workers scaled various nonmetric stimuli by both paired comparison and ratio methods the Thurstonian Case V values were a logarithmic function of the ratio scale values. This result is precisely what is expected if each added unit on a Thurstonian Case V or jnd scale is equivalent to a constant ratio increment rather than a constant increment on the psychological continuum and the ratio scale is valid. Suppose that stimuli A, B, and C yielded Thurstonian scale values of 1, 2, and 3, respectively, and ratio scales values of 3, 6, and 12, respectively. Each Thurstonian unit corresponds to a doubling of the ratio scale value (a constant ratio increment). A logarithmic transformation of the ratio scale values yields values of .48, .78, and 1.08 which are linearly related to the Thurstonian scale values of 1, 2, and 3.

Stevens (1966d) has pointed out that had Thurstone gone further in proposing various cases for the solution of his law and proposed a Case VI in which σ_ψ is assumed to be directly proportional to ψ, paired comparison scales and psychophysical ratio scales would be linearly related. If Thurstone had applied this solution to paired comparison of measurable stimuli of variable intensity he would most likely have proposed a psychophysical power law.

It should be recalled that ROC curves obtained in signal detection experiments frequently indicate that the variance of the SN distribution increases with signal strength. Ekman's law appears to serve a valuable function of unifying data from experiments on such seemingly diverse topics as signal detection, discrimination, magnitude estimation, and paired comparison judgments.

References

Adrian, E. D., & Matthews, R. The action of light on the eye: I. The discharge of impulses in the optic nerve and its relation to the electric changes in the retina. *Journal of Physiology,* 1927, **63,** 378–414.

Banks, W. P. Signal detection theory and human memory. *Psychological Bulletin,* 1970, **74,** 81–99.

Berglund, B., Berglund, U., Engen, T., & Ekman, G. Individual psychophysical functions for twenty-eight odorants. *Perception and Psychophysics,* 1971. **9,** 379–384.

Bernoulli, D. Specimen theoriae novae de mensura sortis. *Commentarii Academiae Scientiarum Imperiales Petropolitanae,* 1738, **5,** 175–192. (Transl. by L. Sommer in *Econometrica,* 1954, **22,** 23–36.)

Blackwell, H. R. Psychophysical thresholds: Experimental studies of methods of measurement. *Bulletin of the Engineering Research Institute,* University of Michigan, No. 36, 1953.

Blough, D. S. A method for obtaining psychophysical thresholds from the pigeon. *Journal of the Experimental Analysis of Behavior,* 1958, **1,** 31–43.

Bond, B., & Stevens, S. S. Cross-modality matching of brightness to loudness by 5-year-olds. *Perception and Psychophysics,* 1969, **6,** 337–339.

Borg, G., Diamant, H., Ström, L., & Zotterman, Y. The relation between neural and perceptual intensity: A comparative study on the neural and psychophysical response to taste stimuli. *Journal of Physiology,* 1967, **192,** 13–20.

Boring, E. G. A chart of the psychometric function. *American Journal of Psychology,* 1917, **28,** 465–470.

Boring, E. G. The stimulus error. *American Journal of Psychology,* 1921, **32,** 449–471.

Brentano, F. *Psychologie vom emperischen Standpunkte.* Leipzig: Duncker & Humblot, 1874.

Churcher, B. G. A loudness scale for industrial noise measurement. *Journal of the Acoustical Society of America,* 1935, **6,** 216–226.

Cohn, J. Experimentelle Untersuchungen über die Gefuhlsbetonung der Farben, Helligkeiten, und ihrer Combinationen. *Philosophische Studien,* 1894, **10,** 562–603.

Cornsweet, T. N. The staircase method in psychophysics. *American Journal of Psychology,* 1962, **75,** 485–491.

Corso, J. F. The neural quantum theory of sensory discrimination. *Psychological Bulletin,* 1956, **53,** 371–393.

Corso, J. F. Neural quantum controversy in sensory psychology. *Science,* 1973, **181,** 467–468.

Davis, H., & Krantz, F. W. International audiometric zero. *Journal of the Acoustical Society of America,* 1964, **36,** 1450–1454.

Delbrück, M. A physicist's renewed look at biology: Twenty years later. *Science,* 1970, **168,** 1312–1315.

Eisler, H. Empirical test of a model relating magnitude and category scales. *Scandinavian Journal of Psychology,* 1962, **3,** 88–96.

Eisler, H. Magnitude scales, category scales, and Fechnerian integration. *Psychological Review,* 1963, **70,** 243–253.

Ekman, G. Discriminal sensitivity on the subjective continuum. *Acta Psychologica,* 1956, **12,** 233–243.

Ekman, G. Weber's law and related functions. *Journal of Psychology,* 1959, **47,** 343–352.

Ekman, G., & Künnapas, T. Measurement of aesthetic value by "direct" and "indirect" methods. *Scandinavian Journal of Psychology,* 1962, **3,** 33–39.   (a)

Ekman, G., & Künnapas, T. Scales of aesthetic value. *Perceptual and Motor Skills,* 1962, **14,** 19–26.   (b)

Ekman, G., & Künnapas, T. A further study of direct and indirect scaling methods. *Scandinavian Journal of Psychology,* 1963, **4,** 77–80.

Elliot, P. B. Tables of d'. In J. A. Swets (Ed.), *Signal detection and recognition by human observers.* New York: Wiley, 1964.

Engen, T., & Tulunay, Ü. Some sources of error in half-heaviness judgments. *Journal of Experimental Psychology,* 1956, **54,** 208–212.

Engen, T. Psychophysics: Discrimination and detection. In J. W. Kling & L. A. Riggs (Eds.), *Woodworth & Schlosberg's experimental psychology.* (3rd ed.) New York: Holt, 1971.

Estes, W. K. The problem of inference from curves based on group data. *Psychological Bulletin,* 1956, **53,** 134–140.

Fechner, G. T. *Element der Psychophysik.* Leipzig: Breitkopf & Härterl, 1860.

Fechner, G. T. *Vorschule der Aesthetik.* Leipzig: Breitkopf & Härterl, 1876.

Fullerton, G. S., & Cattell, J. McK. *On the perception of small differences.* Philadelphia: University of Pennsylvania Press, 1892.

Fuortes, M. G. F., & Hodgkin, A. L. Changes in time scale and sensitivity in the ommatidia of Limulus. *Journal of Physiology,* 1964, **172,** 239–263.

Galanter, E. The direct measurement of utility and subjective probability. *American Journal of Psychology,* 1962, **75,** 208–220.

Galanter, E., & Pliner, P. Cross-modality matching of money against other continua. In H. R. Moskowitz, B. Scharf, & J. C. Stevens (Eds.), *Sensation and measurement.* Dordrecht-Holland: Reidel, 1974.

Garner, W. R. Context effects and the validity of loudness scales. *Journal of Experimental Psychology,* 1954, **48,** 218–224.

Gescheider, G. A. Auditory and cutaneous apparent successiveness. *Journal of Experimental Psychology,* 1967, **73,** 179–186.

Gescheider, G. A., Barton, W. G., Bruce, M. R., Goldberg, J. H., & Greenspan, M. J. The effects of simultaneous auditory stimulation upon the detection of tactile stimuli. *Journal of Experimental Psychology,* 1969, **81,** 120–125.

Gescheider, G. A., & Wright, J. H. Effects of sensory adaptation on the form of the psychophysical magnitude function for cutaneous vibration. *Journal of Experimental Psychology,* 1968, **77,** 308–313.

Gescheider, G. A., Wright, J. H., & Polak, J. W. Detection of vibrotactile signals differing in probability of occurrence. *Journal of Psychology,* 1971, **78,** 253–260.

Gescheider, G. A., Wright, J. H., Weber, B. J., & Barton, W. G. Absolute thresholds in vibrotactile signal detection. *Perception and Psychophysics,* 1971, **10,** 413–417.

Graham, C. H., Brown, R. H., & Mote, F. A., Jr. The relation of size of stimulus and intensity in the human eye: I. Intensity thresholds for white light. *Journal of Experimental Psychology,* 1939, **24,** 555–573.

Green, D. M., & Swets, J. A. *Signal detection theory and psychophysics.* New York: Wiley, 1966.

Greene, L. C., & Hardy, J. D. Spatial summation of pain. *Journal of Applied Physiology,* 1958, **13,** 457–464.

Gregg, L. W. Fractionation of temporal intervals. *Journal of Experimental Psychology,* 1951, **42,** 307–312.

Guilford, J. P. *Psychometric methods.* New York: McGraw-Hill, 1954.

Hanes, R. M. A scale of subjective brightness. *Journal of Experimental Psychology,* 1949, **39,** 438–452. (a)

Hanes, R. M. The construction of subjective brightness scales from fractionation data: A validation. *Journal of Experimental Psychology,* 1949, **39,** 719–728. (b)

Hardy, J. D., Wolff, H. G., & Goodell, H. Studies on pain: Discrimination of differences in pain as a basis of a scale of pain intensity. *Journal of Clinical Investigation,* 1947, **26,** 1152–1158.

Harper, R. S., & Stevens, S. S. A psychological scale for weight and a formula for its derivation. *American Journal of Psychology,* 1948, **61,** 343–351.

Hartline, H. K., & Graham, C. H. Nerve impulses from single receptors in the eye. *Journal of Cellular and Comparative Physiology,* 1932, **1,** 277–295.

Hecht, S. Vision II. The nature of the photoreceptor process. In C. Murchison (Ed.), *Handbook of general experimental psychology.* Worcester, Mass.: Clark University Press, 1934.

Hecht, S., Haig, C., & Chase, A. M. Influence of light adaptation on subsequent dark adaptation of the eye. *Journal of General Physiology,* 1937, **20,** 831–850.

Hecht, S., Shlaer, S., & Pirenne, M. H. Energy, quanta, and vision. *Journal of General Physiology,* 1942, **25,** 819–840.

Hellman, R. P., & Zwislocki, J. J. Monaural loudness function of a 1000-cps tone and internal summation. *Journal of the Acoustical Society of America,* 1963, **35,** 856–865.

Hellman, R. P., & Zwislocki, J. J. Loudness function of a 1000-cps tone in the presence of a masking noise. *Journal of the Acoustical Society of America,* 1964, **36,** 1618–1627.

Hellman, R. P., & Zwislocki, J. J. Loudness determination at low sound frequencies. *Journal of the Acoustical Society of America,* 1968, **43,** 60–64.

Herbart, J. F. *Psychologie als Wissenschaft, neu gegrundet Auferfahrung, Metaphysik, und Mathematik.* Königsberg, Germany: Unzer, 1824.

Horeman, H. W. Relation between brightness and luminance under induction. *Vision Research,* 1965, **5,** 331–340.

Jastrow, J. The psycho-physic law and star magnitudes. *American Journal of Psychology,* 1887, **1,** 112–127.

Jones, F. N. A forced-choice method of limits. *American Journal of Psychology,* 1956, **69,** 672–673.

Kenshalo, D. R., Decker, T., & Hamilton, A. Spatial summation on the forehead, forearm, and back produced by radiant and conducted heat. *Journal of Comparative and Physiological Psychology,* 1967, **63,** 510–515.

König, A., & Brodhun, E. Experimentelle Untersuchungen ueber die psychophysiche Fundamental-formel in Bezug auf den Gesichtssinn. *Sitzungsberichte Preussische Akademie Wissenschaften,* Berlin, 1889, **27,** 641–644.

Krantz, D. H. Threshold theories of signal detection. *Psychological Review,* 1969, **76,** 308–324.

Künnapas, T., & Wikström, I. Measurement of occupational preferences: A comparison of scaling methods. *Perceptual and Motor Skills,* 1963, **17,** 611–694.

Lockhart, R. S., & Murdock, B. B., Jr. Memory and the theory of signal detection. *Psychological Bulletin,* 1970, **74,** 100–109.

Luce, R. D. A threshold theory for simple detection experiments. *Psychological Review,* 1963, **70,** 61–79.

Ludvigh, E., & McCarthy, E. F. Absorption of visible light by the refractive media of the human eye. *Archives of Ophthalmology,* 1938, **20,** 37–51.

Markowitz, J., & Swets, J. A. Factors affecting the slope of empirical ROC curves: Comparison of binary and rating responses. *Perception and Psychophysics,* 1967, **2,** 91–97.

Marks, L. E. Spatial summation in the warmth sense. In H. R. Moskowitz, B. Scharf, & J. C. Stevens (Eds.), *Sensation and measurement*. Dordrecht-Holland: Reidel, 1974.   (a)

Marks, L. E. *Sensory processes*. New York: Academic Press, 1974. (b)

Marks, L. E., & Stevens, J. C. Individual brightness functions. *Perception and Psychophysics*, 1966, **1**, 17–24.

Marks, L. E., & Stevens, J. C. The form of the psychophysical function near threshold. *Perception and Psychophysics*, 1968, **4**, 315–318.

Marks, L. E., & Stevens, J. C. Spatial summation of warmth: Influence of duration and configuration of the stimulus. *American Journal of Psychology*, 1973, **86**, 251–267.

McBurney, D. H. Magnitude estimation of the taste of sodium chloride after adaptation to sodium chloride. *Journal of Experimental Psychology*, 1966, **72**, 869–873.

Merkel, J. Die Abhängigkeit zwischen Reiz und Empfindung. *Philosophische Studien*, 1888, **4**, 541–594.

Miller, G. A. Sensitivity to changes in the intensity of white noise and its relation to masking and loudness. *Journal of the Acoustical Society of America*, 1947, **19**, 609–619.

Miller, G. A., & Garner, W. R. Effect of random presentation in the psychometric function: Implication for a quantal theory of discrimination. *American Journal of Psychology*, 1944, **57**, 451–467.

Munsell, A. E. O., Sloan, L. L., & Godlove, I. H. Neutral value scales: I. Munsell neutral value scale. *Journal of the Optical Society of America*, 1933, **23**, 394–411.

Norman, D. A. Neural quantum controversy in sensory psychology. *Science*, 1973, **181**, 468–469.

Oberlin, K. W. Variation in intensive sensitivity to lifted weights. *Journal of Experimental Psychology*, 1936, **19**, 438–455.

Peck, R. E. The application of thymometry to the measurement of anxiety. *International Journal of Neuropsychiatry*, 1966, **2**, 337–341.

Plateau, J. A. F. Sur la mesure des sensations physiques, et sur la loi qui lie l'intensité de ces sensations à l'intensité de la cause excitante. *Bulletins de l'Academie Royale des Sciences, des Lettres, et des Beaux-Arts de Belgique*, 1872, **33**, 376–388.

Pollack, I., & Norman, D. A. A non-parametric analysis of recognition experiments. *Psychonomic Science*, 1964, **1**, 125–126.

Poulton, E. C. The new psychophysics: Six models for magnitude estimation. *Psychological Bulletin*, 1968, **69**, 1–19.

Pradhan, P. L., & Hoffman, P. J. Effect of spacing and range of stimuli on magnitude estimation judgments. *Journal of Experimental Psychology*, 1963, **66**, 533–541.

Riesz, R. R. Differential intensity sensitivity of the ear for pure tones. *Physical Review*, 1928, **31**, 867–875.

Robinson, D. W., & Dadson, R. S. A re-determination of the equal loudness relations for pure tones. *British Journal of Applied Physics*, 1956, **7**, 166–181.

Ross, S., & Katchmer, L. The construction of a magnitude function for short time intervals. *American Journal of Psychology*, 1951, **64**, 397–401.

Savage, C. W. Introspectionist and behaviorist interpretations of ratio scales of perceptual magnitudes. *Psychological Monographs*, 1966, **80** (19, Whole No. 627).

Savage, C. W. *The measurement of sensation*. Berkeley: University of California Press, 1970.

Scharf, B. Complex sounds and critical bands. *Psychological Bulletin*, 1961, **58**, 205–217.

Scharf, B., & Stevens, J. C. The form of the loudness function near threshold. *Proceedings of the 3rd International Congress on Acoustics, Stuttgart, 1959*, (Vol. I). Amsterdam: Elsevier, 1961.

Sellin, T., & Wolfgang, M. E. *The measurement of delinquency*. New York: Wiley, 1964.

Sivian, L. J., & White, S. D. On minimum audible sound fields. *Journal of the Acoustical Society of America*, 1933, **4**, 288–321.

Stevens, J. C., & Guirao, M. Individual loudness functions. *Journal of the Acoustical Society of America*, 1964, **36**, 2210–2213.

Stevens, J. C., & Mack, J. D. Scales of apparent force. *Journal of Experimental Psychology,* 1959, **58,** 405–413.

Stevens, J. C., Mack, J. D., & Stevens, S. S. Growth of sensation on seven continua as measured by force of handgrip. *Journal of Experimental Psychology,* 1960, **59,** 60–67.

Stevens, J. C., & Marks, L. E. Spatial summation and the dynamics of warmth sensation. *Perception and Psychophysics,* 1971, **9,** 291–298.

Stevens, J. C., & Stevens, S. S. Warmth and cold: Dynamics of sensory intensity. *Journal of Experimental Psychology,* 1960, **60,** 183–192.

Stevens, J. C., & Stevens, S. S. Brightness function: Effects of adaptation. *Journal of the Optical Society of America,* 1963, **53,** 375–385.

Stevens, S. S. A scale for the measurement for a psychological magnitude: Loudness. *Psychological Review,* 1936, **43,** 405–416.

Stevens, S. S. *Handbook of experimental psychology.* New York: Wiley, 1951.

Stevens, S. S. On the brightness of lights and the loudness of sounds. *Science,* 1953, **118,** 576. (Abstract)

Stevens, S. S. Pitch discrimination, mels, and Koch's contention. *Journal of the Acoustical Society of America,* 1954, **26,** 1075–1077.

Stevens, S. S. The measurement of loudness. *Journal of the Acoustical Society of America,* 1955, **27,** 815–820.

Stevens, S. S. The direct estimation of sensory magnitude—loudness. *American Journal of Psychology,* 1956, **69,** 1–25.

Stevens, S. S. On the psychophysical law. *Psychological Review,* 1957, **64,** 153–181.

Stevens, S. S. Problems and methods of psychophysics. *Psychological Bulletin,* 1958, **55,** 177–196.

Stevens, S. S. Cross-modality validations of subjective scales for loudness, vibrations, and electric shock. *Journal of Experimental Psychology,* 1959, **57,** 201–209. (a)

Stevens, S. S. Tactile vibration: Dynamics of sensory intensity. *Journal of Experimental Psychology,* 1959, **57,** 210–218. (b)

Stevens, S. S. Ratio scales, partition scales and confusion scales. In H. Gulliksen & S. Messick (Eds.), *Psychological scaling: Theory and applications.* New York: Wiley, 1960.

Stevens, S. S. The psychophysics of sensory function. In W. A. Rosenblith (Ed.), *Sensory communication.* Boston: MIT Press, 1961. (a)

Stevens, S. S. Is there a quantal threshold? In W. A. Rosenblith (Ed.), *Sensory communication.* Boston: MIT Press, 1961. (b)

Stevens, S. S. The basis of psychophysical judgments. *Journal of the Acoustical Society of America,* 1963, **35,** 611–612.

Stevens, S. S. Matching functions between loudness and ten other continua. *Perception and Psychophysics,* 1966, **1,** 5–8. (a)

Stevens, S. S. Power-group transformations under glare, masking, and recruitment. *Journal of the Acoustical Society of America,* 1966, **39,** 725–735. (b)

Stevens, S. S. On the operation known as judgment. *American Scientist,* 1966, **54,** 385–401. (c)

Stevens, S. S. A metric for social consensus. *Science,* 1966, **151,** 530–541. (d)

Stevens, S. S. Neural events and the psychophysical law. *Science,* 1970, **170,** 1043–1050.

Stevens, S. S. Issues in psychophysical measurement. *Psychological Review,* 1971, **78,** 426–450. (a)

Stevens, S. S. Sensory power functions and neural events. In W. R. Loewenstein (Ed.), *Handbook of sensory physiology.* (Vol. 1). Berlin and New York: Springer-Verlag, 1971. (b)

Stevens, S. S. A neural quantum in sensory discrimination. *Science,* 1972, **177,** 749–762. (a)

Stevens, S. S. Perceived level of noise by Mark VII and dB(E). *Journal of the Acoustical Society of America,* 1972, **51,** 575–601. (b)

Stevens, S. S. *Psychophysics: Introduction to its perceptual, neural and social prospects.* New York: Wiley, 1975.

Stevens, S. S., Carton, A. S., & Shickman, G. M. A scale of apparent intensity of electric shock. *Journal of Experimental Psychology,* 1958, **56,** 328–334.

Stevens, S. S., & Galanter, E. H. Ratio scales and category scales for a dozen perceptual continua. *Journal of Experimental Psychology,* 1957, **54,** 377–411.

Stevens, S. S., & Guirao, M. Loudness, reciprocality, and partition scales. *Journal of the Acoustical Society of America,* 1962, **34,** 1466–1471.

Stevens, S. S., Morgan, C. E., & Volkmann, J. Theory of neural quantum in the discrimination of loudness and pitch. *American Journal of Psychology,* 1941, **54,** 315–355.

Stevens, S. S., & Volkmann, J. The relation of pitch to frequency: A revised scale. *American Journal of Psychology,* 1940, **53,** 329–353.

Stuiver, M. Biophysics of the sense of smell. Unpublished doctoral dissertation, University of Gronigen, Netherlands, 1958.

Swets, J. A. Indices of signal detectability obtained with various psychophysical procedures. *Journal of the Acoustical Society of America,* 1959, **31,** 511–513.

Swets, J. A. Is there a sensory threshold? *Science,* 1961, **134,** 168–177.

Swets, J. A., Tanner, W. P., Jr., & Birdsall, T. G. The evidence for a decision-making theory of visual detection. University of Michigan: Electronic Defense Group Technical Report No. 40, 1955.

Swets, J. A., Tanner, W. P., Jr., & Birdsall, T. G. Decision processes in perception. *Psychological Review,* 1961, **68,** 301–340.

Tanner, W. P., Jr., & Swets, J. A. A decision-making theory of visual detection. *Psychological Review,* 1954, **61,** 401–409.

Tanner, W. P., Jr., Swets, J. A., & Green, D. M. Some general properties of the hearing mechanism. University of Michigan: Electronic Defense Group Technical Report No. 30, 1956.

Teghtsoonian, M. The judgment of size. *American Journal of Psychology,* 1965, **78,** 392–402.

Teghtsoonian, R. On the exponents in Stevens' law and the constant in Ekman's law. *Psychological Review,* 1971, **78,** 71–80.

Thalmann, R. Cross-modality matching in a study of abnormal loudness functions. *Laryngoscope,* 1965, **75,** 1708–1726.

Theodor, L. H. A neglected parameter: Some comments on "A table for calculation of d' and β." *Psychological Bulletin,* 1972, **78,** 260–261.

Thorndike, E. L. Handwriting. *Teachers College Record,* 1910, **11,** No. 2.

Thurstone, L. L. A law of comparative judgment. *Psychological Review,* 1927, **34,** 273–286.

Thurstone, L. L. The phi-gamma hypothesis. *Journal of Experimental Psychology,* 1928, **9,** 293–305.

Thurstone, L. L. *The measurement of values.* Chicago: University of Chicago Press, 1959.

Titchener, E. B. *Experimental psychology. Quantitative.* New York: Macmillan, 1905.

Tonndorf, J., & Khanna, S. M. Submicroscopic displacement amplitudes of the tympanic membrane (cat) measured by a laser interferometer. *Journal of the Acoustical Society of America,* 1968, **44,** 1546–1554.

Torgerson, W. S. *Theory and methods of scaling.* New York: Wiley, 1958.

Urban, F. M. The future of psychophysics. *Psychological Review,* 1930, **37,** 93–106.

Vendrik, A. J. H., & Eijkman, E. G. Psychophysical properties determined with internal noise. In D. R. Kenshalo (Ed.), *The skin senses.* Springfield, Ill.: Charles C Thomas, 1968.

Verrillo, R. T. Effect of contactor area on the vibrotactile threshold. *Journal of the Acoustical Society of America,* 1963, **35,** 1962–1966.

Verrillo, R. T. Vibrotactile sensitivity and the frequency response of the Pacinian corpuscle. *Psychonomic Science,* 1966, **4,** 135–136.

Verillo, R. T. Cutaneous sensation. In B. Scharf (Ed.), *Experimental sensory psychology.* Scott, Foresman & Co., 1975.

von Békésy, G. Über das Fechner'sche Gesetz und seine Bedeutung für die Theorie der akustischen Beobachtungsfehler und die Theorie des Hörens. *Annalen der Physik,* 1930, **7,** 329–359.

von Békésy, G. A new audiometer. *Acta Oto-laryngology,* 1947, **35,** 411–422.

Wald, G. Human vision and the spectrum. *Science,* 1945, **101,** 653–658.

Warren, R. M. A basis for judgments of sensory intensity. *American Journal of Psychology,* 1958, **71,** 675–687.

Warren, R. M. Reply to S. S. Stevens. *Journal of the Acoustical Society of America,* 1963, **35,** 1663–1665.

Warren, R. M. Visual intensity judgments: An empirical rule and a theory. *Psychological Review,* 1969, **76,** 16–30.

Warren, R. M., Sersen, E. A., & Pores, E. A basis for loudness judgments. *American Journal of Psychology,* 1958, **71,** 700–709.

Warren, R. M., & Warren, R. P. A critique of S. S. Stevens' "new psychophysics." *Perceptual and Motor Skills,* 1963, **16,** 797–810.

Weber, E. H. *De pulsu, resorpitione, auditu et tactu: Annotationes anatomicae et physiologicae.* Leipzig: Koehlor, 1834.

Wickelgren, W. A., & Norman, D. A. Strength models of serial position in short-term recognition memory. *Journal of Mathematical Psychology,* 1966, **3,** 316–347.

Wilska, A. Eine Methode zur Bestimmung der Horschwell enamplituden des Trommelfels bei verschiedenen Freguenzen. *Skandinavisches Archiv für Physiologie,* 1935, **72,** 161–165.

Wright, A. A. Psychometric and psychophysical theory within a framework of response bias. *Psychological Review,* 1974, **81,** 322–347.

Yilmaz, H. Perceptual invariance and the psychophysical law. *Perception and Psychophysics,* 1967, **2,** 533–538.

Zuriff, G. E. A behavioral interpretation of psychophysical scaling. *Behaviorism,* 1972, **1,** 118–133.

Zwislocki, J. J. An analysis of some auditory characteristics. In R. D. Luce, R. R. Bush, & E. Galanter (Eds.), *Handbook of mathematical psychology.* Vol. III. New York: Wiley, 1965.

Zwislocki, J. J. On intensity characteristics of sensory receptors: A generalized function. *Kybernetik,* 1973, **12,** 169–183.

Zwislocki, J. J. A power function for sensory receptors. In H. R. Moskowitz, B. Scharf, & J. C. Stevens (Eds.), *Sensation and measurement.* Dordrecht-Holland: Reidel, 1974.

Author Index

The numbers in *italics* refer to the pages on which the complete references are listed.

Ström, L., 146, *164*
Stuiver, M., 18, *169*
Swets, J. A., 56, 58, 59, 63, 66, 67, 69, 73, 74, 75, 77, 79, *166, 169*

T

Tanner, W. P., Jr., 56, 58, 59, 63, 66, 67, 69, 73, 74, *169*
Teghtsoonian, M., 149, 152, 162, *169*
Thalmann, R., 137, 138, *169*
Theodor, L. H., 68, *169*
Thorndike, E. L., 95, *169*
Thurstone, L. L., 42, 86, 94, 95, *169*
Titchener, E. B., 153, *169*
Tonndorf, J., 16, *169*
Torgerson, W. S., 99, 102, 105, 106, 107, 114, *169*
Tulunay, Ü., 117, *165*

U

Urban, F. F., 83, *169*

V

Vendrik, A. J. H., 72, *169*
Verrillo, R. J., 16, 17, 18, *169*

Volkmann, J., 43, 44, 45, 103, 104, 106, 107, *169*
von Békésy, G., 32, 43, 45, *169*

W

Wald, G., 12, 13, *170*
Warren, R. M., 152, 153, 154, *170*
Warren, R. P., 152, *170*
Weber, B. J., 52, 53, 71, *165*
Weber, E. H., 2, *170*
White, S. D., 16, *167*
Wickelgren, W. A., 82, *170*
Wikström, I., 158, *166*
Wilska, A., 15, *170*
Wolff, H. G., 93, 94, *166*
Wolfgang, M. E., 156, *167*
Wright, A. A., 49, *170*
Wright, J. H., 52, 53, 71, 78, 79, 80, 139, 140, *165*

Y

Yilmaz, H., 133, 134, *170*

Z

Zotterman, Y., 146, *164*
Zuriff, G. E., 150, *170*
Zwislocki, J. J., 123, 124, 141, 147, *166, 170*

Subject Index